Exploring the Philosophy of R. G. Collingwood

Also available from Bloomsbury

Aesthetic Theory, Abstract Art, and Lawrence Carroll, by David Carrier
The Philosophy of Henry Thoreau, by Lester H. Hunt
The Philosophy of Susanne Langer, by Adrienne Dengerink Chaplin
The Selected Writings of Eva Picardi, edited by Annalisa Coliva
The Selected Writings of Maurice O'Connor Drury, edited by John Hayes

Exploring the Philosophy of R. G. Collingwood

From History and Method to Art and Politics

Peter Skagestad

BLOOMSBURY ACADEMIC
LONDON • NEW YORK • OXFORD • NEW DELHI • SYDNEY

BLOOMSBURY ACADEMIC
Bloomsbury Publishing Plc
50 Bedford Square, London, WC1B 3DP, UK
1385 Broadway, New York, NY 10018, USA
29 Earlsfort Terrace, Dublin 2, Ireland

BLOOMSBURY, BLOOMSBURY ACADEMIC and the Diana logo
are trademarks of Bloomsbury Publishing Plc

First published in Great Britain 2021
This paperback edition published in 2022

Copyright © Peter Skagestad, 2021

Peter Skagestad has asserted his right under the Copyright, Designs
and Patents Act, 1988, to be identified as Author of this work.

For legal purposes the Acknowledgments on p. ix constitute
an extension of this copyright page.

Cover design by Charlotte Daniels
Cover image: Aerial view of Oxford city centre © A.P.S. (UK) / Alamy Stock Photo

All rights reserved. No part of this publication may be reproduced or
transmitted in any form or by any means, electronic or mechanical,
including photocopying, recording, or any information storage or retrieval
system, without prior permission in writing from the publishers.

Bloomsbury Publishing Plc does not have any control over, or responsibility for,
any third-party websites referred to or in this book. All internet addresses given
in this book were correct at the time of going to press. The author and publisher
regret any inconvenience caused if addresses have changed or sites have ceased
to exist, but can accept no responsibility for any such changes.

A catalogue record for this book is available from the British Library.

Library of Congress Cataloging-in-Publication Data
Names: Skagestad, Peter, 1947-author.
Title: Exploring the philosophy of R.G. Collingwood: from history and
method to art and politics / Peter Skagestad.
Description: London; New York: Bloomsbury Academic, 2020. |
Includes bibliographical references and index.
Identifiers: LCCN 2020031011 (print) | LCCN 2020031012 (ebook) |
ISBN 9781350152908 (hardback) | ISBN 9781350189232 (paperback) |
ISBN 9781350152915 (ebook) | ISBN 9781350152922 (epub)
Subjects: LCSH: Collingwood, R. G. (Robin George), 1889-1943.
Classification: LCC B1618.C74 S59 2020 (print) | LCC B1618.C74 (ebook) | DDC 192–dc23
LC record available at https://lccn.loc.gov/2020031011
LC ebook record available at https://lccn.loc.gov/2020031012

ISBN: HB: 978-1-3501-5290-8
PB: 978-1-3501-8923-2
ePDF: 978-1-3501-5291-5
eBook: 978-1-3501-5292-2

Typeset by Deanta Global Publishing Services, Chennai, India

To find out more about our authors and books visit www.bloomsbury.com
and sign up for our newsletters.

To my son
Erik Ober Skagestad

Contents

Preface and Acknowledgments	ix
List of Abbreviations	xi
Introduction	1
1. The Plan of This Book	2
1 Life and Work	5
1. Biographical Highlights	5
2. Idealism and Realism	10
3. The Reception of Collingwood's Philosophy	13
4. Going Forward	15
Further Reading	15
2 Early Works	17
1. *Religion and Philosophy*	17
2. *Speculum Mentis, or The Map of Knowledge*	27
Further Reading	36
3 Philosophical Method	37
1. Scope and Method	38
2. Philosophical Concepts	40
3. Philosophical Judgments	46
4. Two Skeptical Positions	51
5. Philosophical Inference	53
6. The Idea of System	55
7. The Collingwood-Ryle Exchange	57
8. *The Idea of Nature*—Transition to the Theory of Absolute Presuppositions	59
Further Reading	61
4 Historical Understanding	63
1. Collingwood's Conception of History	64
2. The Re-enactment Doctrine	69
3. Historical Explanation	74

	4. Popper's Situational Analysis	79
	5. Dray's Review of Objections	83
	6. Fairy Tales and Magic	89
	Further Reading	91
5	The Principles of Art	93
	1. What Art Is and Is Not	94
	2. Consciousness and Its Corruption	106
	3. Art as Language	108
	4. The Artist and the Community	111
	Further Reading	114
6	Questions and Answers	115
	1. Critique of the Realists	116
	2. The Logic of Question and Answer	117
	3. Some Critical Observations	122
	4. The Radical Conversion Hypothesis	126
	Further Reading	130
7	The Doctrine of Absolute Presuppositions	131
	1. "Absolute Presuppositions" Defined	132
	2. Metaphysics as the Analysis of Absolute Presuppositions	137
	3. A Case Study: Isaiah Berlin's Critique of the Enlightenment	142
	4. Anti-metaphysics	144
	5. Collingwood's Disagreement with Ayer	147
	6. Illustration: The Existence of God	149
	Further Reading	152
8	Politics, Society, and Civilization	153
	1. Collingwood's Politics	153
	2. Collingwood's Moral Philosophy	158
	3. *The New Leviathan* I: Collingwood's Psychology Revisited	162
	4. *The New Leviathan* II: Society	165
	5. *The New Leviathan* III: Civilization and Barbarism	171
	6. Conclusion	179
	Further Reading	180

Notes	181
Select Bibliography	191
Index	199

Preface and Acknowledgments

The seeds of this book date back many years to when I wrote my doctoral dissertation on Collingwood's metaphysics at Brandeis University in the early 1970s. A year later I published a book comparing and contrasting Collingwood's philosophy of history to that of Sir Karl Popper, whose lectures I had attended at Brandeis. Two years of compulsory military service in my native Norway followed, and upon my discharge my philosophical interests had moved in a different direction. Twenty years ago an invitation to give a paper at an international Collingwood Congress rekindled my interest in Collingwood's philosophy, and the result, finally, is this book.

I am grateful to Bloomsbury Academic's anonymous reviewers, to my old friend and colleague Howard DeLong, and to my wife Elaine for reading earlier drafts of the manuscript and making numerous helpful suggestions for revisions. All remaining errors and omissions are my own responsibility.

At Bloomsbury, I am further indebted to Colleen Coalter, Becky Holland, Zoe Jellicoe, Leela Devi, and Dhanuja Ravi for sure-footedly guiding the manuscript through the editorial and production process.

As ever, I remain indebted to my mentor Alasdair MacIntyre for guiding me, decades ago, through my first baby steps in Collingwood studies.

Finally, Section 3 of Chapter 7 is excerpted from my earlier article 'Collingwood and Berlin: A Comparison', published in the *Journal of the History of Ideas*, vol. 66, no. 1, 2005, 99–112, Copyright 2005 by Journal of the History of Ideas, Inc., and is here reprinted with permission.

Like Collingwood's later works, this book has been written under the cloud of an impending threat to our civilization. During the recent dark years I have given much thought to the question of what students of philosophy can do to defend the practice of rational inquiry as an institution in our society against the powerful forces seeking to trivialize, marginalize, and delegitimize it, if not – *yet* – to suppress it outright. And I have reached the conclusion that the best use I personally can make to this end of my talents and experience, such as they are, is defiantly to carry on the practice of rational inquiry, *as if* its value and importance were beyond dispute. That is part of what I have tried to do in this book.

Peter Skagestad
June 2020

Abbreviations

A	*An Autobiography*
EM	*An Essay on Metaphysics*
EPA	*Essays in the Philosophy of Art*, Donagan, Alan, ed.
EPH	*Essays in the Philosophy of History*, Debbins, William, ed.
EPM	*An Essay on Philosophical Method*
EPP	*Essays in Political Philosophy*, Boucher, David, ed.
FML	*The First Mate's Log*
FR	*Faith and Reason*, Rubinoff, Lionel, ed.
GRU	'Goodness, Rightness, Utility'
IH	*The Idea of History*
IN	*The Idea of Nature*
NL	*The New Leviathan*. Following established convention, references to this work cite paragraph numbers, rather than page numbers.
OPA	*Outlines of a Philosophy of Art*
PA	*The Principles of Art*
PE	*The Philosophy of Enchantment*
PH	*The Principles of History*
RBES	*Roman Britain and the English Settlements*
RP	*Religion and Philosophy*
RUP	'Ruskin's Philosophy', reprinted in EPA
SM	*Speculum Mentis*

Introduction

No longer a neglected philosopher, Robin George Collingwood (1889–1943) has in recent decades become widely recognized as one of the most significant philosophers of the twentieth century. Considered in his lifetime as fighting a rearguard action in defense of an outmoded Idealism, Collingwood is now recognized as a cogent critic of the then-nascent analytic philosophy, while himself a master of rigorous philosophical analysis. Collingwood was fully and consistently committed to reason and to the use of rational argument that is the pride of the analytic tradition, while ambitiously tackling the substantive philosophical issues that analytic philosophers—in his own time as later—have tended to shy away from. And he brought to bear on these issues an unparalleled wealth of knowledge, of history, archaeology, politics, literature, art, and folklore. His early death was one of the tragedies of twentieth-century philosophy. Thus Ray Monk, author of a noted biography of Ludwig Wittgenstein, recently argued that the "continental"/"analytic" divide that has characterized postwar philosophy could have been avoided had Collingwood lived longer. The divide, Monk argued, was largely engendered by Gilbert Ryle, who succeeded Collingwood as Waynflete Professor of Metaphysical Philosophy at Oxford.[1] Had Collingwood not died when he did, Ryle would not have occupied this very influential position.

In his relatively short life, Collingwood made significant and original contributions to all branches of philosophy, and left his mark on metaphysics, epistemology, philosophy of religion, philosophy of language and mind, aesthetics, philosophy of history, ethics, and social and political philosophy. His influence has been correspondingly wide ranging; Collingwood's biographer Fred Inglis sees him as a direct influence on the prominent ethicist Alasdair MacIntyre, among others, and a forerunner of—though not apparently an influence on—the historian of science Thomas Kuhn.[2] The relevance of Collingwood's philosophy for today's thought thus far exceeds what is as yet generally appreciated.

1. The Plan of This Book

In his *Autobiography* Collingwood exhorts those who are interested in his work, whether they agree or disagree with him, to write about the subject matter, not about him (A, 118–19). This exhortation has been notoriously ignored by later writers, for more than one reason. In the case of the philosophy of history, as understood in the English-speaking world, Collingwood, as is pointed out by the editors of the posthumously published *Principles of History*, has set the agenda for the discipline, making it well-nigh impossible to practice the discipline without reference to Collingwood (PH, xiii). Another reason is that, in addition to his published works, Collingwood left behind a massive amount of unpublished, and in most cases unfinished, manuscripts, many of which have since appeared in print. So, a certain amount of reconstruction is required to gain a full understanding of his thought.

There is today a wealth of literature on Collingwood's philosophy, but not to the best of my knowledge any chronologically organized examination of all aspects of his philosophy. Most accounts to date have been thematically organized, relating Collingwood's ideas either to his predecessors or to present-day philosophical concerns, and with one exception confined to certain salient themes within Collingwood's philosophy.[3] These approaches have their merits, but it is the belief of this author that a chronological approach will give a fuller understanding of both the continuity and the evolution of Collingwood's thought. Thus, we review the progression of his thought, starting with this first book *Religion and Philosophy* (1916) and concluding with his final book *The New Leviathan* (1942). It should be noted, however, that Collingwood typically worked on multiple projects simultaneously and over periods of many years. Thus, while *The New Leviathan* was published in 1942, it is the fruit of ideas developed in lectures on moral and political philosophy delivered over a twenty-year period. And while *The Idea of History* was published posthumously in 1946, it was largely written in 1936. So, my objective has been to present Collingwood's philosophical ideas in a roughly chronological order. I say "philosophical" since Collingwood was also a historian and an archaeologist, and his work in these fields falls outside the scope of this study. And, while I have attempted to place Collingwood's philosophy within the context of his contemporaries and predecessors, this does not preclude referencing, where appropriate, Collingwood's relevance to later philosophers.

The only chronologically organized study of Collingwood's philosophy that I am aware of is Lionel Rubinoff's magisterial classic.[4] However, Rubinoff confines himself to Collingwood's metaphysics, whereas the present study aims to address all aspects of Collingwood's philosophy. By aiming at generality, I do not, however, lay any claim to being comprehensive; as the title of this book indicates, this is an exploration of each aspect of Collingwood's philosophy, not a comprehensive account of any of them.

In a letter to the Clarendon Press from 1939, Collingwood himself grouped his work into three series: Philosophical Essays, comprising *An Essay on Philosophical Method* and *An Essay on Metaphysics*; Philosophical Principles, comprising *The Principles of Art* and *The Principles of History*; and Studies in the History of Ideas, comprising *The Idea of Nature* and *The Idea of History*.[5] Why not use this organization—Collingwood's own—as our organizing principle? The grouping of the two *Essays* provides, as we shall see in Chapter 7, a valuable clue to understanding the latter *Essay*, and thus to understanding Collingwood's philosophy more generally. The other two series did not materialize, as *The Principles of History*, *The Idea of Nature*, and *The Idea of History* were all left unfinished at Collingwood's untimely death, and what we today know as *The Idea of History* is that work together with Chapter 1 of *The Principles of History* and various other writings on the philosophy of history. Also, in 1939 Collingwood had not yet begun work on *The New Leviathan*, which we today cannot help seeing as a companion volume to *The Principles of Art*.

While there is, as noted, a large literature on Collingwood's philosophy, most of this literature has not penetrated very far beyond the ranks of academic philosophers. The overriding goal of the present book is to make Collingwood's philosophy, and some of the contentious issues it has raised, accessible to a general audience. Thus, no prior knowledge of philosophy is presupposed, and philosophical jargon has been avoided to the extent possible. Collingwood propounded a number of controversial ideas, and while he was a master of graceful prose, he was not always a careful writer, which is one reason why the interpretation of Collingwood's thought is also fraught with controversy. No one writing about Collingwood can ignore these controversies, or avoid taking stands on the most important of them, but I hope to have avoided getting embroiled in esoteric controversies that are of interest only to professional Collingwood scholars.

My objective in this book is to provide an overview of Collingwood's philosophy, rather than to promote "my" interpretation of his thought. However, given that Collingwood studies have been, and continue to be, a highly controversial field, I cannot avoid embracing particular stances on salient points of contention; two issues in particular stand out as worthy of mention at the outset. First, while I shall argue that Collingwood's thought evolves over time, I join those who reject the thesis, originated by T. M. Knox and later embraced by Alan Donagan, that Collingwood in the late 1930s underwent a radical conversion from idealism to a relativistic historicism. This thesis I regard as having been decisively discredited, most conclusively by James Connelly, as we will see in Chapter 6. Secondly, I will be defending Collingwood's controversial doctrine that historical knowledge consists in the re-enactment of past thoughts. This doctrine, as I understand it, has been largely misunderstood by its numerous critics, as has been argued by William Dray, in particular. This subject will be addressed in detail in Chapter 4.

Thus prepared, the reader is invited to embark on what proposes to be a journey of exploration and discovery.

1

Life and Work

1. Biographical Highlights

For a full and rich account of Collingwood's life, the reader is referred to Inglis's biography; here we shall simply set forth some highlights.[1] Collingwood was born in Coniston, in England's Lake District, in 1889, to parents William Gershom Collingwood and his wife Dorrie Collingwood. Gershom, as Collingwood senior was known, was a painter, writer of fiction and nonfiction, a folklorist steeped in British folktales and Icelandic sagas, an archaeologist, and private secretary to, and biographer of, the critic John Ruskin, cofounder with William Morris of the Arts and Crafts movement. Gershom was also Oxford-trained in the Idealist philosophy of T. H. Green and Bernard Bosanquet, Gershom's tutor at Oxford. Dorrie was also a painter, as well as an accomplished pianist. All this matters because Robin and his three sisters were homeschooled by their parents in Latin, Greek, and math, as well as in drawing, painting, music, archaeology, and practical DIY skills. And sailing, which became Robin's lifelong passion. His sailboat *Swallow* was to be immortalized in the children's books of the Collingwood family friend Arthur Ransome. Wherever possible, learning by doing was emphasized in the children's education.

Since Gershom did not hold down a full-time paying job until 1905, when he accepted a lecturership at University College, Reading, the family was far from wealthy and often short of money, but they appear to have earned enough from Gershom's books and lectures and Dorrie's paintings that they did not suffer deprivation, and Robin seems to have had an exceptionally happy childhood.

At twelve, Collingwood tells us in his *Autobiography*, he came across a copy of Immanuel Kant's *Groundwork for the Metaphysics of Morals*, and, while he found it impossible to understand, he was imbued with a sense that this was something that was vitally important for him to comprehend (A, 3–4). Thus his fate was sealed.

At age fourteen, after a year at the preparatory school Charney Hall, Robin was sent to boarding school at Rugby, where he lived for five years under pigsty conditions in an overcrowded dormitory. Collingwood later described these five years as largely wasted, due to the mind-numbingly regimented schedule, which seemed to him designed to prevent the students from doing any actual thinking (A, 8). He admits, though, that he was on excellent terms with his teachers, and Inglis has observed that he impressed his teachers sufficiently to be appointed head of his house in preference to more senior students.[2] Also, due to a knee injury he was excused from sports and used his free time to practice the violin and teach himself Italian to read Dante. So, not a complete waste. At Rugby he also was baptized and confirmed, as his freethinking parents had not given him a religious upbringing.

Collingwood's daughter Teresa Smith has noted that while Collingwood described himself as a "rebel" at Rugby, he did not rebel against the school's disciplinary regimen or its informal culture, both of which he fit right into. What he rebelled against was the school's pedagogy, which he found inimical to the kind of independent inquiry which his father, under the influence of Ruskin's pedagogical ideas, had inculcated into him.[3]

In 1908 Collingwood enrolled at University College, Oxford, from which he graduated with First Class honors in 1912. His teachers at Oxford included the Realist philosophers John Cook Wilson and H. A. Prichard, as well as the Idealist J. A. Smith, who was to become an important mentor. Collingwood later confessed himself to have fallen under the sway of the Realists and to have remained a Realist until 1916. However, in his student years he also discovered the philosophy of the Italian Idealist Benedetto Croce, who was to remain an important influence, and in 1913 he published a translation of Croce's *Philosophy of Giambattista Vico*. Vico was to become another lifelong influence.

Upon graduating in 1912 Collingwood joined Pembroke College, Oxford, as a fellow and lecturer in philosophy and classics. Later, he also taught the philosophy students at Lincoln College, and by the mid-twenties he estimated he tutored or lectured about forty hours a week. His lectures were completely written out and revised every year. This workload did not prevent him from publishing five books while at Pembroke: *Religion and Philosophy* (1916), *Roman Britain* (1923), *Speculum Mentis* (1924), *Outlines of a Philosophy of Art* (1925), and *An Essay on Philosophical Method* (1933). From 1933 to 1934 he also wrote the posthumously published *The Idea of Nature*. At this time he also established himself as one of Britain's leading archaeologists; thus, in 1913, he became head of excavations at Galava at Amberside, replacing F. J. Haverfield, who had retired the previous year. Collingwood was to return to archaeological digs annually during college vacations for most of his life.

Collingwood's work as an historian and archaeologist falls outside the scope of this book, but is of sufficient importance for his philosophical work to bear emphasizing. Already growing up, Collingwood went on excavations with his father. Since Gershom is known to have accompanied Haverfield on some excavations, it is likely that this is when Robin made Haverfield's acquaintance. At Oxford, he accompanied Haverfield on several excavations, and upon Haverfield's death in 1919 Collingwood volunteered to take over his lectures on Roman history at Oxford. In 1927 he was appointed university lecturer in philosophy and Roman history. Continuing Haverfield's work on the archaeology of Roman Britain, Collingwood established himself as the leading authority on Hadrian's Wall and the adjacent depression known as the Vallum, in particular. In addition, Collingwood's method of question and answer, of which more in Chapter 6, became widely accepted by British archaeologists.[4] In 1930 Collingwood published *The Archaeology of Roman Britain*, followed in 1936 by a revised and enlarged *Roman Britain*, published as Part One of *Roman Britain and the English Settlements*, with J. N. L. Myres, Volume One of the *Oxford History of England*, which was to remain the standard text on the subject for the next thirty years. (Collingwood and Myres were not actually coauthors; Collingwood's *Roman Britain* and Myres's *The English Settlements* were bound together as one volume.) Finally, Collingwood collected and copied almost 1,000 Roman inscriptions; the projected volume *Roman Inscriptions of Britain* was, however, left unfinished at his death and was not published until 1965.

That Collingwood, at least at times, felt more at home in the world of history and archaeology than in that of academic philosophy is evidenced in a letter to his friend de Ruggiero in 1927, in the wake of the disappointing reception of his first major philosophical work *Speculum Mentis*:

> For four months I have been deep in historical studies, and there I find myself among friends and willing collaborators; the return to philosophy means a return to a work in which I become more and more conscious of being an outlaw.[5]

Collingwood spent the First World War in the Intelligence section of the Admiralty. In 1919 he married Ethel Winifred Graham, who was to bear him two children. During his tenure at Pembroke, in 1931, Collingwood's health suffered from an attack of chickenpox, in the aftermath of which he wrote what he himself considered his best book—indeed, the only one he was able to complete to his own satisfaction—*An Essay on Philosophical Method*. In 1935 he succeeded his old mentor J. A. Smith as Waynflete Professor of Metaphysical Philosophy, a promotion that significantly lightened his workload. In 1936 he gave the lectures that were to become the bulk of the posthumous *The Idea of History* (1946), long considered his magnum opus. In 1937 he suffered a breakdown and underwent a fifty-hour course of psychoanalysis. *The Principles of Art* appeared in 1938, and Collingwood suffered his first and second strokes, in March and September of that year, then wrote *An Autobiography*, and took a medical leave from his professorship. In the winter of 1938–9, on his doctor's advice, he went on a voyage to the Dutch East Indies, now Indonesia. His doctor had, however, recommended that he spend his leave writing, and while on board he penned *An Essay on Metaphysics* and one-third of a projected *Principles of History*, intended to be a companion volume to *The Principles of Art*.

Upon his return to England, in the summer of 1939, Collingwood guided a group of students on a Mediterranean voyage, during which he kept a journal to be published as *The First Mate's Log*. By the end of that voyage the Second World War had erupted, which is, in all probability, why Collingwood did not continue work on *The Principles of History*, but instead embarked on his massive treatise on social and political philosophy, *The New Leviathan* (1942), which he explicitly said was his contribution to the war effort. Early in 1941 he suffered his third stroke, which forced him to rein in the scope of *The New Leviathan* to four parts, instead of the projected five. Later that year the Collingwoods divorced, and he married his former student Kathleen Edwardes, twenty-two years his junior, who was to bear him one daughter. In January 1942 Collingwood suffered yet another stroke, leaving his left side paralyzed; he died a year later at the family home in Coniston.

At his death Collingwood left behind a wealth of unpublished material. The task of selecting and editing this for publication was entrusted by The Clarendon Press to Collingwood's pupil and friend T. M. Knox, who published *The Idea of Nature* in 1945 and *The Idea of History* in 1946, while making the controversial decision to leave the bulk of *The Principles of History* unpublished. Part of this book—less than half—was incorporated into *The Idea of History*. Knox wrote a highly controversial preface to this book, more of which in Chapter 6. The manuscript of the *Principles* was long believed to have been destroyed but was discovered at Oxford University Press in 1995 and published in 1999 together with several essays on the philosophy of history. Later publications include a number of Collingwood's lectures and essays, including several essays on folklore and literature that were published together with a long but unfinished book manuscript on folktales, under the title *The Philosophy of Enchantment* (2005).

In his Oxford years Collingwood was no doubt a philosophical outlier; his works were largely ignored by his colleagues—although widely reviewed in nonphilosophical publications—and Collingwood made it clear in his *Autobiography* that he felt isolated in Oxford. This does not mean that he was a loner; he had numerous friends and pupils in the archaeological community, in which he had assumed a leading role. He was actively involved in politics and in church life. He enjoyed long friendships with the Italian philosophers Benedetto Croce and Guido de Ruggiero, whose *History of European Liberalism* he translated from Italian in 1927. At Pembroke he met J. R. R. Tolkien, and their shared interest in folktales became the basis for a lasting friendship. Finally, Collingwood was an extremely popular lecturer, noted both for the clearness of his delivery and for his often mischievous humor and wit.[6] On occasion, his lectures had to be moved to a different college, as Pembroke did not have a lecture hall large enough to accommodate his students.

We have repeatedly referred to Idealists and Realists; it is time to peer behind these labels and ask what they stand for.

2. Idealism and Realism

In Collingwood's formative years—and indeed throughout his career—Oxford and Cambridge philosophy was dominated by a Realist revolt against what was and remains known as British Idealism. This was a movement founded by Thomas Hill Green (1836–82), and which included, among others, F. H. Bradley (1846–1924), J. M. E. McTaggart, and Bernard Bosanquet (1848–1923). Taking the nature of reality to be spirit, rather than matter, these thinkers have been widely, but mostly wrongly, referred to as Hegelians; they were certainly knowledgeable of Hegel, as of Kant, but at the same time they worked within a distinctly British tradition.

Green was primarily an educator and social reformer, but he grounded his social and educational ideas in an Idealist metaphysics. Against the Utilitarians, such as Jeremy Bentham and John Stuart Mill, Green advocated a positive concept of liberty as not simply the absence of restraint or compulsion, but as the ability to pursue enjoyment as a participant in a community. Freedom is "a positive power of doing and enjoying, and that, too, something that we do or enjoy in common with others."[7] The metaphysical reasoning underlying Green's conception of a common good takes the form of a critique of empiricism. Knowledge, Green held, cannot be built up from sense data; if I call something, for instance, "a sensation of white," I am already relating it to a background from which it is picked out, and to an organism that senses it; thus sense data presuppose relations, and only relations are real.[8]

To be real, then, is to belong to a system of relations, which ultimately comprises the order of nature. My awareness of myself as a finite self is at the same time an awareness of my relatedness to a transcendent, infinite reality. But relations are products of the mind and projected on to the objects of sense. So, nature is a product of mind. Each finite mind constitutes nature in so far as it grasps the system of relations to which it belongs, but this grasp is always incomplete, so we have to presuppose an infinite mind which grasps and thus constitutes the whole. This mind is God, aka the Absolute. As Frederick Copleston summarizes Green's conclusion:

> God is the infinite eternal subject; and His complete knowledge is reproduced progressively in the finite subject in dependence, from the empirical point of view, on the modifications of the human organism.[9]

Bradley, who was no doubt the most systematic thinker among the Idealists, departed from Green in important respects. Probably Bradley's most widely read work is his *Ethical Studies* (1876), which reviews, in dialectical progression, "Pleasure for Pleasure's Sake," "Duty for Duty's Sake," and "My Station and Its Duties," to arrive, finally, at "Ideal Morality." His metaphysics, however, is primarily to be found in *Appearance and Reality* (1893). Unlike Green, Bradley has no use for relations. (To be precise, Bradley rejected external relations but tentatively accepted internal relations where a thing is related to something else by its very definition as, for example, husband to wife.[10])

Bradley's point of departure is to argue that the attempt to approach philosophy from talk about substance, qualities, or relations is bound to lead to insoluble muddles. For instance, we may say that a lump of sugar has the qualities of whiteness, hardness, and sweetness. By saying that the lump *is* white and also *is* sweet, we obviously do not mean to equate whiteness and sweetness. Rather, we think of the lump as a substance to which these qualities adhere. However, that substance is not a "something" over and above the whiteness, hardness, and sweetness; rather, it is the way in which these qualities are related to each other. But what is this relation? The quality of whiteness is related to sweetness. So, is being related to sweetness identical with being white? If so, to say that whiteness is related to sweetness is simply to say that whiteness is whiteness. Is being related to sweetness something different from being white? In that case, whiteness is something different from being white![11]

Bradley's solution to this and similar muddles is to take reality as a whole as the entry point into metaphysics. The splitting up of reality into things with qualities and relations belongs to the realm of appearance. To talk about qualities and relations is all right for everyday practical purposes, but it does not get us far in philosophy. Reality is the totality in which all the contradictions generated by appearance are dissolved; this totality Bradley calls the Absolute. The Absolute is an infinite act of experience, a single and all-inclusive experience, which embraces all diversity. Unlike Green, Bradley does not equate the Absolute with God. The Absolute is in a sense spirit, but it is not a person; it is suprapersonal.[12]

Bradley's metaphysics was controversial from the start; among other things, it raised the menacing specter of atheism. A remedy for this was proposed in the form of Personal Idealism, advanced primarily by J. M. E. McTaggart. For McTaggart there was no Absolute; there was only society, or the system of individual selves. McTaggart starts out from the premise that something exists; this much is known by immediate experience. He proceeds to argue that what exists is differentiation. The very fact of perception demonstrates differentiation, as perception inherently involves more than one term. So, something exists and that something is differentiated. What exists cannot be mere qualities, as a quality presupposes a substance. So, substances must exist. These substances must be similar or dissimilar, so relations exist. Now, we have seen Bradley dissolving the concept of relation, but McTaggart has an answer. A relation presupposes two or more terms, and it stands in a derivative relation to each of its terms, so we get an infinite regress, as Bradley had demonstrated. But "these infinite series are not vicious, because it is not necessary to complete them to determine the meaning of the earlier term."[13]

Absolute Idealism was defended against McTaggart's criticism by Bosanquet, but we shall not follow the Idealists further; enough has been said, for present purposes, to illustrate the central ideas of the movement. In Boucher and Vincent's pithy summary: "All the forms of Idealism have at least one common element; they refuse to acknowledge that the material process is the ultimate character of reality—to the extent that reality is known or knowable."[14] The authors also acknowledge that Idealism has not endured a happy fate; it faced wholesale rejection by the generation of Realists that followed. These included G.E. Moore and Bertrand Russell at Cambridge and John Cook Wilson, H. A. Prichard, and H. W. B. Joseph at Oxford. The central tenet of the Realists was that knowledge makes no difference to the object known, with the corollary, hinted at by Russell but explicitly drawn by Prichard, that the study of ethics can make no difference to the conduct of life. As Collingwood resided at Oxford throughout his career, it was primarily the Oxford Realists who became the targets of his criticisms. We shall return to his disagreements with the Realists in Chapter 6; for now, I cannot forbear to recall Alasdair MacIntyre observe in a lecture that Hegel was lucky to have Kant as his opponent, whereas Collingwood had the misfortune to be stuck with Cook Wilson and Prichard.

As a critic of Realism, Collingwood has been generally identified as an Idealist. He himself generally rejected the label, angrily so in private correspondence with Gilbert Ryle, more of which in Chapter 3. This rejection, however, is hardly conclusive, as Collingwood also did not label Bradley an Idealist, preferring instead to refer to "the school of Green" (A, 15). Bradley himself, Collingwood once noted, did not care whether his philosophy was called Realism or Idealism (EPM, 231). Collingwood clearly shares the Idealists' rejection of Empiricism. He agreed with the Empiricists that all knowledge is based on experience, and with the Pragmatists that all thought is for the sake of action. But the mind is an indispensable agent in experience, not a passive receptacle of experience. Experience does not consist in sensation simply, but in bringing concepts to bear on our sensations. Here, as in many other respects, there is a striking parallel to the American Pragmatist Charles Peirce, who identified the basic building blocks of knowledge as percepts, rather than sensations. Also, as we shall see in Chapter 3, Collingwood articulated and deployed a dialectical method, explicitly derived from Hegel and Bradley, but also in important respects different from Hegel's.

Collingwood parts company with the Idealists over the Absolute. There is no Absolute for Collingwood, as we shall see. Philosophy, for him, is entirely backward looking; all philosophy can ever do is summarize the progression of consciousness to the present day. In this respect Collingwood was fond of quoting Hegel: "This is as far as consciousness has come." A second major difference, which will be explored in detail in Chapters 4, 6, and 7, is Collingwood's commitment to a *rapprochement* between philosophy and history, a *rapprochement* which at times may sound like a complete fusion. Collingwood is here following in the footsteps of the Italian Idealists Croce, de Ruggiero, and Giovanni Gentile, before Gentile joined the Italian fascist party.[15] But again, Collingwood was an independent thinker; while influenced by the Italians, he was by no means their pupil and refused, for instance, to embrace Croce's *complete* absorption of philosophy into history.

3. The Reception of Collingwood's Philosophy

Collingwood, we have noted, was philosophically isolated at Oxford, and his books received mixed reviews in philosophical journals upon their publication. His first major work, *Speculum Mentis*, was met with a wall of silence.[16] While *An Essay on Philosophical Method* and *The New Leviathan* were on the whole well received, *An Autobiography* and *An Essay on Metaphysics* met with a shocked response for their overtly polemical tone. However well received in general, *An Essay on Philosophical Method* provoked a blistering response from Gilbert Ryle, of which more in Chapter 3. *The Principles of Art* received rave reviews, as did the posthumous *The Idea of History*. As noted by David Boucher, Collingwood's books were largely ignored by the philosophical journals with the exception of *Mind*,[17] but were widely and on the whole favorably reviewed in nonphilosophical publications. With the exception of the first *Essay*, they were addressed to a general audience, and they must have sold well enough for Oxford University Press to keep publishing them and to keep them in print continuously for decades.

The postwar years, however, saw little interest for Collingwood's philosophy, with the exception of his philosophy of history. Upon its publication in 1946, *The Idea of History* attracted widespread acclaim. Thus, no one writing about philosophy of history in the English-speaking world could ignore Collingwood's contribution to the field, whether they regarded it favorably or with hostility. Some of this literature will be discussed in Chapter 4. But political philosophy had largely disappeared from the scene and with it Collingwood's contributions in *The New Leviathan*. And seen through the lens of the analytic philosophy which dominated Anglo-American academia for a quarter of a century, Collingwood's metaphysics, epistemology, and philosophy of mind and language necessarily appeared simply confused. An example of this, noted by Boucher, is the first major monograph on Collingwood's philosophy to appear, Alan Donagan's *The Later Philosophy of R.G. Collingwood* (1962), which is sharply critical of Collingwood on points where, Boucher argues, Donagan has simply failed to understand Collingwood (EPP, 2).

Two highly sympathetic studies of Collingwood appeared less than a decade later, Louis Mink's *Mind, History, and Dialectic* (1969) and Lionel Rubinoff's *Collingwood and the Reform of Metaphysics* (1970), followed by my own modest contribution *Making Sense of History* in 1975, and W. J. van der Dussen's magisterial *History as Science: The Philosophy of R.G. Collingwood* in 1981. A huge literature on Collingwood's thought has later arisen, of which this book's bibliography offers only a sampling. It is telling, in this respect, that while G. J. Warnock's *English Philosophy since 1900*, published in 1958, does not mention Collingwood, A. J. Ayer's *Philosophy in the Twentieth Century*, appearing in 1982, devoted an entire chapter to Collingwood, the *only* philosopher to be honored with his own chapter.[18]

Interest in Collingwood's political philosophy was rekindled by the appearance, in 1989, of David Boucher's *The Social and Political Thought of R.G. Collingwood*, followed by Boucher's edition of a number of Collingwood's essays on political philosophy. In 1994, the Centre for Collingwood Studies was founded at Boucher's University of Wales, and that same year Boucher and James Connelly joined forces to found the Collingwood Society and the journal *Collingwood Studies*, later *Collingwood and British Idealism Studies*. And in recent decades, beginning with *The New Leviathan* in 1992, five of Collingwood's major works have been reissued in new editions, with critical introductions and a wealth of supplementary, previously unpublished material.

4. Going Forward

In what follows we shall examine Collingwood's works in a roughly chronological order which will show the gradual progression of his thought over time, with the caveat that Collingwood typically worked on several projects at a time. Thus his last book, *The New Leviathan*, was twenty years in the making, while the posthumous *The Idea of History* was largely written in 1936, but was based on a series of lectures originally given in 1926, and subsequently revised over the following decade, while Collingwood was also at work on *An Essay on Philosophical Method*. With the exception of *The Idea of History* we shall follow the order of publication; thus we begin with his earliest works and progress through philosophical method, history, art, logic, and metaphysics, to conclude with Collingwood's social and political philosophy.

Further Reading

Fred Inglis, *History Man: The Life of R.G. Collingwood*.
David Boucher and Andrew Vincent, *British Idealism: A Guide for the Perplexed*.
Peter Johnson, *R.G. Collingwood: An Introduction*, Chapter One.

2

Early Works

In this chapter we shall look at Collingwood's first two books, *Religion and Philosophy* and *Speculum Mentis*. The contours of Collingwood's mature philosophy take shape only in the latter of these, but the former can be usefully regarded as a kind of preface, presaging several individual themes that were to occupy a central position in Collingwood's later thought.

1. *Religion and Philosophy*

It was Collingwood's view that all intellectual activity has for its object one and the same thing, namely, the totality of historical fact. This view led him, in his earliest book *Religion and Philosophy* (1916), to regard religion, theology, science, history, and philosophy as essentially identical, and to dismiss the boundary lines ordinarily drawn between them as due to simple misconceptions of the inquiry or experience under consideration. Later, this view was to undergo considerable modifications: The conviction that the object of all inquiry is one and the same was never surrendered, but Collingwood came to see that the form and manner in which the mind knows its object is subject to significant variation. This new conception was given a comprehensive statement in Collingwood's second book, *Speculum Mentis* (1924), wherein art, religion, science, history, and philosophy are arranged in a hierarchy, wherein each higher stage renders explicit what was only implicitly known on the stage below. This implies that philosophy, rather than revealing something novel and hitherto unknown, renders more truly known that which in a sense we knew already. In Collingwood's later works, especially in *An Essay on Philosophical Method* (1933) and *An Essay on Metaphysics* (1940), the attempt is made to render this conception more precise by replacing the distinction between form and content with the distinction between forms of judgment, or proposition.

Religion and Philosophy was Collingwood's first book, written, we are told (A, 93), with the purpose of refuting the psychological approach to the study of religion, as represented, for example, by William James in *The Varieties of Religious Experience* (RP, 131 n), although James is mentioned only once, and not for the purpose of refutation. As against psychologism Collingwood proposes a natural religion approach, attempting to treat Christianity as "a critical solution of a philosophical problem" (RP, xiii). The details need not concern us here, although this critique foreshadows Collingwood's frequently repeated insistence, in later works, that psychology is not properly a science of the mind, but only of feeling (A, 92–5, EM, 112–21). But in the course of deriving the truths of revelation from philosophical premises, Collingwood covers a number of philosophical topics of interest for understanding his later work. Specifically, I wish to draw attention to his discussions of the relationship between thought and action, the relationship between philosophy and history, and the nature of reference.

a. Thought and Action

"Thought" and "will," Collingwood argues, are not the names of mental entities, but are predicative expressions, qualifying actions. Thinking and willing are not things we do with our thought and will, in the sense that we walk with our legs. We always think or will something definite; what we will is always an action, for instance walking. Willing and walking are then not two different operations, one mental and one physical, but are one and the same, namely the act of walking freely performed. Thinking is not something over and above this action; in thinking we are conscious of what we will, that is, of what we do; the consciousness of walking is nothing different from the act of walking consciously performed. Thought and will, therefore, consist simply in the free and conscious execution of actions. In this sense, "the mind *is* what it *does*" (RP, 34); not in the sense that there are specifically "mental" actions, but in the sense that all actions involve presence of mind in so far as they are freely and consciously performed.

When I am conscious of walking, we might say that walking is the object of my consciousness, but this is not to imply that there are here two distinct entities, consciousness as a subject and walking as an object; there is only the conscious activity of walking. The same relation, Collingwood argues, holds for all cases where we speak of a "subject" and an "object"; there is really only the conscious activity, which is differently referred to as the consciousness of an object or as the object of consciousness. Thinking is always thinking of a definite object, and an object is always an object of thought. "All consciousness is the consciousness of something definite, the thought of this thing or that thing; there is no thought in general but only particular thoughts about particular things. The *esse* of the mind is not *cogitare* simply, but *de hac re cogitare*" (RP, 100). The object of a thought is not an "idea," in the sense of an image or likeness of the real thing; the object of a thought *is* that thing, in so far as it is thought of: "My thought of the table is certainly not something 'like' the table; it is the table as I know it" (RP, 101). The mind and its object are one and the same.

There is an interesting parallel here to Charles Peirce's description of the mind, in 1868, with the Shakespearean phrase "his glassy essence," meaning you can look *at* the mind only by looking *through* it.[1] But although Collingwood was obviously familiar with the work of Peirce's friend James, I know of no evidence that he was familiar with Peirce's writings.

In communication, Collingwood notes, two people share the same piece of knowledge, not similar pieces of knowledge but the same piece. But if, in consciousness, the mind is its object, does it not follow that two minds, when conscious of the same object, are one and the same? It does, Collingwood affirms. If two people are conscious of the same object, they have the same knowledge, and thus to that extent share the same mind (RP, 101). Collingwood is not here denying the uniqueness of the individual. Each of us participates in a variety of knowledge situations and a variety of practical projects, and the totality of these constitutes my uniqueness as an individual. But I do not know alone, and I do not will alone:

> Man does not struggle with either his intellectual or his moral problems in solitude. He receives each alike from his environment, and in solving them he is doing other people's work as well as his own. (RP, 103)

Collingwood is here broaching an idea that was to become prominent in his later thought. Historical knowledge, he was to argue, is possible because and to the extent that the historian is able to re-enact the thought of the historical agent. By "re-enactment" is meant thinking the agent's thought, not one like it but the very same thought.[2] This influential and controversial doctrine will be examined in Chapter 4.

The mind and its object are the same; but what are we to say when two people perceive the same object differently or place incompatible constructions on one and the same fact? The distinction between fact and construction is, according to Collingwood, false. When we speak of two people placing different constructions on the same fact, what we mean is that at least one of them is in error as to what that fact is. To the extent that he is in error, he does not know the fact which is known to the other; this is different from saying that they know the same fact but construe it differently. The difference between the two constructions is the difference between the fact and something erroneously believed to be a fact.

We shall only note in passing the problem raised for the theory of error: If, in knowledge, the mind is identical with its object, what is the mind identical with when in error? The important point which Collingwood is making is this: The mind cannot be studied in abstraction from its activity of knowing; this activity, in turn, cannot be studied in abstraction from the objects known. What precisely is it that is being denied? In the context of *Religion and Philosophy*, this discussion has an obvious polemical edge against the psychology of religion, that is, against the attempt to study the religious consciousness without raising such questions as whether or not God exists. Since God is the object of the religious consciousness, God must also be the object of any study of that consciousness.

But the implications are more far-reaching. What is denied, in the special case of religion, is the possibility of separating the first-order study of facts and the second-order study of consciousness. The second-order study must include within it the first-order study, or it cannot be pursued at all. In *Religion and Philosophy*, as we shall see shortly, this argument is extended to the field of historical knowledge, but it is not developed in its full generality until *Speculum Mentis*. It is argued in the latter work that each activity of the mind necessarily involves giving an account of that activity. If that account is a true one, it is not something additional to the activity accounted for; it is an integral element of that activity, and it is subject to progressive change, as the activity itself changes. But the mind can also give itself a false account of its activity, and it can reinforce its error by posing a distinction between the mind and its concrete activities, purporting to give an account of the former but not of the latter. It will thereby become immune to correction by what takes place on the level of concrete activity, that is, on the level of facts. This is how philosophy may deteriorate from genuine reflection on experience to dogmatic apriorism. In each particular form of activity, the reflection to which the activity gives rise may produce its own particular dogmatism:

> [I]n all these dogmatisms there is a distinction between the direct form of consciousness (art, religion &c.) and the reflective form (aestheticism, theism &c.), and this appears as the distinction between direct or primary experience, as the apprehension of the object and reflective or secondary experience, as the return of the mind upon itself to study its own primary experience. Such a distinction between primary and secondary experience is the infallible mark of dogmatism in all its varieties. (SM, 255)

To avoid misunderstanding, what is being denied here is not the distinction between first-order and second-order thinking per se, a distinction which Collingwood was to make extensive use of in his later work. What is denied is that the second-order thinking can be completely abstracted from the first-order thinking; on the contrary it must include the first-order thinking within itself. To give an example, aesthetics may be regarded as first-order thinking about art. In the philosophy of art we may raise and consider various questions about aesthetics: What questions should aesthetics raise? What is the purpose of aesthetics? Who are its audience? Who is qualified to pursue aesthetics? To tackle such questions is second-order thinking about first-order thinking about art. Collingwood's point is that such questions cannot be fruitfully pursued or satisfactorily answered unless one *also* thinks about Shakespeare or Eliot, Turner or Cézanne, Mozart or Beethoven, and so on. Thinking about thinking about art must at the same time be thinking about art.

Immediately, Collingwood is here polemicizing against the Oxford Realists, the school of Cook Wilson, Prichard, and Joseph. That school is not of any great intrinsic interest, but it should be noted that Prichard in particular set the tone for a great deal of twentieth-century ethical theory by arguing that moral philosophy should not be concerned with prescribing value judgments or decisions. What is or is not the moral thing to do can be discovered only on the level of direct, immediate experience; the task of moral philosophy is merely to elucidate what goes into this experience.[3] Prichard thus counts as one of the founders of the school of ethical intuitionism, in which he was preceded by G. E. Moore and followed by W. D. Ross as outstanding representatives. Later, linguistic philosophy—conceived as a strictly second-order study of how we speak about, say, rights, or truth, or other minds—is so far the heir to the Realism which Collingwood was concerned to combat.

But secondly, something of wider importance is at issue; Collingwood is not merely opposing a particular school, but is opposing the entire movement which may, in the broadest sense, be called "analytical" as opposed to "speculative." This movement is restricted neither to Oxford, nor to the British Isles. It was exemplified in the abandonment of ethics as a normative science for ethics as the elucidation of moral concepts and judgments—an abandonment which has fortunately been reversed since the 1972 appearance of John Rawls's *A Theory of Justice*. It is exemplified also in the substitution of "philosophy of science" for "natural philosophy" and of "analytical" for "speculative" philosophy of history.

b. Philosophy and History

The philosophy of history was until the mid-nineteenth century understood chiefly as the philosophical reflection on historical events, the reflection on history as res gestae. When this conception was challenged by a succession of thinkers, most notable of whom were Wilhelm Dilthey in Germany, F. H. Bradley in England, and Benedetto Croce in Italy, their challenge was due not so much to a dissatisfaction with traditional philosophy as to certain concerns arising outside philosophy. Among the many conspicuous cultural events of the nineteenth century was the rise of historical-critical scholarship as a cultural movement, challenging traditional beliefs and values, especially in the realm of religion. Analytical philosophy of history, the reflection on *historia rerum gestarum*, emerged in part as the demand that the critical historians exhibit their own credentials before proceeding to the task of iconoclasm. The dilemma of analytical philosophy of history emerges most clearly in the work of Croce. According to the later Collingwood, Croce unequivocally rejected the conception of philosophy of history as a reflection on the course of history; such reflection, he maintained, is either the business of historians or something wrongly believed to be the business of historians. What is left for the philosopher is reflection on the activity of historians, but this too, Croce argued, is nothing additional to historical research, but is an element in it. Croce concluded that there is no autonomous realm for philosophy; philosophy must as a whole be incorporated into history as its "methodological moment" (IH, 201).

In *Religion and Philosophy*, without explicitly mentioning Croce, Collingwood largely accepts Croce's premises, but is unable to accept the philosophical skepticism implied by the conclusion. There are two ways, Collingwood suggests, of understanding history. History conceived as merely the external chronicle of events cannot impugn or throw doubt on the conclusions of speculative thought, because it abstains from raising the questions to which these conclusions are answers. On the other hand, history conceived· as the attempt to understand past events by rendering them meaningful to the present cannot, properly speaking, absorb philosophy, since it is itself conditional upon philosophical presuppositions. In either case, history cannot absorb or replace philosophy as speculative thought.

Having guarded himself against the philosophical skepticism of Crocean historicism, Collingwood turns volte-face and attacks the contrary, anti-historicist position. Two versions of the position are considered: It may be held *either* that speculative thought cannot be based upon historical facts, because the latter are themselves too insecurely ascertained, *or* that historical and philosophical truths are truths of different orders, so that each is irrelevant to the other. The former argument fails on the same grounds as all varieties of skepticism; it is a "fantastic and hypercritical position," which ends up refuting itself (RP, 44). If no historical evidence can justify philosophical inferences, neither can the evidence of memory justify the inference by which the skeptical position is itself reached: "whether the facts are two thousand years or two minutes distant in time makes no real difference" (RP, 45).

The second argument is given more serious consideration. The argument may be taken two ways. It may be taken to imply merely that, once you recognize a premise as purely historical and untainted by philosophy, you cannot proceed to draw a philosophical conclusion. In this sense the argument, though true, is a tautology: All it says is that "you cannot extract from an argument more than its premises contain" (RP, 45). The problem of how to identify a purely historical premise or a purely philosophical conclusion is left untouched. (Collingwood does not seem to notice that the argument so dismissed is the very same one which he himself has just advanced against historicism.)

But the anti-historicist argument may be taken in a different sense:

> It may, secondly, be interpreted to mean that when we cite instances in support of philosophical views the philosophical conclusion depends not on the historical fact but on the "construction," as it is called, which we put upon the fact. We look at the fact in the light of an idea; and the philosophical theory which we described as proved by the fact is due not to the fact but to the idea we have read into it. (RP, 45–6)

For instance, of two persons, one may believe in the theory of human selfishness, and the other in altruism; they may both observe a third person perform a certain action, and each may construe the action as a confirming instance of his or her own theory. Should we not then say that the fact of the action itself, as distinct from the two different constructions placed on it, is irrelevant to the truth or falsity of either theory? Far from it, Collingwood insists: Of the two persons, the egoist and the altruist, one is right and the other is in error, and which is which depends on the fact and not in the least on the construction placed on it by either. The difference between the two constructions is simply the difference between a historical fact and a historical error.

> Thus the distinction between fact and the construction put upon it is false; what we call construction is merely our attempt to determine further details about the fact. And since the question of whether C was acting selfishly or not is a question of historical fact, the doctrine that people act in general selfishly or altruistically is based entirely on historical fact, or on something erroneously imagined to be historical fact. The attempt to dissociate philosophy and history breaks down because, in point of fact, we never do so dissociate them. One simply cannot make general statements without any thought of their instances. (RP, 46)

The last sentence strikingly anticipates a central doctrine of *An Essay on Philosophical Method*, namely the doctrine that philosophical judgments are essentially categorical. That is to say, philosophical judgments, though universal, are assertions of facts and stand under the test of facts. The point of this doctrine is to cut across the a priori-empirical dichotomy; the same thing is intended in *Religion and Philosophy*.

c. Religion and Theology

It might be thought, Collingwood suggests, that the task of theology is merely to determine the nature of God, for which purpose it may assume God's existence, as physics assumes the existence of matter and proceeds to determine its nature. But this, he argues, will not do, for two reasons. First, the physicist makes no general assumption concerning the existence of matter; she defines matter in a determinate manner and then goes on to inquire whether this definition is instantiated, whether, that is, this particular kind of matter exists. Secondly, when it is said, wrongly, that physics assumes the existence of matter, the kernel of truth in this statement is that the existence of matter in general is a metaphysical question, which physics may legitimately excuse itself from raising. This vitiates the analogy between physics and theology. The questions raised by theology are no less ultimate than those raised by metaphysics—they are, according to Collingwood, one and the same—so theology cannot be excused from raising and answering metaphysical questions. Theology, then, is obliged to provide a proof of the existence of God; what should such a proof look like? Collingwood's answer is that proving the existence of God is nothing different from determining God's nature; if a statement to the effect that God has such-and-such a nature is true, it is eo ipso true that God exists: "To distinguish between the question, 'What do I mean by God?' and the question, 'Does God exist, and if so what is he like?' is impossible, for the two questions are one and the same" (RP, 62).

The point that is being made here is that the serious employment of a referring expression, such as "God," in a subject-predicate statement presupposes the belief that the referring expression is instantiated. If I believe God to have such-and-such a nature, this belief necessarily presupposes my belief in God's existence. In that case I shall be satisfied of God's existence to the extent that I am satisfied of what is God's nature. This position is certainly defensible, so long as "God" is the subject-expression whose instantiation is in question. A familiar problem with atheism is that atheists are notoriously unsuccessful in explaining exactly what it is that they claim does not exist. But Collingwood goes on, secondly, to make the quite different point that assigning a meaning to *any* referring expression presupposes that the thing referred to actually exists. This is a far more doubtful position and especially telling is Collingwood's chosen example of the dragon which, it is asserted, exists in Fairyland. But

Collingwood does not avoid attaching a perfectly definite meaning to the word "dragon," and he is not using the word in a fairy-tale context. To that extent, Collingwood succeeds in actually exemplifying precisely what he is concerned to deny—namely that we can employ quite meaningful referring expressions without presupposing that the thing referred to exists.

Despite these reservations, I believe Collingwood is making one very important and perfectly correct point—namely, that there are special subject-expressions which are of such a kind that we cannot seriously employ them without making the presupposition that they are instantiated. "God" is a case in point, although, as Collingwood was to make clear in his later works, the existence of any particular God does not thereby follow. (As Descartes already noted, "I" is another. I might not exist, but in that case I would not be able to use the pronoun "I.") In the special case of such expressions, there can be no difference between asserting the existence of the reference and asserting certain propositions in which the expression occurs as subject. This claim will not be pursued now, but will be argued in our discussion of *An Essay on Philosophical Method*, where Collingwood makes this argument with greater caution and clarity.

As Collingwood was to note later, in a footnote in *Speculum Mentis*, his earlier book failed to recognize the distinction between explicit and implicit knowledge and thus led him into an excessively intellectualistic or abstract attitude toward religion (SM, 108 n). In private notes from about 1918 Collingwood dismisses *Religion and Philosophy* as an example of "New Realism" and pronounces himself ready to "repudiate the whole thing" (EPM, Editors' Introduction, xxii–xxiii). And we know, from Collingwood's *Autobiography*, that his disenchantment with Realism took place *after* the publication of *Religion and Philosophy* (A, 29 ff).

On the other hand, in the above-cited footnote about *Religion and Philosophy*, Collingwood also notes: "With much of what that book contains I am still in agreement" (SM, 108 n). Also, we have noted that *Religion and Philosophy* announced: (i) the thought-action unity, (ii) the unity of two minds knowing the same object, (iii) the dogmatism inherent in purely second-order thought, (iv) the rejection of the analytic-empirical dichotomy—all of them prominent themes in Collingwood's later thought.

Lacking in *Religion and Philosophy* was a dialectical method. For that, we turn to Collingwood's first truly mature work, *Speculum Mentis*.

Lionel Rubinoff has described the relationship between the two books by saying that *Speculum Mentis* makes explicit the truth that was implicit in *Religion and Philosophy*'s explicit error:

> Thus *Speculum Mentis* is not simply a repudiation of *Religion and Philosophy*; it is also an attempt to supply the conceptual framework from which the explicit aim of *Religion and Philosophy* may be finally realized. In short, *Religion and Philosophy* is not simply negated but is rather superseded by *Speculum Mentis*.[4]

2. *Speculum Mentis, or The Map of Knowledge*

A far more ambitious work than *Religion and Philosophy*, *Speculum Mentis*— "The Mirror of the Mind"—is a kind of phenomenology or, in Collingwood's words, "a critical review of the chief forms of human experience" (SM, 9); in this book, five forms of human experience are reviewed, and it is shown, in each case, how the form of experience in question breaks down under the tension between its implicit and explicit aspirations. This tension can be rationally resolved only by making the transition to a new form of experience, which renders explicit the implicit aspirations of the former. So we view the mind passing through the successive stages of art, religion, science, history, and philosophy, until philosophy finally is reabsorbed into each concrete form of experience as its self-consciousness. As David Boucher has noted, these five forms of experience had already been singled out by the Italian Idealist Giovanni Gentile, to whom Collingwood was in many respects indebted, but Boucher also notes that Collingwood gave these forms of experience his own original treatment.[5]

Collingwood's point of departure in *Speculum Mentis* is the dilemma posed by the fragmentation of Western culture in the wake of the Renaissance and Enlightenment disassembly of the Christian culture of the Middle Ages. In the Middle Ages the roles of individuals were defined by institutions, above all the church. Their roles were thereby also limited, and there were severe penalties from breaking out of those limits, but for ordinary men and women the institutions conferred a sense of belonging, as well as of wholeness as human beings (SM, 23–4). And this wholeness was mirrored in the wholeness of the culture; there was no such thing as church architecture, religious art, religious poetry, or religious philosophy; architecture, art, poetry, and philosophy were all pursued in service to religion. This wholeness was broken up by the Renaissance and Enlightenment, which by degrees fragmented our culture and thereby fragmented us as human beings:

> Today we can be as artistic, we can be as philosophical, we can be as religious as we please, but we cannot ever be men at all; we are wrecks and fragments of men, and we do not know where to take hold of life and how to begin looking for the happiness which we know we do not possess. (SM, 35)

We clearly recognize here Max Weber's "disenchantment" and Emile Durkheim's "anomie." The solution, Collingwood holds, does not consist in turning back to the medieval way of life; the Renaissance had to happen and would only happen again if we were to succeed in recreating the medieval world: "If we went back to the middle ages, we should only return to childhood, and the throes of adolescence would still be to come" (SM, 36). It is imperative, rather, to work our way through adolescence to full adulthood. And a first step, Collingwood proposes, is to construct a map of knowledge, which is defined as follows:

> It is to be a statement of the essential nature or structure of each successive form of experience, based on actual knowledge of that form from within, and concentrated upon the search for inconsistencies, rifts which when we put a strain on the fabric will widen and deepen and ultimately destroy it. (SM, 46)

As an aside, we note that we here see an early adumbration of Collingwood's later account of presuppositional change, fully articulated in 1940, as we shall see in Chapter 7. For now, we turn to Collingwood's review of the successive forms of experience.

The progression is this: Art is a form of questioning, which requires religion for its answer. But the answer is in various ways incoherent; the attempt at rendering it coherent produces a new question, in the form of science, the answer to which is found in history; this answer in its turn is incoherent; what it tries to say can actually only be said by philosophy. The special problems of philosophy, forcing its reabsorption into concrete experience, offer complications which would lead us far afield from the present inquiry.

What is of special interest in *Speculum Mentis* for our overall understanding of Collingwood's philosophy is, first, the explicitly *dialectical* method, in the Hegelian sense of the term. Briefly, thought evolves through later stages denying or negating earlier stages, but the negation is never simple. The later stage contains within it the earlier stage as that which is being denied and can only be understood as containing it. For instance, within Christendom, atheism can only be understood as the repudiation of the Christian God; nineteenth-century democratic movements can only be understood as the repudiation of absolute monarchy and so on. The dialectical method is spelled out in detail in *An Essay on Philosophical Method*, but it is *practiced* throughout *Speculum Mentis*.

Secondly, what is of special interest in this work is its analysis of knowledge as a process of questions and answers, rather than as a body of propositions. This analysis is found in Collingwood's discussions of art and science as the specifically questioning activities of the mind. Their common denominator is their explicit pretension to abstain from categorical assertion; they are both, presumably, thought content held in suspension of judgment, that is, supposal or hypothesis.

a. Art

In his characterization of art, Collingwood takes as his point of departure Croce's theory of art as pure imagination, or thought content without an object:

> The aesthetic experience cares nothing for the reality or unreality of its object. It is neither true nor false of set purpose: it simply ignores the distinction. There is no such thing as the so-called artistic illusion, for illusion means believing in the reality of that which is unreal, and art does not believe in the reality of anything at all. Its assertions are not real assertions but the very suspension of assertion; ... (SM, 60)

So far, Collingwood is merely following Croce. Croce was quite right, Collingwood holds, in characterizing the explicit pretensions of art, but he made the error of construing this attitude as self-contained and self-sufficient, thereby precluding any explanation of how anything different from art can ever arise out of art:

> Once the mind has succeeded in attaining a condition in which it neither asserts nor denies but only represents objects to itself intuitively or imaginatively, there is no reason why it should ever pass out of this

condition. The ability to assert or deny is an ability which it could never acquire. (SM, 76)

But, in fact, Collingwood holds, art does give rise to religion; in religion, the mind asserts the reality of the object of imagination which in art is merely contemplated; art is therefore both logically and temporally prior to religion. Art thus is *explicitly* pure imagination; *implicitly*, it is assertion. In so far as there is such a thing as religion, it can have come into being only by a transformation of the artistic attitude. This transformation, Collingwood argues, comes about through the attempt to resolve a certain inconsistency inherent in the artistic experience, an inconsistency inherent in the very attitude of supposal.

Supposal purports to be merely the suspension of assertion; but, in fact, supposal is only one moment of a thought-complex the outcome of which is assertion:

> The fact is that imagination never exists *in vacuo*, and therefore the problem of how it is to escape from its vacuum is an unreal problem, and insoluble because it is unreal. Supposal and assertion are not two independent chapters in the history of the mind; they are two opposite and correlative activities which form as it were the systole and diastole of knowledge itself. (SM, 77)

The concrete union of the two is found in the act of questioning, of which they form the two opposite moments. Collingwood's analysis of questioning is approached first from the perspective of assertion. In the process of acquiring knowledge we never make a "bare assertion"; our assertions are always answers to questions:

> A crude empiricism imagines that knowledge is composed wholly of assertion: that to know and to assert are identical. But it is only when the knower looks back over his shoulder at the road he has travelled, that he identifies knowledge with assertion. (SM, 77)

This is the error allegedly made by empiricist and realist philosophers who, having no firsthand acquaintance with research, identify knowledge with its corpse, as it lies buried in textbooks and encyclopedias.

The analysis is, secondly, approached from the perspective of the question. Assertion always issues from a question; it is therefore already present in the question, though not *as* assertion. The thought-content of the assertion is present, though it is not yet held to have a real object. Questioning, therefore, is assertion held in suspension, in other words, it is supposal. Genuine questioning looks forward to an answer, that is, an assertion. This is where art diverges from genuine questioning:

> In art, on the other hand, the suspending of assertion seems to be an end in itself, and does not look forward to its own negation, the renewal of assertion. Art, as pure imagination, may be paradoxically defined as a question which expects no answer: that is, a supposal. (SM, 78–9)

In this sense, art is a philosophical error, consisting in the abstraction of the moment of supposal from the act of questioning, to which it belongs. In general, mere supposal and mere assertion are opposite philosophical errors, both ignoring the organic unity of supposal and assertion in the act of questioning. These errors are either overcome by the critical self-consciousness of their implications, or they are reinforced and ossified by the dogmatic affirmation of their explicit content. In the latter case, we get the dogmatic affirmation of supposal in aesthetic and scientific philosophy or the dogmatic affirmation of assertion in religious and historical philosophy. These dogmatisms can be avoided only by the recognition that art and science are the questions to which religion and history, respectively, are the answers.

In conclusion, art fails because it is of the essence of truth that it be made explicit and subjected to discussion and criticism, but art explicitly only imagines, while it falls to religion to make explicit assertions (SM, 109).

Having examined the case of art in some detail, we can deal with the other forms of consciousness more briefly.

b. Religion

Religion, already in its primitive forms, asserts the reality of the objects of imagination. With the growth of religion the assertive element, which is at its center, gives birth to the community of believers, that is, the church:

> If a number of minds are engaged in imagining, they have no common ground, for each man's imaginations are his own. But if they are engaged in asserting, they at once become a society, for each asserts what he believes to be not his own but common property, objective reality. (SM, 116)

I cannot forbear to point out, albeit as an aside, that these words almost eerily echo Charles Peirce's earlier definition of reality:

> The real, then, is that which, sooner or later, information and reasoning would finally result in, and which is therefore independent of the vagaries of me and you. Thus, the very origin of the conception of reality shows that this conception essentially involves the notion of a COMMUNITY, without definite limits, and capable of a definite increase of knowledge.[6]

Religion retains many of the elements of art, such as images and rituals, but these are now asserted as real. In fact, the images, rituals, and formulas of religion are *symbols*, but religion systematically mistakes them for their meaning. Thus, religion commits the believer to statements that are literally untrue, as when, in the Eucharist, one says that the bread is the body of Christ, or when we say that God is our heavenly father. Of course the bread is not anybody's body, God is not literally a father, and certainly does not reside up in the sky. And yet these statements symbolize a meaning that *may* be true, but the distinction between the symbol and the meaning is hidden from religion and becomes explicit only in science (SM, 121–3).

In failing to distinguish between symbol and meaning, religion becomes embroiled in a self-contradiction. Because the believer is committed to the truth of statements that are literally false, the believer has to withdraw from discussion and criticism, leaving that aspect to theology, while taking refuge in faith. But this is self-contradictory, because to claim the truth of anything is to claim that it will withstand criticism: "Rational truth—and all truth is rational—is essentially that which can justify itself under criticism and in discussion" (SM, 131). Ultimately, by taking its language literally instead of metaphorically, religion lands itself in this self-contradictory position (SM, 153).

c. Science

Collingwood goes on to apply his analysis of supposal and assertion to a critique of the prevalent philosophies of science of his day. Put very briefly, the critique is this. Explicitly, modern science understands itself as merely hypothetical; it confines itself to making assumptions and drawing out their implications, without attempting to make any categorical statements as to how things in the world actually are. The explicit self-understanding of modern science, to which Collingwood is referring, includes a diversity of highly influential philosophical and intellectual movements, such as the fictionalism of Vaihinger, the hypothetico-deductivism of Poincaré and Duhem, and the positivism of Mach, Schlick, and their successors, among whom rank some of the founders of quantum physics, such as Bohr and Heisenberg. Against all these heroes of modern science, Collingwood points out that there is one thing they have overlooked—namely, that if science depends entirely on the making of assumptions, then the categorical assertion of what assumptions have actually been made cannot be indifferent to science. The whole venture of science, as an activity of making and following out assumptions, depends, in the last resort, on a basis of historical fact. This conclusion is, of course, highly controversial, but we can on this occasion bypass the controversy, as nothing of major import in Collingwood's philosophy depends upon it being resolved in his favor.

Science fails, then, by explicitly asserting abstractness, whereas implicitly it rests on concrete individual facts. The latter are the province of history.

d. History

History offers us the concreteness that science failed to deliver. In history, we confront the concrete fact, something which we did not find in art, religion, or science. However, individual facts turn out to be abstractions and thus chimera. What is concrete is reality in its completeness, and it can be known only in its completeness. We understand each individual fact only by understanding its relations to other facts. These other parts must be understood in their relations to yet other facts and so on. So, no part of reality can be truly known in isolation from *all* the other parts. But we cannot grasp the totality of facts in an instant, in a single cognition; our historical knowledge has to be built up piecemeal, fact by fact. This poses a dilemma: since we can only study history by studying its parts, and we cannot understand the parts without knowing the whole, history turns out to be unknowable:

> If universal history is an absolute and perfectly-organized individual whole, such that every part in it determines every other part, there is no escape from the conclusion that ignorance or error concerning any one part involves an essential and radical ignorance or error concerning every other. (SM, 232)

And yet we obviously do know historical facts. How to resolve the dilemma? One—apparently commonsensical—answer would be that we can, and in fact do, understand individual historical facts in isolation. But a fact isolated from the other facts that it relates to has lost its concreteness, which consists in just those relations to other facts. Such a study of isolated facts is a study of abstractions, which brings us back to the province of science, with its problems (SM, 233).

The object of history, the totality of facts, thus appears to be something that cannot *become* known; either it is known at the outset, or it is unknowable. Collingwood's solution is that we escape the dilemma if there is an object that is changed by being known, so that what we know in the end is not the same thing that we were previously ignorant of. Now such an object is the human mind: "The world of facts which is explicitly studied in history is therefore implicitly nothing but the knowing mind as such" (SM, 245). So history is implicitly philosophy: we can study the world of facts only by studying the knowing mind.

e. Philosophy

Collingwood now appears to have arrived at a dangerous position, where philosophy is the supreme form of knowledge, supplanting art, religion, science, and history. An apparently arrogant and hubristic position, as well as one poorly befitting a proficient artist, an accomplished historian, and an observant Christian, all of which Collingwood was. It is also a position that was belied by Collingwood's announcement, early in the book, that there can be no impartial judge of the various forms of experience (SM, 43). But recall Collingwood's rejection of the distinction between first-order and second-order study. The remainder of *Speculum Mentis* is devoted to analyzing and rejecting aesthetic philosophies, philosophies of religion, science, or history, which are based on such a distinction. To recall, the "distinction between primary and secondary experience is the infallible mark of dogmatism in all its varieties" (SM, 255). So, philosophy cannot be the second-order study of other forms of thought; it can study these forms of thought only by *being* these forms of thought. The philosopher can study art, religion, science, and history only by being an artist, a religious thinker, a scientist, or an historian. These forms of knowledge are not to be rejected or abandoned, but to avoid error

2. Speculum Mentis, or The Map of Knowledge

they need to be self-consciously pursued. So, in the end, there can be no map of knowledge; to be true to its object, the map would have to be knowledge itself (SM, 309).

Speculum Mentis is reminiscent of—and fairly clearly inspired by—Hegel's famous *Phenomenology of Mind*. In the end, however, Collingwood's book is a reductio: what Hegel attempted, however noble the effort, simply cannot be done. This may leave philosophy itself in a limbo, as argued by Louis Mink: "The great climax of the drama of development turns out to be nothing but the playwright stepping in front of the closed curtain to remind the audience of what it already has seen."[7] Yet something has been accomplished: The wholeness of culture, and thereby of us as individuals, toward which modernity is striving can be accomplished, and can only be accomplished, through the increased self-awareness of each form of experience, an awareness in which each form recognizes, and thus transcends, its separateness from our culture as a whole.

What is the place of *Speculum Mentis* in Collingwood's oeuvre? In *An Autobiography* in 1938 he referred to it as "a bad book in many ways," but then he re-read it for the first time since it was published and found it much better than he had remembered. Specifically, he noted in a footnote, there was "not a great deal that needs to be retracted" (A, 56 and n).

Lionel Rubinoff has proposed that *Speculum Mentis* sets forth Collingwood's overall philosophical system—the ramifications of which were worked out through the remainder of his career.[8] In support of this claim Rubinoff mentions that *Speculum Mentis* was Collingwood's first book after the First World War, which is when Collingwood, as per his *Autobiography*, recognized the need for a new orientation in philosophy. Primarily, though, the interpretation rests on Rubinoff's finding, in *Speculum Mentis*, the idea of a "scale of forms," implicit in this work, but later made explicit in *An Essay on Philosophical Method* and central to Collingwood's thought going forward. By this is meant a hierarchical progression of thought, from lower to higher, where each higher step contains within it the lower step as that which the new step denies. This idea, to which we will return in the next chapter, is not made explicit in *Speculum Mentis*, but it is certainly reasonable to see the above progression of thought forms as exemplifying a scale of forms, wherein religion contains pure imagination as that which it denies, and so forth up the ladder. Collingwood himself references a "dialectical series," "a series of terms, each one of which is an erroneous description of the next" (SM, 206). Also, the editors of the New Edition of *An*

Essay on Philosophical Method have pointed out that the concept of a scale of forms was explicitly introduced by Collingwood in lectures in 1923, even if the name did not appear in *Speculum Mentis* (EPM, Editors' Introduction, xxv).

Louis Mink describes *Speculum Mentis* as "in certain ways the most illuminating of [Collingwood's] books."[9] Jan van der Dussen describes it as "the best worked out and the most important of Collingwood's philosophical books," while taking exception to Rubinoff's claim that it represents a "master plan" for his subsequent works. Collingwood's mind, he holds, was too versatile to conform to any such plan.[10] In the same vein James Connelly, while largely sympathetic toward Rubinoff, concludes that he "ends up by attempting to prove too much."[11]

Religion and Philosophy challenged the distinction between purely first-order and second-order inquiry—a central theme in Collingwood's thought throughout his life. It also introduced the idea of the unity of two minds knowing the same thing, an idea central, as we shall see, to Collingwood's later philosophy of history. As Collingwood noted in *Speculum Mentis*, the earlier book failed to recognize the implicit-explicit distinction, which was also to occupy a central place in his thought going forward.

One important idea which is made explicit in *Speculum Mentis*, but developed in detail only in later works is the idea that assertions are always answers to questions (SM, 77). Again, in his *Autobiography*, Collingwood credits this recognition with inspiring his philosophical re-orientation, so its appearance this early is an important clue to the evolution of his thought, a topic to which we will return in Chapter 6.

Further Reading

Louis Mink, *Mind, History, and Dialectic: The Philosophy of R.G. Collingwood*, Chapter Two.

Lionel Rubinoff, *Collingwood and the Reform of Metaphysics: An Essay in the Philosophy of Mind*, Chapters Three and Four.

3

Philosophical Method

Most of Collingwood's works are remarkably accessible—deceptively accessible, it has been suggested.¹ Unfortunately, this cannot be said of *An Essay on Philosophical Method* (1933), and yet an understanding of the central themes of this work is indispensable to an understanding of Collingwood's subsequent works. How highly Collingwood himself thought of it is evidenced in his *Autobiography*, where he described the *Essay* as his "best book in matter; in style I may call it my only book, for it is the only one I have ever had the time to finish as well as I knew how,…" (A, 18). The editors of the New Edition of the *Essay* praise it as "one of the most sustained attempts within the philosophical tradition to articulate a conception of philosophy as a first science and to defend the thesis of the autonomy of philosophy" (EPM, xcvii). The *Essay* is possibly also Collingwood's most difficult book, in spite of—or perhaps because of—its elegant and fluent style, which was to earn it A. J. Ayer's faint praise of being "a contribution to belle-lettres rather than philosophy," a fact also noted by Collingwood's editors (EPM, xxxix).² Bernard Williams, who was otherwise quite sympathetic toward Collingwood and praised his philosophical writing as "unrivalled in its brilliance" in twentieth-century British philosophy, nonetheless dismissed the *Essay* as "mostly a dull and dated book."³ It is my hope that the pages to follow will prove both Ayer and Williams wrong. The problem may be both that the central doctrines of the *Essay* are themselves novel and unfamiliar, and that the medium in which they are presented may appear forbidding to most present-day readers.

The *Essay* is at the outset cast in the form of a proposed revision of the logic found in the textbooks of the day, among which Collingwood cites the logic book of Johnson, but may also intend Cook Wilson's. These books were the last expression of that conception of logic which emerged in the Renaissance, following the decline of medieval formal logic, and which included, besides formal logic, a number of topics more properly belonging to metaphysics, psychology, semantics, or scientific method. When Collingwood proposes his reform of "logic," this must not therefore be understood in terms of the present-day sense of "formal logic"; precisely, how it is to be understood, remains to be determined.

At this stage we may note, as was also noted at the end of Chapter 2, that central to the *Essay* is Collingwood's dialectical account of philosophical concepts in terms of a "scale of forms." Each philosophical concept, according to this account, forms a step in a hierarchical ladder of concepts, in which each higher rung contains the immediately lower rung within it, as that which it denies, so that it summarizes the whole sequence of lower rungs within it. This account will be examined in detail in Section 2 of this chapter, but as it runs as a thread through Collingwood's later thought, it bears highlighting at the outset.

The *Essay* may be conveniently analyzed under five main topics: the scope and method of philosophy in general; the nature of philosophical concepts; the nature of philosophical judgments; philosophical inference; and the role of system in philosophy.

1. Scope and Method

Philosophy, according to Collingwood, does not seek to discover novel facts, but to render more intelligible what in a sense we know already. The discovery of this principle is attributed to Socrates:

> [T]he principle that in a philosophical inquiry what we are trying to do is not to discover something of which until now we have been ignorant, but to know better something which in a sense we knew already; ... the difference itself has been a familiar fact ever since Socrates pointed it out. (EPM, 11)

No specific reference is given; Collingwood may be referring to the Socratic doctrine set forth, for example, in the *Meno*, to the effect that learning is recollection. In the form in which Collingwood states the principle, it is, however, more immediately reminiscent of Aristotle's formulation of his solution to the paradox which Socrates had attempted to solve by the doctrine of recollection, cited by Collingwood:

> I imagine there is nothing to prevent a man in one sense knowing what he is learning, in another not knowing it. The strange thing would be, not if in some sense he knew what he was learning, but if he were to know it in that precise sense and manner in which he was learning it.⁴

What Collingwood is saying is, however, something different from what was held by either Socrates or Aristotle. In the *Meno*, Socrates was giving an account of the a priori nature of mathematical knowledge, while Aristotle, in the *Posterior Analytics*, was concerned to explain how knowledge can be gained through syllogistic inferences, where the conclusion is wholly contained in the premises. Neither held that philosophy is characterized by a peculiar manner of knowing, which is what Collingwood is arguing. Collingwood is aware of the difference and duly notes his departure from Socrates. The latter was right, he argues, in recognizing that both mathematics and philosophy presuppose preexistent knowledge, but wrong in drawing the conclusion that they are simply identical forms of knowledge. This error, Collingwood holds, was corrected by Plato in his distinction between mathematics and dialectic:

> The difference is stated by saying that in mathematics the mind "goes from hypothesis not to a principle but to a conclusion," whereas in dialectic it "goes from hypotheses to a non-hypothetical principle." (EPM, 13)

In mathematics, it is held, the reasoning proceeds in one direction only: from hypotheses to conclusions; in dialectic, on the other hand, the process of reasoning is reversible. The mind can return upon itself and question its own hypotheses:

> In dialectic we not only draw the consequences of our hypotheses, but we recollect that they are only hypotheses; that is, we are free to "cancel the hypothesis," or assume the opposite and see what follows from that. (EPM, 14)

This method Collingwood makes his own. Its significance is this: Philosophy, unlike mathematics, is never merely hypothetical; in philosophy we are not bound to accept whatever conclusions follow from our hypotheses. Philosophical reasoning is a two-way traffic between the hypotheses by which we seek to render experience intelligible and the experience by which we check the accuracy of our hypotheses; by this dual process of reasoning we seek to raise the hypotheses to the level of categorical principles. This notion will be unwrapped in some detail in our consideration of Collingwood's analysis of philosophical judgments. For the moment a possible objection should be considered: Is this process of reasoning not circular, in that the hypothesis is checked by the experience which it has itself conditioned? Philosophy is supposed to render experience more intelligible; the experiential test of a philosophical hypothesis must be the test of experience *as* rendered intelligible by this hypothesis, since it would make little sense to test the hypothesis against an experience which is held to be not fully intelligible. But this appears to beg the question, unless we have an independent standpoint from which to judge of what is more and what is less intelligible. If that standpoint is given only by the hypothesis which is in question, each hypothesis will be self-confirming.

Collingwood's reply to this difficulty is found in his notion of the philosophical scale of forms. To understand that notion, we must review Collingwood's analysis of the philosophical concept.

2. Philosophical Concepts

a. Overview

This analysis takes its point of departure in the traditional classificatory scheme of genus and species, as it is found in the old-fashioned logic books. Collingwood provisionally adopts this scheme, but only for the purpose of subjecting it to thoroughgoing revision. In traditional logic, a concept stands for a genus by denoting a class and including in its intension the common properties shared by all the members of the class; in the same way, the species subdivide the class into mutually exclusive and exhaustive subclasses, the members of each sharing properties not found in the others:

> Thus every individual present in the generic class will be present in one, and only one, of the specific classes, which are thus exclusive in relation to each other and exhaustive in relation to the generic class. (EPM, 28)

For instance, the dog Niki (not Collingwood's example) belongs to the species dog and *therefore* not to the species cat; moreover, she belongs to the class of mammals, *not* that of birds or fishes, to the class of vertebrates, *not* that of mollusks or crustaceans, and finally, to the kingdom of animals, not that of plants. At each level of the hierarchy membership in one class precludes membership in any of the other classes at that level.

Now the trouble is that there are perfectly common and familiar concepts which plainly resist such classification. The concept of art divides into, for example, poetry and music; but these are not mutually exclusive, for a song must be said to belong to both. A single song is one individual, not two; yet it belongs to the two different species of poetry and music. Concepts of this kind, Collingwood holds, are common enough in ordinary discourse, and they are endemic to philosophical discourse. Examples are given from ethics and logic. In ethics, we divide the genus good into the species pleasant, expedient, and right; we do not thereby mean to suggest that an expedient action is necessarily unpleasant, or that a right action is necessarily inexpedient. Similarly, in logic we distinguish between judgment and inference, but an inference is also a judgment, and a judgment for which we have reasoned grounds is also an inference. And so forth. It is not merely that in philosophy we have some recalcitrant concepts; the whole field of philosophy seems to resist classification according to genus and species. Collingwood does not draw the conclusion that this classification is in general faulty, but argues, rather, that it must be subjected to certain modifications before it can be applied to the concepts of philosophy.

Initially, this point is made by saying that philosophical concepts denote overlapping classes. Now philosophers may—and frequently do—try to avoid recognizing this by ignoring mixed cases and studying only pure cases: for example, veridical perception untainted by illusion, or things good in themselves as distinct from relative goodness. This gambit Collingwood labels the fallacy of *precarious margins*: the fallacy of supposing that the overlap is limited in scope and beyond it lies a marginal region uncontaminated by the overlap (EPM, 48). This is precarious because there is no guarantee that the overlap will not infuse the entire region covered by the concept. This fallacy may be avoided by falling into the opposite fallacy of concluding that, since the two concepts have the same extension, they are really one and the same concept. This Collingwood labels the fallacy of *identified coincidents* (EPM, 49). Both fallacies are instances of the fallacy of *false disjunction*: "the principle that when a generic concept is divided into its species there is a corresponding division of its instances into mutually exclusive classes" (EPM, 49). This principle, Collingwood holds, while true in the exact and empirical sciences, is false in philosophy.

The initial claim is subsequently revised: The overlap is not one between the classes denoted, but between the *intensions* of concepts, that is, what the concept *means* rather than the objects it *refers to*. This overlap is not random and haphazard, but exhibits a definite structure, which Collingwood describes as a *scale of forms*. As noted earlier, this scale is a kind of hierarchy of concepts, in which each concept overlaps in a definite manner with the one above and the one below it. The employment of "above" and "below" here may cause some puzzlement. The idea, put in the terminology of genus and species, is this: Each genus is supposed to possess a generic essence— the property that makes it the genus it is—which is differently realized in its various species. The various species exhibit differences in kind, but to the extent that they embody different realizations of the generic essence, they also differ in degree. Hence, the appropriateness of the hierarchical gradation.

But the hierarchy exemplified by the scale of forms can also be understood— and is understood by Collingwood—in a second way: the higher form of the concept is higher by virtue of having developed out of the lower forms. Thus the scale is not just a hierarchy, but also a process of development; more of this below.

This is of course so far highly abstract. One of Collingwood's examples may make this idea a little clearer. Let us assume, as above, that the good is divided into the pleasant, the expedient, and the right. The three clearly differ qualitatively. They exhibit different kinds of good. Collingwood's claim is, in the first place, that they also differ quantitatively: the expedient is better—or *more* good—than the pleasant, and so with the right and the expedient. This is what is meant by saying that the generic essence is realized in varying degrees. This is so far simple enough. But Collingwood also claims, in the second place, that the generic essence is in a sense identical with the specific forms in which it is realized. This means that when we say that the expedient action is better than the pleasant action, or that the right action is better than the expedient action, the relation "better than" expresses not merely a difference in degree of goodness—which is eo ipso a difference in kind between goodness and relative badness—but expresses at the same time a difference in degree of pleasure or expediency. Pleasure, it is held, is attainable only by aiming at expediency, and expediency is attainable only by aiming at the right. This idea forms the crux of the twin notion of the scale of forms and the overlap of intensions. The intension of each term is diffused in specifically different ways up and down the scale:

> Thus each term, which in itself is simply one specific form of goodness, has also a double relation to its neighbours: in comparison with the one below, it is what that professes to be; in comparison with the one above, it professes to be what that one is. (EPM, 87)

If this sounds familiar, it is because it is obviously a further elaboration of the implicit-explicit distinction that was at the heart of *Speculum Mentis*, as seen in the previous chapter.

The above is admittedly a compressed account of Collingwood's analysis of philosophical concepts, but one important conclusion already emerges. The concept of a scale of forms makes it possible to answer the objection, noted earlier, of circularity in Collingwood's account of philosophical method. There is no need of an external standpoint from which to judge the adequacy of a philosophical hypothesis. Each stage of the reasoning process provides a standpoint from which to judge all the preceding ones. Each new hypothesis gives a reinterpretation of experience, thereby creating new data by which to test the hypothesis; but the original data, the uninterpreted experience, is not simply discarded, but is preserved within the new experience, as that which is now denied. In Collingwood's words:

> The overlap consists in this, that the lower is contained in the higher, the higher transcending the lower and adding to it something new, whereas the lower partially coincides with the higher, but differs from it in rejecting the increment. (EPM, 91)

Put concretely, the moral experience of which regularianism—rule ethics—is the theory is different from that of which utilitarianism is the theory. But there is still a continuity between them, as the utilitarian experience is preserved within regularianism as part of the data of which regularianism takes account. From the point of view of regularianism, utilitarianism can be fully understood and refuted, but not vice versa. "Each term in the scale, therefore, sums up the whole scale to that point. Wherever we stand in the scale, we stand at the culmination" (EPM, 89). Thus, as noted, the scale of forms denotes a process, as well as a hierarchy. Historically, regularianism succeeds utilitarianism, and offers the advantage of hindsight, by which the earlier stage can be understood. The point here is that the test of a philosophical hypothesis lies not only in the extent to which it makes sense of the moral experience to which it has itself given rise, which would be circular, but also in the extent to which it succeeds in making sense of its predecessors. Thus, the experiential basis against which philosophical theories are to be tested includes the historical experience of thought.

The scale-of-forms analysis bears an obvious affinity to Hegel's dialectic; Collingwood himself, as we have seen, referred to it in *Speculum Mentis* as "dialectic"; and when the *Essay* was published *The Times Literary Supplement* referred to it as "for all its brevity, one of the finest restatements in British philosophy of a Platonic and Hegelian metaphysic."[5] In a manuscript from 1933, the year the *Essay* appeared, Collingwood credits Bradley with having formulated the scale of forms, and notes that Bradley was in this particular respect indebted to Hegel, while firmly drawing the line at labeling Bradley a Hegelian (EPM, 243–5). It has been noted by both David Boucher's and Collingwood's editors that Benedetto Croce departed from Hegel by holding that only philosophical concepts related by opposition can stand in a dialectical relation, concepts related by mere distinction cannot. Collingwood's view is that the concepts forming a scale of forms are related by both opposition and distinction; thus, his dialectic is a modification of both Croce's and Hegel's (EPM, xxxi).[6]

b. Some Context: Hume's Fork and Russell's Theory of Descriptions

The preceding section is, of course, highly abstract; it will be helpful to raise the question, what exactly is it that Collingwood is denying? For an answer we need to go back to David Hume, who in 1748 concluded his *Enquiry Concerning Human Understanding* with this famous paragraph:

> If we take in our hand any volume; of divinity or school metaphysics, for instance; let us ask, *Does it contain any abstract reasoning concerning quantity or number?* No. *Does it contain any experimental reasoning concerning matter of fact and existence?* No. Commit it then to the flames: for it can contain nothing but sophistry and illusion.[7]

Hume was concerned only with divinity and school metaphysics, but "Hume's Fork," as it has come to be known, was later generalized to all discourse by the Viennese logical empiricists and, to a somewhat lesser degree, by their British counterparts, the early analytic philosophers such as Bertrand Russell, L. Susan

Stebbing, and Gilbert Ryle. If all discourse has to be either exact reasoning, as in logic and mathematics, or else empirically verifiable, that leaves little for philosophy to do, beyond the logical analysis of language.

The twentieth-century version of Hume's Fork may be found in Russell's famous Theory of Descriptions, originally published in 1905. Russell pointed out a number of oddities, including the asymmetry between the propositions "The present King of England is bald"—when Russell wrote this, there was a King of England—and "The present King of France is bald." If the first of these propositions is false, then "The present King of England is not bald" is true. But if the second proposition is false, as in fact it is, it does not follow that "The present King of France is not bald" is true. This proposition is actually also false because there is no present King of France! Russell's solution is that the similar grammatical form of the two sentences conceals a different logical form. Specifically, and somewhat simplified, "The present King of France is bald" can be rewritten:

i. There is an entity which is now King of France and is bald.

Whereas "The present King of France is not bald" can be rewritten:

ii. There is an entity which is now King of France and is not bald.[8]

"The present King of France," while grammatically the subject of the statements, is logically a predicate, and in the above paraphrases can be seen to be so. Since both i and ii falsely assert that there is at present a King of France, they are not strictly contradictory and so can both be false.

Gilbert Ryle, in his 1931 essay "Systematically Misleading Expressions," restated the Theory of Descriptions—strangely, without actually mentioning Russell—and applied it to a number of cases, the most interesting for present purposes being abstractions and universals. Statements like "Jones hates the thought of going to the hospital" and "The idea of taking a holiday has just occurred to me" *appear* to be about a thought and an idea, respectively, and this appearance has led philosophers to speculate at length about what sort of things thoughts and ideas are. But this appearance is misleading—misleading to philosophers, that is, since non-philosophers are not in the least misled. To steer the philosophers right, Ryle rewrites the first statement as "Jones feels distressed when he thinks of what he will undergo if he goes to the hospital," which is about Jones and not about a thought, and the second statement as "I have just been thinking that I might take a holiday," which is about me and not about an idea.[9]

Similarly, we routinely use expressions like "Unpunctuality is reprehensible" or "Virtue is its own reward." Expressions like these, according to Ryle, have led philosophers to posit two sorts of objects, particulars like Jones and Smith, and universals, like Unpunctuality and Virtue. This seems to Ryle obviously absurd, since no one would think a universal, such as unpunctuality, merits reproof; rather, unpunctual people do. Again, the absurdity can be avoided by turning the grammatical subject into a predicate; thus: "Whoever is unpunctual deserves that other people should reprove him for being unpunctual" and "Whoever is good, gains something by being good."[10] Through this elimination of universals, another major province of philosophy goes by the board, and Ryle concludes that the analysis of meaning along the preceding lines is "the sole and whole function of philosophy."[11]

Well and good, but what has any of this got to do with Collingwood? J. Connelly and G. D'Oro, in their superb Introduction to the new edition of the *Essay*, note that what Russell and Ryle were engaged in was the reduction of concepts to empirical classes (EPM, lxxxi ff). Thus, "dog" simply *means* all the dogs there are, "cat" *means* all the cats there are, and so forth. The Theory of Descriptions only works on this assumption. This reduction, if successful, would leave no subject matter for philosophy, as Ryle clearly saw. Every object of inquiry would belong either to the exact or to the empirical sciences—as per Hume's Fork. While admitting that concepts in the natural sciences are definable by their extension, Collingwood argues, as we have seen, that philosophical concepts resist such classification, thus leaving philosophy untouched by the Russell-Ryle offensive and staking out an autonomous subject matter for philosophy. Thus the scale of forms is, inter alia, a refutation of Hume's Fork and thereby also of Russell's Theory of Descriptions. Ryle was to object strenuously, as we shall see in Section 7.

3. Philosophical Judgments

a. Quality

Judgments, or propositions—in the *Essay* Collingwood uses the two words interchangeably—are in general either affirmative or negative. If I ask, "Where did I leave my purse?" and reply, "Not in the taxi, I am sure," this answer has some affirmative implications, but can be considered simply negative, in that it tells me nothing about where I did, in fact, leave my purse (EPM, 105). In philosophy, by contrast, negative answers to questions typically do imply affirmative answers to those questions. If I dissent from a philosophical view, it is not the case simply that I consider it wrong; it is also the case that I have in mind—however vaguely or inchoately—some alternative view which I wish to affirm. I may not immediately be able to state this alternative view, but by dissenting from the view that has been put forth I place myself under an obligation. This principle, which Collingwood claims to follow from the Socratic principle that we never proceed from sheer ignorance to sheer knowledge but always come to know better what in a sense we knew already, Collingwood labels the principle of *concrete negation*, which he contrasts with the fallacy of *abstract negation*, the fallacy of simply dissenting without having anything affirmative in mind.

Collingwood also proposes a principle of *concrete affirmation*. Whenever I affirm a philosophical position, there is always a specific philosophical position I am concerned to deny. Outside of philosophy affirmative statements also have negative implications, namely each affirmative statement denies all the statements that are inconsistent with it. For instance, when I say, "The Battle of Hastings was fought in 1066," I am of course denying that the Battle of Hastings took place in 1087, but this denial is not part of the meaning of my assertion since I am equally denying that the battle took place in any other year you may name (EPM, 107). In philosophy, however, since philosophical concepts belong in a scale of forms, the philosophical judgment affirms the highest or truest form of the concept attained to date, thereby denying all the inferior forms of the concept that are summarized in the proximate form, since each step on the scale summarizes the whole scale up to that point (EPM, 108). Consequently to affirm a philosophical position is implicitly to deny some specific other position, and if we do not understand what, specifically, a past philosopher was concerned to deny, we also do not understand what he or she was affirming.

To take an example familiar to students of philosophy, Immanuel Kant's *Groundwork* is scarcely intelligible except as the denial of some form of utilitarianism; hence, in ethics anthologies J. S. Mill's *Utilitarianism* is usually placed before the *Groundwork*, even though it was written some seventy-five years later.

b. Quantity

Judgments are generally divided into universal, as "All humans are mortal," particular, as "Some mammals are human," and singular, as "Socrates is human." Philosophical judgments are universal, but it will come as no surprise that they are a special type of universal judgments. Collingwood begins by noting that every universal judgment implies a set of particular as well as singular judgments, and goes on to note three different ways in which universal judgments are formed.

First, we start from singular instances: Socrates, a human, is mortal; Plato is mortal; Aristotle is mortal; and so on. After a while we suspect that it is no coincidence that these humans are mortal, and we conclude that they are mortal *because* they are human, and thus that all humans are mortal. Such generalization by enumeration is common in ordinary thinking, although frowned upon by logicians and not admitted into scientific thinking (EPM, 112). Secondly, we start not from the singular, but the particular. After judging that each particular kind of mammal is mortal we conclude that all mammals are mortal. This is the procedure that is normal in empirical science. Thirdly, we begin by judging that S, as such, is P, and conclude from that that each instance of S is P, and therefore that this individual S is P. This is the procedure in the exact sciences.

None of these works in philosophy. Noting, for instance, that many right acts promote happiness and concluding from this that this promotion of happiness is what makes them right is to commit the fallacy of identified coincidents. Secondly, we might follow the example of the empirical sciences and try to find the generic essence of, say, knowledge by observing what all species of knowledge have in common. This procedure, however, would only reveal the minimum condition for knowledge, not the generic essence. Thirdly, we can follow the example of the exact sciences and assume, for instance, that pleasure is the motive for all actions and then impose this principle on each species of action. We would then have to argue, for instance, that the martyr derives pleasure from his suffering, and while this is not necessarily false, it ignores the different roles that pleasure plays in different types of action (EPM, 113–14).

Collingwood's solution is that the philosopher needs to use all three methods at once. No philosophical judgment can be accepted unless it can be arrived at by both generalization and scientific induction, and can in turn form the basis for deducing individual facts.

c. Modality

Judgments in the exact sciences are hypothetical, not categorical. The judgment that every square has its diagonals equal does not presuppose or imply that there are any squares. It is entirely possible that no one has ever drawn, or otherwise formed, a perfectly straight line, in which case there would not be any squares. But it would still remain true that every square has its diagonals equal, meaning that if there were any squares, they would have this property. Collingwood does entertain the possibility that figures may have to exist and be perceived, in order for geometry to be possible; but, if so, the recognition of this necessity is not itself part of geometry. Collingwood does not, however, mention arithmetic or algebra, where we arguably do make categorical judgments.

Judgments in empirical science may at first appear categorical, as empirical science deals with facts, but this appearance turns out to be deceptive. Take tuberculosis, as the term is used in medicine. It is not a collective term covering all the infinite variety of conditions that can be caused by tubercle bacillus. Rather, it refers to a "standard case" characterized by certain specific properties. Now, while it is true that these properties have been chosen in the course of examining numerous individual cases, it remains possible that no one individual case exhibits all of the properties included in the term "tuberculosis." And yet the concept of tuberculosis remains useful in diagnosing and treating the individual cases. As in exact science, empirical science depends on certain categorical judgments being made—for instance, the measurement of a patient's temperature at a particular time. But these judgments, while indispensable to medicine, are not themselves part of medical science. Again, Collingwood is here making a controversial claim; it could certainly be argued that the data of any science *are* part of that science.

Philosophical judgments, by contrast, are categorical. This follows, in a sense, from the initial methodological rule that all philosophical assumptions may be "canceled" by reference to actual experience. If philosophical assumptions were merely hypothetical, like those of mathematics, there would be nothing to check them against. In mathematics, once we have made an assumption, we are bound to accept whatever follows from it; the process of reasoning is irreversible. In philosophy, however, each assumption is subject to checking, which is made possible by the fact that what we derive from the hypotheses is something which in a sense we knew already. When it is said, therefore, that philosophical judgments are categorical, what is meant is not, of course, that they are a priori or incorrigible, but, on the contrary, that their truth or falsity is affected by what is or is not the case.

More specifically, what is meant is that the subject of a philosophical judgment is assumed to be something real. For instance, we cannot seriously talk about the nature of reality or the properties of virtue without assuming that there is such a thing as, respectively, reality or virtue. Collingwood finds support for this thesis in Plato's statement that dialectics requires a "non-hypothetical starting point" and in Aristotle's statement that the subject matter of metaphysics is reality or being. But the most conspicuous—and most controversial—historical example is the Ontological Proof of God's existence, originally formulated in the eleventh century by St. Anselm of Canterbury and later restated by Descartes. Anselm's Proof, according to Collingwood, has a dual origin, in Plato's doctrine that a thought is always a thought of something, and in the Neo-Platonist idea that God in His being combines existence and essence. Combining the two ideas, Anselm concluded that, whenever we think of God, we think of Him as necessarily existing, so that God's existence cannot be denied without a kind of absurdity. But Anselm's God, again according to Collingwood, is nothing else than Plato's necessary being, the necessarily existing object of thought, so the object of theological thought is also the object of metaphysical thought (EPM, 125). Furthermore, what is true of metaphysics is true of all philosophy, and Collingwood cites logic as an example.

Logic, he argues, is not possible except on the presupposition that its subject matter actually exists. For instance, if a logician states that all universal judgments are hypothetical, this is a universal judgment which supplies an instance of itself, and so is necessarily false. It is not formally contradictory, but what is asserted in the judgment is inconsistent with the fact of the judgment being made. This is what is known today as a *pragmatic* inconsistency, most famously exemplified by Descartes's "I do not exist" which, though not formally inconsistent, nonetheless cannot be truly asserted. Similarly, logic contains reasoning about reasoning and arguments about arguments, and so cannot without some sort of absurdity deny the reality of reasoning or of arguments:

> Logic, therefore, stands committed to the principle of the Ontological Proof. Its subject-matter, namely thought, affords an instance of something which cannot be conceived except as actual, something whose essence involves existence. (EPM, 131)

The theological significance of the Ontological Proof is treated somewhat lightly; Collingwood does state that the Proof "does not prove the existence of whatever God happens to be believed in by the person who appeals to it" (EPM, 12). I take the significance to be the following. God is defined by His believers as a being than whom nothing greater can be conceived. To seriously admit such a concept into one's vocabulary and make it the subject of serious assertions—that is, putatively true or false statements—require the belief that the concept is actually instantiated. Put otherwise, the belief in God's existence is a *presupposition* (more of these in Chapter 7) for raising the question of the truth or falsity of any statement wherein "God" appears as the subject term. The believer cannot deny God's existence without contradicting his own belief, and the nonbeliever, in denying God's existence, fails to deny that which the believer asserts, because his concept of "God" is a different one from that held by the believer. The nonbeliever simply fails to satisfy the preconditions for employing the conceptual scheme to which "God," as defined above, belongs. The Proof does not, therefore, consist in formally deducing the existence of God from the definition of "God," but in transcendentally deducing God's existence as a necessary precondition for seriously employing that concept.

It could be objected here that God might have a "literary" existence; in other words, just as scholars may seriously employ the name "Hamlet" without presupposing that Hamlet has physical existence, so we might employ the word "God" without presupposing that God has physical existence. I am not aware that Collingwood considered this possibility.

4. Two Skeptical Positions

In line with his own advice to philosophers to make clear what it is they are denying, Collingwood next addresses two skeptical positions, which he labels "critical" and "analytical" philosophy.

Critical philosophy, as described by Collingwood, disavows any positive doctrines and claims to confine itself to exhibiting fallacies and inconsistencies in other philosophies. Presumably, its criticism is purely formal and does not presuppose any positive doctrine concerning the subject matter of philosophy. Critical philosophy is open to two objections. First, by disavowing any positive doctrines and claiming to move on a strictly formal plane, the critical philosopher admits to having no interest in the substantive problems which other philosophers have been trying to solve. Consequently, she will lack the sympathetic understanding that is a prerequisite for evaluating how adequately other philosophers have solved their problems. The detection of inconsistencies misses the point of philosophical criticism, because inconsistencies are most often found in those philosophers who have tackled the most serious problems, and who have made the most earnest attempts at solving them. By ignoring the problem situation, critical philosophy renders itself unable fairly to assess the merits or demerits of rival philosophies (EPM, 139). In the first place, then, critical philosophy, even when taken at its face value, is undesirable. But, in the second place, it cannot be taken at face value. Its claim to pure, non-constructive criticism is untenable. Its critical activity presupposes that philosophy ought to be free from contradictions; this is a positive conception of philosophy, which must be defended by constructive philosophical arguments (EPM, 140).

Unfortunately, Collingwood does not tell us who the critical philosophers are whom he has in mind. The Oxford Realists, however, are fairly obvious targets, since the objections to critical philosophy are reiterated, in the *Autobiography*, as objections to the Realists in particular (A, 22, 49). His characterization of analytical philosophy is more explicit: The analytical philosophers are Bertrand Russell, G. E. Moore, and most especially L. S. Stebbing. Analytical philosophy is, on the one hand, more agnostic than critical philosophy: not only does it propound no positive doctrine, it propounds no negative doctrine either. On the other hand, it is also less agnostic: It holds that we can find the correct answers to philosophical questions; these answers, however, are not given in philosophical propositions, but in the propositions of science and common sense. All philosophy can do is analyze these propositions and show what they "really" mean (EPM, 142).

Collingwood is not writing off this view as a mere error; it is a half-truth, which is true in what it affirms, but in error concerning what it denies. Collingwood grants that the analysis of pre-philosophical propositions is indeed the task of philosophy, but claims that the analytical philosophers are mistaken in their analysis of analysis itself. Philosophical analysis does not exclude the affirmation of positive doctrine, but necessarily implies it. Three kinds of propositions enter into any philosophical analysis: the data to be analyzed, the results of the analysis, and the principles according to which the analysis is conducted. The data are not philosophical propositions; they are propositions of science or of common sense. Nor, on the analytical view, are the results philosophical propositions; they are the same propositions of science or of common sense, understood for what they really mean. It follows that the only component of analysis which properly belongs to philosophy is the body of principles according to which the analysis is carried out. In so far as the analytical philosopher purports to be doing philosophy at all, there devolves upon her the obligation to enunciate and justify those principles, that is, to propound positive philosophical doctrines: "[The] principles constitute a theory concerning the nature and method of philosophy; this is a philosophical theory, and a constructive one;" (EPM, 144–5).

Like critical philosophy, analytical philosophy in the end defeats itself.

5. Philosophical Inference

The exact sciences proceed deductively, from axioms to conclusions. The axioms themselves do not require demonstration, either, as in the older view, because they are self-evident, or, as in the modern view, because the axioms are simply assumed, not asserted to be true. Either way, the reasoning in the exact sciences is "irreversible" in Collingwood's terminology. "The conclusions are logically dependent on the axioms; there is no reciprocal dependence of the axioms on the conclusions;" (EPM, 153).

Philosophy differs from the exact sciences in two respects. First, its axioms cannot be simply assumed; since, as already argued, philosophical judgments are categorical, the axioms have to be asserted as true. But what is the justification for asserting them? Are they self-evident truths? According to Collingwood, nothing like this has been claimed by the major philosophers of the past, and he instances Descartes's "I think, therefore I am," which is the starting point for his philosophy, but is neither a self-evident truth nor an assumption. It is actually established by a proof, to wit, the proof that, having set out to doubt everything dubitable, Descartes was driven to the conclusion that he, the doubter, must be something, otherwise there would be no doubt (EPM, 156).

The conclusion to which Collingwood is driven is that philosophical reasoning, unlike mathematical reasoning, has to be reversible: "the principles establishing the conclusions and the conclusions reciprocally establishing the principles" (EPM, 160). Collingwood recalls here the Socratic principle that philosophical reasoning can only lead to conclusions which in a sense we knew already. Instead of imparting new knowledge, philosophy brings us a better understanding of what we already knew. But this allows experience to act as a check on our philosophical axioms: If their conclusions do not advance our preexisting knowledge, the axioms are, to just that extent, unsatisfactory. As Collingwood puts it, we have anticipations of the conclusions of philosophy before reasoning begins, and our philosophical conclusions can be checked against these anticipations (EPM, 163).

As Giuseppina D'Oro paraphrases Collingwood:

Whereas, say, a geometrical proof would not be invalidated by the fact that the results of that proof were unexpected, failure to do justice to experience, be this ethical, scientific or esthetic, casts doubt on the adequacy of the argument which was meant to explain how this experience is possible.[12]

Collingwood next contrasts philosophy with the inductive sciences. Here, we begin with an hypothesis, which we check against data, and through this process the hypothesis becomes progressively more probable, but it can never cross the line into certainty. The data, by contrast, are certain, and no hypothesis can affect their certainty. So, inductive reasoning, like the deductive reasoning of the exact sciences, is irreversible: we can reason from data to hypothesis, not the other way around (EPM, 167). Philosophical reasoning, once again, begins with axioms and draws conclusions which are then checked against experience. But the experience does not consist of "data" with which the philosophical conclusions must agree; rather, they must *explain* the experience: "Consequently, when we ask whether a moral theory tallies with moral experience we are asking whether the theory makes intelligible the moral experience which we actually possess" (EPM, 172).

There is a striking similarity here to John Rawls's later concept of "reflective equilibrium." According to Rawls we test an ethical theory, such as a theory of justice, by deducing practical conclusions from it and checking these against our "pre-theoretic intuitions" on the subject. To the extent that the conclusions of the theory agree with our pre-theoretic intuitions, the theory is validated, and the intuitions are no longer pre-theoretic—we now have reasons for them. If the conclusions of the theory clash with one or more intuitions, neither the theory nor the intuitions trump the other. We may revise either the theory or the intuitions until they come in agreement. So the theory is testable: if it clashes with all our intuitions it is a nonstarter. But it is not falsifiable by individual cases, and it may on occasion override particular intuitions.[13]

D'Oro illustrates Collingwood's point with Kant's Categorical Imperative. Everyone, Kant claims, knows the difference between acting for the sake of duty, doing the right thing because it is the right thing, and acting in accordance with duty, but for other motives, such as expedience or pleasure. The Categorical Imperative explains why we can make this distinction, and also enables us to articulate it. Thus, the Categorical Imperative "makes intelligible the moral experience which we actually possess."[14]

6. The Idea of System

In the *Essay* Collingwood considers four objections to the idea of system in philosophy. A system claims finality, completeness, objectivity, and unity, but none of these is attainable. No system to date has been final; each has been succeeded by another system. The current scope of human knowledge is such that no single person can encompass it all. Each philosophical system has simply expressed the personal opinion of a single philosopher. And lastly, philosophical problems are so diverse that each can only be tackled in isolation from all other problems.

All four objections, Collingwood holds, are false. Since human knowledge is constantly growing and changing, no branch of knowledge can claim finality. As Collingwood was fond of quoting Hegel: This is as far as consciousness has come. This does not prevent scientists from trying to present mathematics or medicine in a systematic form. This systematization is not an obstacle to continued process, but rather a stepping-stone toward progress. As Collingwood had earlier put it in his 1928 lectures (IH, 428), in order to progress we must, from time to time, take stock of where we are, and for that purpose we need to give our current state of knowledge a systematic form. This is the function of system in philosophy, as well as in other branches of knowledge. Collingwood grants that this task may be harder in philosophy than in science or history, as philosophical concepts and judgments are interconnected to such a degree that incorporating new insights may require remaking the whole body of philosophical knowledge from its foundations. The lesson, however, is not that philosophers may be excused from this task, but rather that it requires more patience in philosophy than in other branches of knowledge (EPM, 180).

To the second objection Collingwood grants that no one person can master the sum total of human knowledge, but counters that one person may adequately survey all of modern philosophy and that this is all that is needed for the construction of a philosophical system. (We note, as an aside, that Collingwood wrote this in 1933, when he could hardly have anticipated the veritable explosion in philosophical literature that has taken place over the past half-century.) Even so, a critic may object, the construction of a philosophical system is too vast a task for any one person to undertake. Quite so, Collingwood responds, and no one person has ever undertaken it. Any philosopher who has ever attempted system-building has always built on the foundation of the thoughts of his predecessors, with whom he sees himself as a collaborator in a collective effort. It follows that there can be no such thing as a private, personal, and self-contained philosophical system (EPM, 182).

The third objection has thus already been answered. Each philosopher, when engaged in system-building, is only contributing a relatively small part to a collective effort. But in that case, the critic may object, can this philosopher really be said to be engaged in system-building, if all he or she is contributing is bits and pieces of a system? Well, in order to contribute effectively the philosopher must form an idea of exactly how her contribution fits into the whole; that is, she must address the general question of what philosophy is (EPM, 183–4).

Finally, the fourth objection is that the system-builder, by imposing a false unity on the diversity of philosophical topics, is thus succumbing to rigid and ready-made formulas that are detrimental to the flexibility required for philosophical problem solving. Collingwood obviously holds no brief for rigid and ready-made formulas, but responds that the methodical avoidance of rigidity itself requires something in the nature of a system (EPM, 185).

Having completed the purely negative task of rebutting the four objections, Collingwood turns to the positive task of outlining the true task of system in philosophy. And this he finds in the scale of forms introduced earlier in this chapter. Each philosophy, each step on the scale of forms, assimilates into itself a previous philosophy of which it is the denial, and so it summarizes all the steps on the scale up until this point. There is thus no claim to finality; in advocating my system I am simply asserting that this is the point we—the community of philosophers—have reached to date. Similarly, there is no claim to completeness; each philosophy is only a moment in the history of thought, summarizing and reinterpreting previous philosophies up to that point. The objectivity of a philosophical system is provided by the problem situation in which each philosopher finds himself; the set of problems which he needs to address is something he finds, not something he invents. And finally, uniformity and flexibility are not necessarily mutually opposed; the recognition of a scale of forms opens up the possibility of a uniform flexibility, which is neither rigid nor random (EPM, 191–2).

Collingwood's *Essay* contains a wealth of thought, of which the preceding is a mere sampling. Enough has been said, however, to place the remainder of his corpus in its proper perspective.

7. The Collingwood-Ryle Exchange

The Ontological Proof is widely thought to be refuted by Kant's famous objection that existence is not a predicate: Once I have completely described something, I add nothing by saying that the thing so described exists. Collingwood mentions Kant's objection but without seriously discussing it, noting only that with Hegel's rejection of Kant's subjective idealism, the Proof "has never again been seriously criticized" (EPM, 126). The Proof had, in fact, been criticized on broadly Kantian grounds two years earlier by Ryle, in the paper mentioned in Section 2b, "Systematically Misleading Expressions," as well as by Russell.[15] In his paper, Ryle argued that statements like "God exists" or "Satan does not exist" cannot be "about" God or Satan, respectively, the way "I am sleepy" is about me. Ryle argues this by analogy with statements like "Unicorns do not exist" or "Carnivorous cows do not exist," which he analyzes in the following way:

> "Unicorns do not exist" seems to mean what is meant by "nothing is *both* a quadruped *and* herbivorous *and* the wearer of one horn" (or whatever the

marks of being a unicorn are). And this does not seem to imply that there are some quadrupeds or herbivorous animals. So "carnivorous cows do not exist" ought to be rendered "nothing is both a cow and carnivorous", which does not as it stands imply that anything is either.[16]

It is worth noting that there is nothing here that Collingwood needed to deny since, in the *Essay*, he was making a claim specifically about *philosophical* concepts, not about unicorns or cows. Ryle came back in 1935 with his paper "Mr. Collingwood and the Ontological Argument,"[17] in which he methodically and effectively demolished a series of positions which were never defended by Collingwood. In this paper, Ryle takes considerable pains to establish that "there is no way of establishing *a priori* particular matters of fact."[18] Collingwood of course never denied this. Collingwood's central philosophical thesis is mentioned once in Ryle's paper, in a parenthesis, and only to be immediately dismissed as unintelligible:

> Though on p. 136 Mr. Collingwood distinguishes between the categorical singular judgements of history and the categorical universal (judgements) of philosophy. I cannot make head or tail of this. After the labours Mr. Collingwood has taken to distinguish between (general) hypothetical propositions and categorical it is upsetting to find that apparently some judgement may be universal and so (I suppose) expressible in purely general terms and yet categorical in the sense of referring to something actually existing.[19]

Collingwood never publicly responded to criticisms, but he did write to Ryle privately, stating inter alia:

> I believe that such propositions as "God exists", "mind exists", "matter exists", and their contradictories, do not assert or deny particular matters of fact; … and what, I suppose, I am objecting to is a question-begging assumption that Hume was right when he divided all possible subjects of discourse into (a) ideas & the relations between them, and (b) matters of fact …[20]

Ryle responded that the proposition "No universal propositions are categorical," which Collingwood had argued against, was simply a tautology, a response which Collingwood dismissed as begging the question. No resolution was reached, and there is no evidence that Ryle really understood Collingwood's position.

8. *The Idea of Nature*—Transition to the Theory of Absolute Presuppositions

According to T. M. Knox, the editor of Collingwood's posthumous publications, the main body of *The Idea of Nature* (1945) was written in between 1933 and 1934 as an attempted application of Collingwood's theory of philosophical method to the problems of the philosophy of nature. In 1939 and later, the manuscript was, however, extensively revised, and the concluding section on Collingwood's own cosmology was replaced by a brief finale, announcing the transition from the idea of nature to the idea of history.[21] The extensive revision of the manuscript may be taken as evidence of a radical change in Collingwood's thought during this period. "Radical" is a relative term; what I will argue is that *The Idea of Nature* proved a recalcitrant touchstone for the theory of philosophical method, and revealed the need for a revision and expansion of the theory, a project which was to be carried out in *An Essay on Metaphysics*.

For the most part, *The Idea of Nature* exemplifies the dialectical scale of forms described in *An Essay on Philosophical Method*: one cosmologist poses a certain definite question concerning nature, and his successors see his answer as inadequate because the question was wrongly put. So the inadequacy of the first answer forces the next generation not simply to find a different answer, but to rephrase the question in a more fruitful way. In this way, the progress of cosmology is seen not to consist in a mere accretion of facts, but in gradual conceptual innovation on the pattern of a dialectical scale of forms, as that idea was explained in the *Essay*. This process is extensively documented with examples from the entire history of cosmology. One example will suffice here.

Thales was the first in recorded history to ask the question, "what is nature?," and to him the question meant "what kind of thing is nature made of?," on the presupposition that nature itself is made of one of the kinds of stuff of which things *in* nature are made. His answer, it is well known, was "water." For a variety of reasons, this answer seemed unsatisfactory to his successor Anaximander, who repeated the question, but whose answer shows that the question was now given a different twist. Nature, according to Anaximander, is made of "apeiron," an undifferentiated something. This answer shows that his question was not quite the same as that of Thales; when asked what nature is made of,

Anaximander was not looking for the kind of stuff that things in nature are made of, but something different in kind. This raises a new problematic; the question now arose as to how nature, and hence the things in nature, could be made of something radically different from the stuff we find in nature. The focus has shifted from the material to the process of coming into being. When, therefore, Anaximander's successor Anaximenes raised the question "what is nature?" and came up with the answer "vapor," he might seem to be returning to the problematic of Thales, by focusing on a stuff found in nature, but the question, properly understood, is a different one from Thales's. Anaximenes has inherited from Anaximander the problem of how things come into being, and the question of the raw material is now subsidiary to the question of the process. Vapor is chosen because it is obviously malleable to condensation and rarefaction, and so accounts for both the raw material and the process. And so on. The answer given by each generation gives rise to a different question, the answer to which is also the answer to the original question, as rephrased within the new problematic. From the higher term on the scale, though not from the lower, the process is seen as a cumulative one (IN, 31–40).

If the entire history of cosmology could have been written in this way, Collingwood's philosophical method would have shown itself spectacularly successful, and no revision would seem to be called for. But such is not the case. The process is, according to Collingwood, discontinuous at certain points, where an entirely new problematic emerges, which in important respects does not preserve the earlier problematic within it. (It may be noted parenthetically that this is the observation later made by Thomas Kuhn, who drew clearly relativist conclusions from it.[22]) In the history of Western cosmology, we have in fact three distinct ideas of nature, and Collingwood does not attempt to account for the transitions between them by the scale of forms. The Greeks held that everything in nature is animate, Renaissance science held that nature is a machine, while twentieth-century science holds that nature is a process (IN, 3–13). These views, it seems, emerged as radical innovations—in Kuhn's terminology, "paradigm switches"—and not as rational outcomes of the preceding question-and-answer complexes. So, to Renaissance cosmology, Greek cosmology is simply erroneous, and to modern cosmology, Renaissance cosmology is simply erroneous. We seem to be forced to the conclusion that these ultimate ideas of nature are simply brute, unintelligible, historically given data. This is, of course, the immediately most plausible conclusion to be drawn from the last sentence of the book: "We go from the idea of nature to the idea of history" (IN, 177). So interpreted, *The Idea of Nature* represents a radical break with *An Essay on Philosophical Method*, and Collingwood would, at this stage appear as a prominent proto-Kuhnian.

This conclusion, I think, would be rashly drawn, but I defer further discussion of the question to Chapter 6, where more context will be provided. At this stage I will content myself with saying that what I take Collingwood, at the end of *The Idea of Nature*, to be saying is something like this: "So far, the radical changes in the idea of nature are left on the level of the merely empirical, i.e. real but unexplained. Let us proceed to explain them and render them intelligible." This seems to be point of Collingwood's quote from Hegel toward the end of the book: "*Bis hierher ist das Bewusstseyn gekommen*, 'That is as far as consciousness has reached'" (IN, 174). This, as we shall see in Chapter 7, is the projects undertaken in *An Essay on Metaphysics*. Meanwhile, in the interest of chronology, we turn now to Collingwood's philosophy of history.

Further Reading

Peter Johnson, *R.G. Collingwood: An Introduction*, Chapter Two.
Louis Mink, *Mind, History, and Dialectic: The Philosophy of R.G. Collingwood*, Chapter Three.

4

Historical Understanding

In his *Autobiography*, Collingwood famously summarized his life's work as "in the main an attempt to bring about a *rapprochement* between philosophy and history" (A, 77), and he went on to claim that "The chief business of twentieth century philosophy is to reckon with twentieth century history" (A, 79), meaning thereby not the events of the twentieth century, but twentieth-century historiography. It was Collingwood's contention, frequently repeated, that just as natural science had come into its own in the seventeenth century, so now history had recently come into its own as a science (IH, 209), meaning thereby "a body of systematic and orderly thinking about a determinate subject matter" (EM, 4). Collingwood was aware that the word "science" was already commonly used to refer to natural science, a usage he duly noted and deplored as slang usage. Whereas history in the past had been a "scissors-and-paste" affair, where historians simply copied the testimony of their "authorities," or at most questioned whether particular statements made by authorities were true or false, scientific historians treated testimony simply as evidence from which, along with coins, pottery, and ruins, the historian inferred what had happened. The modern historian thus was his/her own authority (IH, 137).

For the first couple of decades after his death Collingwood was almost exclusively thought of as a philosopher of history, and the editors of the posthumous *Principles of History* go as far as crediting Collingwood with "effectively [setting] the agenda for those working in [English-language philosophy of history] ever since his untimely death in 1943."[1] His reputation in the field rested partly on the *Autobiography* from 1939, but even more on *The Idea of History*, published in 1946, that is, three years after Collingwood's death. The latter work consists of two parts: The first part, Collingwood's intended *Idea of History*, is a series of lectures from 1936, tracing the history of historiography and philosophy of history from Greco-Roman times to the twentieth century. The second part, the "Epilegomena," consists of seven lectures and manuscripts selected by the editor T. M. Knox, dating from 1935 to 1939, and all but two of them previously unpublished. In 1939, right after finishing *An Autobiography* and while working on *An Essay on Metaphysics*, Collingwood began a book called *The Principles of History* while on sick leave in the Dutch West Indies, now Indonesia, but he completed only about one-third of the projected volume. Exactly why he did not finish it is a subject for debate, but the most plausible explanation is that the outbreak of the Second World War led him to invest all his energies in his major work of political philosophy, *The New Leviathan*, of which more in Chapter 8.

Although Collingwood had authorized the unfinished *Principles of History* for posthumous publication, Knox decided to include only part of it, less than one half, in *The Idea of History*.[2] The unpublished manuscript was long feared to have been destroyed, but in 1995 the manuscripts for Chapters Two and Three were discovered at Oxford University Press, and these were published in 1999 together with Chapter One, which Knox had included in *The Idea of History* and which was copied from that work. A number of shorter manuscripts were also included in the new volume. When *The Idea of History* was published in a revised edition in 1993, the editor included two important lecture series from 1926 and 1928. To these sources we may add a number of papers on philosophy of history which Collingwood published in his lifetime, most of which were collected by William Debbins in a volume published in 1965.

1. Collingwood's Conception of History

It is essential to bear in mind in what follows that Collingwood is not a philosopher telling historians what to do. As we have seen, Collingwood was an expert on Roman history as well as on the archaeology of Roman Britain. In his philosophy of history Collingwood is speaking as a philosopher and an historian, telling the rest of us what historians in fact do.

Following Gambattista Vico's insistence that society is more knowable than the natural world, because it is human made, and in studying society we study the work of our own minds, Collingwood held that history is the self-knowledge of the human mind (IH, 10, 209; A, 107–19). All history, Collingwood held, is the history of thought, including of course the history of ideas, but more generally of thought as expressed in human actions, be it in politics, warfare, trade, navigation, or agriculture (IH, 115). But there is no history of physical events, as such. Geology, for instance, while it studies processes, is a natural science, not history. There is an analogy between the geologist's and the archaeologist's interpretations of stratified rock sites, but there is also an important difference: "The archaeologist's use of his stratified relics depends on his conceiving them as artifacts serving human purposes and thus expressing a particular way in which men have thought about their own life;" (IH, 212).

The historian makes a distinction between what may be called the "outside" and the "inside" of an event. Examples of the outside are "the passage of Caesar, accompanied by certain men, across a river called the Rubicon at a certain date, or the spilling of his blood on the floor of the senate-house at another." Examples of the inside are that which can only be expressed in terms of thought: "Caesar's defiance of Republican law, or the clash of constitutional policy between himself and his assassins" (IH, 213). Only the latter are of interest to historians.

Human biological nature is of interest to historians only in so far as it enters into human thought; in an oft-quoted passage:

> Thus, the historian is not interested in the fact that men eat and sleep and make love and thus satisfy their natural appetites; but he is interested in the social customs which they create by their thought as a framework within which these appetites find satisfaction in ways sanctioned by convention and morality. (IH, 216)

The main body of *The Idea of History* is devoted to the history of historical thought. Although the Greek world was profoundly anti-historical, as exemplified by Plato's writings, Herodotus, and to a lesser degree Thucydides, managed to resist the anti-historical tenor of their time. The basis for history was thought to be eyewitness testimony, but Herodotus did not blindly accept their testimony. Trained, like all free Greek men of his time, to examine witnesses in court cases, Herodotus questioned the testimony of his witnesses. But this placed serious limitations on the scope of history. History could only be Greek history, and it could only be the history of the recent past, from which there were eyewitnesses still living (IH, 25). So, the historian cannot choose his subject matter; it is simply given to him as the events to which there are living eyewitnesses. Moreover, the next generation of historians cannot build on and improve on the work of the previous generation because now the eyewitnesses are dead, and all the evidence is gone (IH, 27).

The Hellenistic period ushered in by the conquest of Alexander the Great broadened the intellectual horizons of the Greeks; they now became conscious of living not just in a city or a nation, but in a *world*, that included Greeks and Barbarians. The scope of history was thereby expanded, but at a cost: a world history could not be written by questioning eyewitnesses:

> It was necessary to construct a patchwork history whose materials were drawn from "authorities," that is, from the works of previous historians who had already written the histories of particular societies at particular times. This is what I call the "scissors-and-paste" historical method. (IH, 33)

Collingwood grants that this method is not entirely uncritical, since one may question individual statements made by an authority, but it does presuppose a general trust in one's authorities.

Among Roman historians Tacitus is singled out for harsh criticism; this of interest because Collingwood here invokes the idea that was to become known as the centerpiece of his philosophy of history, the re-enactment doctrine: "History cannot be scientifically written unless the historian can re-enact in his own mind the experience of the people whose actions he is narrating. Tacitus never tried to do this …" (IH, 39). Exactly what this means will be the subject of the next four sections of this chapter.

The advent of Christianity ushers in a new era in historiography. Christian historiography has four characteristic features: (i) It is a universal history, going back to the origin of man. (ii) Human actions reveal, not human wisdom, but the workings of Providence. (iii) It seeks meaningful patterns in history, such as dividing history into history before Christ and history after Christ. (iv) It subdivides these into smaller units, so Christian history is characterized by epochs or periods (IH, 49–50).

Historical method, however, remains a scissors-and-paste affair, up to the modern era. Collingwood takes the reader on a fascinating tour through Medieval, Cartesian, Enlightenment, and Romantic historical thought, until finally the conception of "scientific" history emerges in the nineteenth century. Scientific history does not treat sources as "authorities," but simply as evidence. When faced with a statement by a supposed authority, the scientific historian does not simply ask "Is it true?," but "What does it mean?" and "Why did this person make this statement?" As an exponent of scientific history Collingwood instances F. H. Bradley who, in 1874, published *The Presuppositions of Critical History*. The context of this essay, Collingwood tells us, was the rise of critical biblical scholarship in the nineteenth century. While exploding the accounts of miracles in the New Testament, the critical historians unintentionally cast doubt on the biblical narrative as a whole. If the accounts of the miracles are not to be believed, why believe the rest of the gospel narratives? Why believe that Jesus ever existed? (IH, 136). History, Bradley noted, is inferred from testimony, but the historian needs a criterion for what counts as testimony (IH, 137). In Bradley's words, "what counts as testimony depends upon what the historian can infer from his own experience."[3] While Collingwood applauds this conclusion, he complains that Bradley interprets it too narrowly, too "positivistically," by limiting the historian's experience to the state of the natural science of his time. Experience in this sense is something the historian brings ready-made to his inquiry, and which cannot be affected by the inquiry (IH, 138–9). What he needs, instead, is to bring to bear his total experience, including the experience of the historical inquiry, of re-enacting the agent's experience in his own mind.

The scientific historian is autonomous vis-à-vis her sources; these sources are not "authorities," but evidence, which the historian questions and criticizes:

> So far from relying on an authority other than himself, to whose statements his thought must conform, the historian is his own authority and his thought autonomous, self-authorizing, possessed of a criterion to which his so-called authorities must conform and by reference to which they are criticized. (IH, 236)

The historian also uses her imagination to interpolate what must have happened, where there are gaps in the evidence: "The historian's authorities tell him of this or that phase in a process whose intermediate phases they leave undescribed; he then interpolates these phases for himself" (IH, 237).

A famous and humorous illustration of the historian's use of evidence is the murder mystery "Who killed John Doe?," where the Rector's neighbor John Doe is found dead at his desk, stabbed in the heart through his back. Collingwood shows how the Inspector solves the mystery by asking a number of pointed questions, in a particular order. The most telling one is this: When the Rector's daughter confesses to the murder, the Inspector does not ask whether her statement is true; rather he asks, "Why did she make the confession?" and "Whom does she suspect?" (IH, 271). This line of questioning is paradigmatic of the scientific historian's attitude toward testimony.

Collingwood's emphasis on the role of present evidence in historical inquiry has often been noted, and some of his utterances on the subject may appear to imply a skepticism about the past. Thus, in his 1928 "Outlines of a Philosophy of History" he says, "if the purpose of history is to know the past, to become acquainted with things as they actually happened, ... then history is certainly an illusion" (IH, 483). The historian knows the past only in so far as present evidence allows it: "The only knowledge that the historian claims is knowledge of the answer which the evidence in his possession gives to the question he is asking" (IH, 487). Again, in *The Idea of History* Collingwood states that "the subject-matter of history is not the past as such, but the past for which we possess historical evidence" (IH, 202). Finally, in *An Essay on Metaphysics* (1940), after noting that metaphysical statements carry the tacit "rubric" "it is, or was, absolutely presupposed that," Collingwood goes on, "History has its own rubric, namely, 'the evidence at our disposal obliges us to conclude that' such and such an event happened" (EM, 56). Now, Collingwood may be making a perfectly innocuous observation here; thus, in the 1928 essay he reminds us of the somewhat obvious point that the past is what *has happened* and thus is not now happening; in that sense the past is not actual (IH, 439–40). It can nonetheless be known—objectively known—by being re-enacted in the present.

But something more controversial may be intended. Since the evidence available to the historian changes from one generation to the next, the vantage point of each historian "is valid only for him and people situated like him" (IH, 108). In the same vein, "every new generation must rewrite history in its own way" (IH, 248). Leo Strauss has noted that Collingwood's acknowledgment of the relativity of historical knowledge falls short of relativism only because Collingwood also firmly believed in the progress of knowledge over time. Indeed, Collingwood did write,

> We can easily conceive the work of medieval history as being done better than it was done in the eighteenth century, but we cannot conceive of it being done better than it is in our own times, because if we had a clear idea

of how it could be done better we should be in a position to do it better, and this better way of doing it would be an accomplished fact. (H, 108–9)

Strauss comments, "He could therefore believe that if historical knowledge is relative to the present, it is relative to the highest standpoint which has ever existed."[4] Collingwood thereby rules out the possibility of degeneration or decay, a serious flaw in Strauss's view.[5] But Collingwood could be understood to make the quite different claim that, if our historical knowledge has declined since the eighteenth century, we would not today be in a position to know this—a far more plausible position.

This gives a very general idea of Collingwood's conception of history. We now get down to particulars.

2. The Re-enactment Doctrine

No part of Collingwood's thought has generated more interest or controversy than his doctrine that historians in their work re-enact the thought of the historical agents. There is today a massive secondary literature on the subject, of which the present writer cannot presume to have done more than scratch the surface. Even so, the reader will notice vastly more footnote references here than in any other chapter in this book. The idea was first broached in the 1928 lectures on the philosophy of history, repeatedly mentioned in passing throughout *The Idea of History*, and discussed in detail in Epilegomenon §4 in that work, as well as in the *Autobiography*.

The idea of re-enactment is this: every rational, and hence intelligible, action performed by an historical agent has a definite thought content. The agent found himself in a situation which he perceived a certain way; given his interests and purposes this situation posed a problem, and his action represents a solution to that problem. The historian understands the action in so far—and only in so far—as he can grasp the situation as the agent saw it and reason his way to the action as a reasonable solution to that problem. Suppose, for instance, the historian wants to understand a certain edict in the Theodosian Code, that is, not just understand what it says, but understand its historical significance: "In order to do that he must envisage the situation with which the emperor was trying to deal, and he must envisage it as the emperor envisaged it" (IH, 283). After looking at the various alternative causes of action available to the emperor, the historian must decide upon the emperor's course of action as the best course of action: "Thus he is re-enacting in his own mind the experience of the emperor; and only in so far as he does this has he any historical knowledge, as distinct from merely philological knowledge, of the edict" (IH, 283).

Now, according to Collingwood's monistic philosophy of mind, familiar to us from Chapter 2, the content of a thought cannot, even for purpose of analysis, be separated from the act of thinking that thought. So, Theodosius's, or Euclid's, thought has an objective content, but I cannot grasp that content without performing, say, Euclid's act of thinking, not an act "like" it, but the very same act. To the common-sense objection that the same act of thought cannot be performed by two persons separated in time by 2,000 years, Collingwood asks us first to consider the case of a person who thinks "the angles are equal" for five seconds. Is this one act of thought, or five, ten, or twenty? Clearly, he holds, it is a single act of thought sustained over five seconds. Now consider a slightly different case:

> Suppose that, after thinking "the angles are equal" for five seconds, the thinker allows his attention to wander for three more; and then, returning to the same subject, again thinks "the angles are equal." Have we here two acts of thought and not one, because a time elapsed between them? Clearly not; there is one single act, this time not merely sustained, but revived after an interval. (IH, 286)

As I understand Collingwood, there is only one way to think the thought content "the angles are equal"; whenever I think "the angles are equal" I perform the same act of thinking, and whenever two persons, however separated in time, think "the angles are equal," they are performing the very same act of thinking:

> If [Euclid] thought "the angles are equal" and I now think "the angles are equal," granted that the time interval is no cause for denying that the two acts are one and the same, is the difference between Euclid and myself ground for denying it? There is no tenable theory of personal identity that would justify such a doctrine. (IH, 287)

It is easy to misconstrue re-enactment as a subjective intuitive or empathetic—or even telepathic—identification of the historian with the historical agent, as it has been misconstrued by many commentators. So, for instance, W. H. Walsh writes: "To say that the historians must penetrate behind the phenomena they study is one thing; to hold that such penetration is achieved by an intuitive act is something very different." And he goes on to raise the rhetorical question, "Can we find any reason for accepting so extravagant a view?"[6] Likewise, Patrick Gardiner equates re-enactment with "'insight', sometimes 'intuition' or 'empathy', and sometimes 'recreating past experience' (Collingwood) or 're-experiencing somebody else's thought' (Dilthey's 'das Nacherleben')."[7] Karl Popper, of whom more in Section 4, refers to re-enactment as "the sympathetic repetition of the original experience."[8] Finally, Collingwood's one-time student Isaiah Berlin has credited Collingwood with believing in "a capacity to transport ourselves into the minds of persons or periods historically remote from us, a transcendental, timeless flight across the barrier of time, ..."[9] That these are misunderstandings is abundantly clear from Collingwood's discussion of how to interpret Plato's *Theaetetus* without knowing the context in which Plato wrote it. The historian of philosophy none the less has to reason his way through Plato's argument, not one "like" it, but the very same one. How is this possible?

> In Plato's mind, this existed in a certain context of discussion and theory; in my mind, because I do not know that context, it exists in a different one, namely that of the discussions arising out of modern sensationalism. Because it is a thought and not a mere feeling or sensation, it can exist in both these contexts without losing its identity, although without some appropriate context it could not exist. (IH, 301)

So, the historian of philosophy does not share Plato's feelings or sensations, and to that extent does not know what it was like to be Plato. In an oft-quoted passage Collingwood makes the same point quite poetically:

> We shall never know how the flowers smelt in the garden of Epicurus, or how Nietzsche felt the wind in his hair as he walked on the mountains; we cannot relive the triumph of Archimedes or the bitterness of Marius; but the evidence of what these men thought is in our hands; and in re-creating these thoughts in our minds by interpretation of that evidence we can know, so far as there is any knowledge, that the thoughts we create were theirs. (IH, 296)

The same point is made in the *Autobiography* in the context of re-enacting Lord Nelson's refusal to take off his decorations at the Battle of Trafalgar, a refusal expressed in the words "in honour I won them, in honour I will die with them." To understand those words, Collingwood holds, he must be able to think them for himself; however, in so doing, he does not become Lord Nelson. Nelson's thought, though present in Collingwood's mind, is at the same time known to have been thought by Nelson on the eve of a sea battle ninety years earlier. This knowledge makes it, in Collingwood's wording, an "incapsulated" thought, a thought that does not answer any question that arises for himself in real life. The question "shall I take off my decorations?" simply does not arise for Collingwood (A, 113). Collingwood concludes: "Historical knowledge is the re-enactment of a past thought incapsulated in a context of present thoughts which, by contradicting it, confine it to a plane different from theirs" (A, 114).

It must be admitted that Collingwood may invite misunderstanding when he refers to action as having an "outside" and an "inside"; the historian must see the action from the inside, *as* an action, not from the outside, as a mere event (IH, 213). This could easily be misconstrued to mean that the historian must get inside the agent's mind, by intuitively or empathetically identifying with the agent. But it is clear from the above that all it means is seeing the action from the agent's perspective, seeing the problem as the agent saw it, and reasoning to the agent's conclusion. The following passage, criticizing Tacitus, is more damaging:

> History cannot be scientifically written unless the historian re-enacts in his own mind the experience of the people whose actions he is narrating. Tacitus never tried to do this: his characters are seen not from inside, with understanding and sympathy, but from outside, as mere spectacles of virtue or vice. (IH, 39)

Collingwood here admittedly *seems* to conflate (i) re-enactment, (ii) seeing the character from the inside, and (iii) understanding and sympathy. If so, this certainly was not his considered view. Bearing in mind that this text was never authorized for publication by Collingwood, we may take this passage as a careless formulation of the rather innocuous observation that understanding and sympathy are *prerequisites* for re-enactment, not constitutive of it.

To show that re-enactment, as Collingwood meant it to be understood, is not limited to intellectual history, Leon Goldstein has used an example from Collingwood's own historical work on Roman Britain, namely the problem of the Vallum, an earthwork south of Hadrian's Wall and continuous with it.[10] The question was, what was this earthwork for? The chief facts, Goldstein quotes from Collingwood, were

> that the Vallum in its original shape was a formidable obstacle to traffic, but incapable of military defense, and so designed, indeed, as to look ostentatiously unmilitary; that this obstacle is carried with remarkable thoroughness, admitting no interruption whether from hard rock subsoil, morass, or ravine, right across the country from Tyne to Solway, close behind the Wall; that, according to the latest results of excavation, it was made at the same time as the Wall, itself; and that the only original ways across it are solid causeways opposite the Wall forts and perhaps also opposite the milecastles, each surmounted by a stone gateway. In sum, the Vallum is a second obstacle parallel to the Wall and provided with a corresponding series of controlled openings for traffic, differing from it in its deliberately unmilitary design. (RBES, 133)

Collingwood concludes that, while the Wall served as military defense, the Vallum served the purpose of custom collection. Collingwood adds significantly: "There is no proof that this explanation of the Vallum is correct. All that can be claimed for it is that it fits the facts" (RBES, 134). Note that there is no testimony available here; Collingwood notes the physical features of the Vallum, and from this evidence, along with knowledge of Roman administration gathered from other sources, he infers what the Vallum was for. He does not know the names, or even necessarily the titles, of those who planned the construction of the Vallum, and they left no written evidence of their thinking. Nonetheless Collingwood re-enacts their thoughts by seeing the Vallum as the solution to a problem they had—the problem of keeping the military defense and the civil administration of the border separate. This example gives us a much broader understanding of re-enactment than might be gleaned from the examples given in *The Idea of History* and *An Autobiography*.

Both Jan van der Dussen and Margit Hurup Nielsen have observed that the re-enactment doctrine was originally widely interpreted as a methodological injunction and in that respect almost universally rejected.[11] This "received view" was questioned in 1956 by Alan Donagan. Using both the example of interpreting the Theodosian Code, described earlier, and the reading and interpreting a passage from an ancient philosopher, Donagan concludes that

Collingwood's wording in both examples indicate that his "subject may be, not historical method, but what historical method achieves." In support of this he cites Collingwood's statements: "Only in so far as he does this [i.e. re-enacts] has he any historical knowledge" and "Nothing short of that will make him the historian of that author's philosophy." Donagan concludes that Collingwood is concerned not with prescriptions, but with what historical knowledge consists in.[12]

This completes our initial sketch of the re-enactment doctrine. The following four sections will examine a number of specific issues that have arisen within the context of the doctrine.

3. Historical Explanation

Opinions vary as to whether Collingwood intended his re-enactment doctrine as a theory of historical explanation or only as a theory of what historical knowledge consists in. In other words, once we have re-enacted the experience of an historical agent, have we thereby *explained* the action, or have we merely ascertained what the action *was*? Collingwood certainly occasionally expressed himself as if it were both, as in this famous—or perhaps notorious—passage:

> ... there is no such thing as the further stage of philosophical or scientific history which discovers their causes or laws or in general explains them, because an historical fact once genuinely ascertained, grasped by the historian's re-enactment of the agent's thought in his mind, is already explained. For the historian there is no difference between discovering what happened and discovering why it happened. (IH, 176–7)

In Collingwood's perhaps most famous example, once we know exactly what Caesar did when crossing the Rubicon, we also know why he did it. That is, *what* he did was openly challenging the constitution of the Roman Republic, and that is also *why* he crossed the river. Re-enactment, it seems, both ascertains and explains. As a theory of historical explanation it has often been contrasted with what is variously known as "the covering-law model,"[13] "the Hempel thesis," or "the Popper-Hempel thesis."[14] The locus classicus for this thesis is the noted logical empiricist philosopher of science Carl G. Hempel's 1942 paper "The Function of General Laws in History."

An explanation of an event, according to Hempel, consists of the following:

(1) a set of statements asserting the occurrence of certain events $C_1, \ldots C_n$ at certain times and places;
(2) a set of universal hypotheses, such that

   (a) the statements of both groups are reasonably well confirmed by empirical evidence,
   (b) from the two groups of statements the sentence asserting the occurrence of event E can be logically deduced.[15]

The statements in (1) contain the determining conditions for the event; the statements in (2) contain the general laws on which the explanation is based. For instance, to explain the cracking of a car radiator on a cold night, one would list the determining conditions, such as that the car was left outside overnight, that the radiator was full of water, that the ambient temperature dropped to 25°F and so on. "Finally, this group would have to include a quantitative law concerning the change of pressure of water as a function of its temperature and volume."[16]

Hempel stresses that the letters E and C stand for *kinds* of events; one cannot fully explain individual events, such as the San Francisco earthquake or the assassination of Julius Caesar because neither can be fully described in every detail. However, there is in this respect no difference between history and the natural sciences: "both can give an account of their subject-matter only in terms of general concepts, and history can 'grasp the unique individuality' of its objects of study no more and no less than can physics or chemistry."[17]

Explanations are in practice often incomplete, in that the general laws involved are not stated. This may be because the general laws are considered inessential since they are assumed to be generally known, as when we explain the burning of a barn by the fact that a burning cigarette was dropped in the hay. A different case, quite common in history, is when the complexity of the situation makes it difficult to state all the underlying conditions with sufficient precision, as when we explain the success of a political movement by its taking advantage of widespread racial prejudice,[18] or the migration of the Dust Bowl farmers to California by continual droughts and sandstorms in the Dust Bowl.[19] In such cases, where complete explanations are not feasible, historians construct an "explanation sketch" which indicates the laws and underlying conditions only vaguely, in a manner to be "filled out" to arrive at a complete explanation: "This filling-out requires further empirical research, for which the sketch suggests a direction."[20]

Hempel explicitly contrasts his concept of historical explanation with "*the method of empathetic understanding.*"[21] This method, he argues, is of value only as a heuristic, to suggest an explanation, which still needs to be tested by empirical evidence.

Hurup Nielsen, in a review of an earlier book of mine, questioned the relevance of Hempel's covering-law model to Collingwood, who wrote before Hempel's landmark paper appeared toward the very end of Collingwood's life.[22] However, Hempel's concept of explanation was spelled out already in J. S. Mill's *System of Logic*, and Dray has noted that Collingwood attacked something very much like it as nineteenth-century positivism, and that it can be traced as far back as to Hume's discussion of causation.[23]

Hempel's thesis initially gained widespread acceptance among philosophers, so much so that, in 1957, Dray could refer to it as the "accepted doctrine."[24] The most extensive and detailed defense of the thesis was made by Patrick Gardiner in 1952; however, Gardiner's point of departure was not Hempel's article, but Karl Popper's *The Open Society and Its Enemies*. In that work Popper argued that historical explanations tacitly assume laws, which are not stated because they are generally quite trivial:

> If we explain, for example, the first division of Poland in 1772 by pointing out that it could not possibly resist the combined power of Russia, Prussia, and Austria, then we are tacitly using some trivial universal law such as: "If of two armies which are about equally well armed and led, one has tremendous superiority of men, then the other never wins." (Whether we say here "never" or "hardly ever" does not make, for our purposes, as much difference as it does for the Captain of H.M.S. *Pinafore*.)[25]

The parenthetical comment is puzzling: The difference between "never" and "hardly ever" is of course the difference between a universal law and a generalization, and no doubt there are exceptions to this one. Why Popper considered this distinction unimportant is unclear to me. Be that as it may, in a footnote Popper objects to Morton White ascribing the thesis to Hempel, because Popper formulated it already in 1934 in *Logik der Forschung*, a book that was reviewed by Hempel in 1937.[26]

Gardiner's account differs from Hempel's in two important respects. First, rather than insisting on universal laws as the basis for explanations, he allows for "generalizations" and "regularities." Thus, "Generalizations about revolutions, class-struggles, civilizations, must *inevitably* be vague, open to a multitude of exceptions and saving clauses, because of the looseness of the terms they employ."[27] Gardiner is here explicitly granting what Popper appeared to parenthetically imply, that historical explanations rely on generalizations which allow for exceptions, rather than on actual laws.

Secondly, and like Popper, Gardiner grants that there is a different kind of explanation historians use, which does not depend on universal laws, but rather on knowing the agent's purposes and plans: "For we view human behavior not only in its reactive aspect, but also under the aspects of being purposive, calculated, planned."[28] In this context Gardiner notes that historians sometimes refer "to what Professor Popper has called 'the logic of the situation,' i.e. in terms of what it would be reasonable to do in such-and-such circumstances, and with such-and-such objectives in view."[29] This may sound Collingwoodian, and I shall argue that it is, but Gardiner sharply distances himself from Collingwood's "inside"/ "outside" metaphor, which he finds "artificial and misleading." "Misleading, because the introduction of a spatial metaphor gives the impression that what are called the 'insides' of events are queer objects, invisible engines that make the wheels go round."[30] Gardiner distances himself further from Collingwood by arguing that explanations from the agent's reason for action can be seen as dispositional explanations—that is, explanations in terms of what is generally done in the agent's situation—thus conforming to Hempel's explanation sketches.[31]

Gardiner's arguments were criticized at length by Dray in 1957. One of his many arguments goes as follows. The covering-law theorist may grant that historians do not as a rule consciously and explicitly employ laws in their explanations, they may be challenged to supply one to justify their use of "because." For instance, a historian may explain the fact that Louis XIV died unpopular by "his pursuits of policies detrimental to French interests," yet deny that he is committed to the law "Rulers who pursue policies detrimental to their subjects' interests become unpopular."[32] Now the logician may ask why the historian refuses to commit himself to this law, and the historian may reply that he did not mean to imply that *any* policies contrary to the subjects' interests lead to unpopularity, only policies of this particular kind: "e.g. involvement of the country in foreign wars, the persecution of religious minorities, the maintenance of a parasitic court, and so on."[33] The logician may now simply reformulate the law as "Rulers who involve their countries in foreign wars, who persecute religious minorities, and who maintain parasitic courts become unpopular."[34] But the historian may reject this one as well; a ruler may do these things, and yet do other things to stave off unpopularity. The logician may then incorporate this qualification into the law, and so on. It may be thought that the historian is at least committed to the "law." "Any ruler pursuing policies and in circumstances exactly like those of Louis XIV would become unpopular." Dray concludes that it is odd to call this a "law" as it appears to apply only to Louis XIV.[35]

Dray goes on to argue that "the explanation of individual human behavior as it is usually given in history has features which make the covering law model peculiarly inept."[36] In contrast to the covering-law model Dray introduces what he calls "rational" explanations, and he notes that his discussion "may be regarded in part as an attempt to 'make sense' of what Collingwood, in particular, has to say about historical understanding" but without any close textual discussion.[37] "[W]hat we very often want," he goes on, citing an example from the historian Trevelyan, "is a reconstruction of the agent's *calculation* of means to be adopted toward his chosen end in light of the circumstances in which he found himself."[38] The calculation need not have been formulated in propositions; in fact, the agent need not have performed it at all:

> [I]n so far as we say an action is purposive at all, no matter at what level of conscious deliberation, there is a calculation which could be constructed for it: the one the agent would have gone through if he had had time, if he had not seen what to do in a flash, if he had been called upon to account for what he did after the event, &c.[39]

Rational explanations, as understood by Dray, in explicit contrast to Gardiner, explain actions as "the thing to have done for the reasons given" as opposed to "the thing that is done on such occasions," as in the covering-law model.[40]

Dray defends the "empathy" method against Hempel's criticisms, but warns against terms like "projection," "identification," "imagination," "insight," "intuition," and so on, which may give the false impression that historical explanation "goes beyond the limits of empirical inquiry."

> As I have pointed out already, it [rational explanation] has an inductive, empirical side, for we build up to explanatory equilibrium *from the evidence*. To get inside Disraeli's shoes the historian does not simply ask himself: "What would I have done?"; he reads Disraeli's dispatches, his letters, his speeches, &c.—and not with the purpose of discovering antecedent conditions falling under some empirically validated law, but rather in the hope of appreciating the problem as Disraeli saw it.[41]

We have already referenced Popper's situational logic as a type of rational explanation; the following section will be devoted to an examination of its relation to Collingwood's re-enactment doctrine.

4. Popper's Situational Analysis

The topic before us was subject to a detailed examination in my earlier book *Making Sense of History*; what follows is in the main a highly compressed account of that discussion. Karl Popper was one of the most prominent philosophers of the twentieth century, who made contributions to metaphysics, epistemology, philosophy of science including probability theory, and social and political philosophy. And philosophy of history and the social sciences. The relationship of his theory of historical explanation to Collingwood's is thus of great interest to students of Collingwood's thought.

Popper's point of departure is his "three-worlds" epistemology. The first is the physical, or material, world and the second is the subjective, or mental, world. The third world is "the world of objective contents of thought, especially of scientific and poetic thoughts and of works of art."[42] This third world, Popper admits, bears some resemblance to Plato's world of ideas, and to Hegel's objective spirit. But it resembles most closely "the universe of Frege's objective contents of thought."[43] This comparison would easily suggest itself anyway, since both the expression "third realm" and "objective thought=content" have gained their philosophical currency from Frege's writings. In his classic 1918 paper "The Thought: A Logical Inquiry," Frege introduced his concept of a third realm in order to identify mathematical and logical objects as something distinct from either the physical symbols or the subjective, psychological ideas attending the symbols. The objects inhabiting the third realm he called *Gedanken*, that is, objective thought-contents, closely corresponding to what he had referred to in an earlier, 1892 paper, cited by Popper, as "sense," thought contents which make up a common store of thought that can be transmitted from one generation to the next.[44]

Popper gives this inventory of his third world:

> Among the inmates of my "third world" are, more especially, *theoretical systems*; but inmates just as important are *problems* and *problem situations*. And I will argue that the most important inmates of this world are *critical arguments*, and what may be called—in analogy to a physical state or to a state of consciousness—the *state of a discussion* or the *state of a critical argument*; and, of course, the contents of journals, books, and libraries.[45]

I have argued elsewhere that Popper's third world bears strong similarities to Charles Peirce's concept of "sign," a major difference being, however, Popper's lack of interest in the physical embodiment of third-world objects—a shortcoming also noted by the philosopher and media theorist Paul Levinson, who is otherwise very sympathetic toward Popper.[46]

Thus armed, Popper turns to the problem of historical understanding: "My thesis is that the main aim of all historical understanding is the hypothetical reconstruction of a historical *problem-situation*."[47] This thesis is then illustrated with an historical example, to wit, the problem of understanding Galileo's stubborn defense of his unsuccessful theory of the tides.

Briefly, Galileo held that the tides were caused by periodical accelerations and retardations in the rotational velocity of the Earth. The problem of historical explanation is: Why did Galileo advance such an odd theory, instead of accepting what everybody else believed, and that Kepler's laws had just confirmed, namely that the tides are due to the influence of the moon? The usual psychological interpretations in terms of Galileo's vanity, or dogmatism, or jealousy toward Kepler are irrelevant in Popper's view; the explanation is to be found elsewhere: "I claim that the first and all-important step is to ask ourselves: *what was the (third-world) problem* to which Galileo's theory was a tentative solution? And what was the situation—the logical *problem situation*—in which this problem arose?"[48] Popper then proceeds to explain Galileo's theory as a perfectly justified attempt at exploiting to the full the explanatory potential of a few simple ideas, namely Copernican astronomy and his own two laws of the conservation of motion. Furthermore, in a situation where the forerunners of modern enlightenment were combating medieval obscurantism, it was perfectly rational to stick to the principle of simplicity of explanation, rather than to invoke the mystical forces attributed to the moon by astrologers. By so understanding the rationality of Galileo's "dogmatism," we have explained it historically:

> Thus we are led by an analysis of Galileo's problem situation to justify the rationality of Galileo's method in several points in which he has been criticized by various historians; and thus we are led to a better *historical understanding* of Galileo. Psychological explanations which have been attempted, such as ambition, jealousy, or aggressiveness, or the wish to create a stir, become superfluous. They are here replaced by a third-world situational analysis.[49]

So far, so good. Popper points out, as had Joseph Agassi before him, that there is considerable resemblance between Popper's situational analysis and Collingwood's concept of re-enactment.[50] But Popper also takes pains to distinguish his "third-world" method from Collingwood's supposed "second-world" method. After granting that he can go with Collingwood a long way, Popper continues:

> We part company over the issue of the second and third worlds; the issue of choosing a subjective or an objective method. (We agree on the significance of problem situations.) Collingwood's psychological way of putting things is by no means merely a matter of formulation. Rather, it is an essential part of his theory of understanding.[51]

And again, referring to Collingwood's famous example of interpreting the Theodosian Code:

> Collingwood makes it clear that the essential thing in understanding history is not the analysis of the situation itself, but the historian's mental process of re-enactment, the sympathetic repetition of the original experience. For Collingwood, the analysis of the situation serves merely

as a help – an indispensable help – for this re-enactment. My view is diametrically opposed.[52]

Enough has been said in the preceding to make it clear that this is simply a misunderstanding of Collingwood, albeit a widespread one. Re-enactment is not a mental process or a sympathetic repetition; it is a logical reasoning from the situation and the agent's goals and purposes to his action.

There remains a real issue of contention between Popper and Collingwood. Commenting on his reconstruction of Galileo's problem situation, Popper emphasizes the distinction between the agent's object and the historian's meta-level. Labeling Galileo's problem situation P_1 and the historian's problem of understanding P^u, Popper warns:

> It is only too easy to mix these two up, for if we formulate the historian's problem by asking "What was Galileo's problem?," the answer seems to be "P_1," but P_1 (as opposed to "Galileo's problem was P_1") seems to belong on the object level rather than the meta-level, and so the two get confused.[53]

Popper proceeds to advance the contention; "*But there are, in general, no problems common to the different levels.*"[54] In support of this contention he notes that the meta-level is richer than the object level; it contains units not found on the object level. This, of course, is also what Collingwood noted by saying that the agent's thought is "incapsulated" in the historian's thought: The historian always has knowledge that was not available to the agent. But it simply does not follow from this difference that the agent's problem cannot *also* be the historian's problem. In Popper's example, Popper's problem was "Why did Galileo hold on to a discredited theory?" and he solved it by pointing to Galileo's principle of simplicity of explanation and his opposition to astrology. By concluding that Galileo's stance was rational given this problem situation, Popper himself essentially reasoned from Galileo's problem to Galileo's solution, which is exactly what re-enactment is.

This, as noted, was highly compressed. When I spelled out the above in greater detail in my earlier book, it was met with misgivings from Jeremy Shearmur, but was in the main accepted by Hurup Nielsen, who was critical of my book on grounds unrelated to this discussion, and by van der Dussen, who, however, faulted me for having made no mention of the important concept of "incapsulation," and who later supplemented my argument with an argument that related the re-enactment doctrine to Frege's analysis of indirect speech.[55]

5. Dray's Review of Objections

In his magisterial *History as Re-enactment* Dray has reviewed and subjected to detailed discussion six major objections to the re-enactment doctrine: (i) intellectualism; (ii) rationalism; (iii) perception, appetite, and emotion; (iv) the history of art and metaphysics; (v) the natural world; and (vi) social factors. We shall look at each, in turn.

a. Intellectualism

By taking historical understanding to consist in the re-enactment of past thought, Collingwood has frequently been charged with having an overly intellectualist conception of history. Dray finds this criticism in, among other places, Walsh's *Philosophy of History* and Peter Winch's *The Idea of a Social Science*.[56] We have already seen, in Goldstein's example of the Vallum, that this criticism is groundless, in that "thought," to Collingwood, overwhelmingly encompasses *practical* reasoning. Dray grants that Collingwood invites criticism by equivocating on the word "reflective." Only reflective thought can be re-enacted, as Collingwood put it in "The Subject Matter of History": "A reflective act, he continues, is 'one which is performed in the consciousness that it is being performed and is constituted what it is by that consciousness'" (IH, 308).[57] This formulation certainly invites the charge of intellectualism, but Dray notes that there is little trace of this doctrine elsewhere in *The Idea of History*. In fact, Collingwood makes it clear in a number of places that re-enactment is not restricted to deliberate or planned acts. In fact, Greco-Roman history is criticized for attributing too much to deliberate plan or policy, "this drawing from Collingwood the remark that 'to a very great extent people do not know what they are doing until they have done it, if then'" (IH, 42).[58]

Dray's hypothesis is that, in "The Subject Matter of History," Collingwood was initially operating with a special, technical sense of "reflective" and then, when he came to defining the term, without noticing it he slipped into the ordinary sense of "reflective" as captured in the above definition. This was a momentary slip, and there is nothing in the re-enactment doctrine that requires that the acts to be re-enacted are reflective in the ordinary sense of the word. An act may be done on the spur of the moment and may still be re-enactable provided the agent, with hindsight, can see it as the solution to a recognizable problem.[59]

b. Rationalism

This objection is that the re-enactment doctrine, by reasoning from the agent's problem to a solution, assumes an unwarranted degree of rationality on the part of historical agents: "For it either assumes that people act much more rationally than it is plausible to believe they do, or it excludes from the subject-matter of history much of what normally engages the attention of historians."[60] Collingwood himself, Dray notes, seems to have been of two minds as to how much rationality should be attributed to historical agents:

> On the one hand, he commends Hegel for having applied the "very fertile and valuable principle" that "every historical character in every historical situation thinks and acts as rationally as that person in that situation can think and act"; and he brands the attitude of Enlightenment historians to the past as "unhistorical" because they assumed the irrationality of all earlier times. (IH, 116, 77–8)[61]

On the other hand, Collingwood declares "that it is 'only by fits and starts, in a flickering and dubious manner, that human beings are rational at all'" (IH, 227).[62]

Collingwood's personal opinion aside, in what respects and to what extent does the re-enactment doctrine require us to attribute rationality to historical agents? We re-enact by reasoning from the agent's problem situation to her solution; she must be deemed rational in the sense of having had good reasons for acting as she did, *given* her beliefs and purposes. The historian must find the implicit argument in her action to be sound.

> But since that argument derives its conclusions from beliefs of the agent which may have been quite erroneous, and takes account of whatever purposes the agent in fact had, no matter how foolish or even monstrous they may have been, the claim to understand the action by grasping the soundness of the argument is clearly compatible with the judgment that, objectively speaking, the action is very irrational indeed.[63]

So actions, to be re-enactable, need only be subjectively rational. But this does not commit Collingwood to the claim that *all* human actions are subjectively rational, since he nowhere claims that all human actions are understandable.[64] If we none the less make this metaphysical assumption, there are four kinds of action that will be problematic from a re-enactment standpoint: (i) confused actions, for instance making a logical error while calculating consequences; (ii) inadvertency, for example, bringing about unintended consequences; (iii) achievements, one does not, say, win a race by intending to; and (iv) arbitrary action, when the person has insufficient reason to act as she did.[65]

c. Perception, Appetite, and Emotion

Dray here recalls Collingwood's famous disclaimer:

> We shall never know how the flowers smelt in the garden of Epicurus, or how Nietzsche felt the wind in his hair as he walked on the mountains; we cannot relive the triumph of Archimedes or the bitterness of Marius; but the evidence of what these men thought is in our hands; (IH, 296)

The reason we shall never know these things, presumably, is that they are not thoughts and so cannot be re-enacted. Now, Dray grants that we cannot know Nietzsche's feeling in its immediacy, but we may know from evidence *that* Nietzsche felt the wind in his hair. Collingwood admits such knowledge to enter into a re-enactment as a premise, but holds that the perception itself is not re-enactable.

> To that extent, at least, a limit has to be recognized here to the applicability of Collingwood's theory of historical understanding as re-enactment, a limit which many of his pronouncements certainly give the appearance of ignoring.[66]

Dray wrote this before the manuscript of *The Principles of History* was discovered, but opined, in the preface to the paperback edition, that there was nothing in it that called for "any significant change in the arguments of the present book." David Boucher has later drawn a different conclusion, noting that *The Principles of History* incorporates the theory of imagination developed in *The Principles of Art* after completion of *The Idea of History*:

> In The *Principles of Art* Collingwood builds a bridge between feeling and intellect by formulating a theory of imagination. ... Imagination, then, makes feelings recoverable in a way that he did not envisage, or perhaps chose not to acknowledge, in *The Idea of History*.[67]

Boucher acknowledges that bringing imagination within the compass of re-enactment would require a reworking of the re-enactment doctrine and conjectures that Collingwood's inability to rework that doctrine may have been the reason why he did not go through with his original plan to include re-enactment in *The Principles of History*.

d. History of Art and Metaphysics

As we shall see in the next chapter, in art the artist does not set out with the intention to produce a specific effect in her audience. Art is the expression of an artist's immediate experience, which she could not have known prior to having and simultaneously expressing that experience. Dray notes Heikki Saari's observation that we can understand the thoughts expressed in a work of art by studying it, even though they are not expressed in propositional form, but objects that such understanding is intuitive, whereas re-enactment is ratiocinative.[68]

Dray does not address Collingwood's own tackling of the problem in *The Idea of History*. The artist, he holds, knows very well what he is doing; he is starting out with a definite problem, that of translating his immediate experience into a work of art:

> In this sense the artist knows very well what he is doing and what he is trying to do. The criterion of his having done it rightly is that, when it is done, it should be seen as expressing what he wanted to express. All that is peculiar to him is the fact that he cannot formulate his problem; if he could formulate it, he would have expressed it; and the work of art would have been achieved. (IH, 314)

Collingwood concludes that there can be a history of art, but none of artistic problems. But surely this is an example of what the historian David Hackett Fischer has termed "the fallacy of the overwhelming exception."[69] If the artist's problem cannot be identified ahead of his solution, it is difficult to see how any re-enactment is possible.

The case of metaphysics will be discussed in detail in Chapter 7; we can here deal with it briefly. Making a presupposition is not an act of thought, so if metaphysics is the history of absolute presupposition, this history cannot be re-enacted. But more of this later.

e. The Natural World

History, in Collingwood's view, is the history of human actions, so the physical world enters into it only derivatively, as something people perceive and react to. This does not mean that he considers the physical world unimportant; writing about Roman Britain, he notes: "These differences in respect of relief, soil, and climate between the highland and lowland zones have deeply affected the lives of their respective inhabitants" (RBES, 3).[70] But these factors have affected the inhabitants through their perception of them and reaction to them. Likewise, the eruption of Vesuvius in 79 CE became an historical event "in so far as people were not merely affected by it, but reacted to this affection in various ways" (A, 128 n 1).[71] And in *The Idea of History* he writes:

> The fact that certain people live, for instance, on an island has itself no effect on their history; what has an effect is the way they conceive that insular position; whether for example they regard the sea as a barrier or as a highway to traffic. (IH, 200)[72]

So, what causes an action is not the situation the agent finds himself in, but his decision on how to deal with the situation. Dray notes that both Donagan and Mink found this view quite acceptable; he himself finds it paradoxical. Writing as an historian, Collingwood cited actual differences in soil and climate as the causes of cultural differences between highland and lowland. As for the eruption of Vesuvius, the experience of the agents may have caused their reactions to it. But that experience was in turn caused by the eruption, and if causation is admitted to be transitive, we have to conclude that the eruption of Vesuvius caused the actions of the agents.[73]

Dray cites Mink's example of the Alps as a constraint on the movement of people:

> Strictly speaking, the geographical location and configuration of the Alps have not been the cause of anything in history. It is men's awareness of and beliefs about the Alps which have been the constraining and effective factors in human events.[74]

Borrowing a principle from Hart and Honoré, Dray suggests that when agents misperceive their situation, we take the agent's perception to be the cause of the action, whereas, when the agents perceive the situation correctly, it is the situation that counts as the cause:

> If the Alps are correctly regarded as a barrier to travel by men of a low level of technology, it will be the Alps themselves, not their thought about them, which will be regarded as the cause of their staying where they are. But if the Alps are regarded as the way to heaven and people start climbing them, it is more likely to be their "thought" which will be said to cause them to act.[75]

But although the Alps may cause human actions, this causal power is still "conditional upon appropriate decisions being made by the agents involved."[76]

f. Social Factors

Edward Hallett Carr, among others, has charged Collingwood with the "serious error" of restricting history to the actions of individuals. Dray grants that Collingwood's examples of re-enactment are examples of individual actions. Similarly, in "The Subject-Matter of History," Collingwood lists only actions of individual agents. However, he praises Vico for "having achieved for the first time 'a completely modern idea of what the subject-matter of history is', namely, 'the genesis and development of human societies and their institutions', the 'process whereby human beings build up systems of language, customs, law, government, etc'" (IH, 65).[77] Also, Collingwood's own historical writings deal as much with town, village, and province life as with the actions of individuals.

A related question is whether Collingwood was a methodological individualist—that is, whether he believed that social phenomena are reducible to the actions of individuals, as claimed by both Donagan and Saari. Dray argues that Collingwood regarded social phenomena as the *resultants* of the actions of individuals, but not *reducible* to them: "He typically represents what happened in history as largely a resultant of what individuals willed, the human past, on his view, being largely a story of unintended consequences."[78] For instance: "In *The New Leviathan*, for example, he insists that 'civilization' is something that can happen to people only collectively, not individually" (NL, 283).[79]

This has been only the briefest recapitulation of Dray's very detailed argumentation, but hopefully sufficient to show that, while there are limits to the applicability of the re-enactment doctrine, these limits are not nearly as narrow as some of Collingwood's critics have maintained. Some of the issues considered here will be further elucidated by a look at Collingwood's unfinished "Folktales" manuscript, also dating from 1936.

6. Fairy Tales and Magic

While delivering the lectures that were to become *The Idea of History*, Collingwood was also at work on a book on the unlikely topic of the history of fairy tales, another project left unfinished and published posthumously, along with related material, as *The Philosophy of Enchantment* (2005). Fairy tales represent the "folk memory" of a culture; they have been handed down through generations—or even millennia—of telling and re-telling by countless storytellers. These tales are, as it were, the relics of a culture's customs and beliefs, and their history can be reconstructed by a method akin to that of archaeology (PE, 118). The subject matter of fairy tales is something called magic, so in order to understand fairy tales we must understand what the anonymous authors took magic to be. How do we do that?

> All historical knowledge involves the recreation in the historian's mind of the past experience which he is trying to study. If magic were a form of belief or custom peculiar to primitive people and absolutely foreign to the mind of civilized man, the civilized historian could never understand it. (PE, 128–9)

This is clearly the re-enactment doctrine, but now with a new twist:

> In order to understand fairy tales, therefore, we must give an account of magic which will show that in its essence it is a thing familiar to ourselves, not as a spectacle, but as an experience; something which we habitually do, something which plays a part in our social and personal life, not as a mere survival of savagery, but as an essential feature of civilization. (PE, 129)

What is being re-enacted here is not mere thought, but a total *experience*, and for this to be re-enacted there must be something essentially the same in the historian's experience. So, the next question is, what *is* magic?

Along with his younger contemporary Evans-Pritchard, Collingwood rejected what was at the time the standard interpretation of the magic of the so-called primitive people—the interpretation formulated by Levy-Bruehl and Sir Edward Tyler and popularized, above all by Sir James Frazer in *The Golden Bough*. This was the theory that magic is essentially attempted, but sadly mistaken, science. The savage, in this view, believes that by sticking pins into an effigy of his enemy he directly harms the enemy, that by performing sowing dances and rituals he causes the grain to grow and so on. In other words, the savage imagines nonexistent cause-effect relationships. The problem with this view, Collingwood writes, is that these same savages had sufficient causal knowledge to practice metallurgy, boat-building, agriculture, and animal breeding: "If 'the savage' really thought in this pre-logical way, he could never have mastered, as he has done, the principles of hunting and fishing, agriculture and stock-farming, metallurgy and carpentry; ..." (PE, 188).

Collingwood is equally dismissive of Sigmund Freud's diagnosis of magic, in *Totem and Taboo*, as neuroses (PE, 156–69). It should be noted that Collingwood consistently expressed the greatest admiration for Freud as a *psychologist*; the problem was Freud's trespassing on the field of anthropology, where he had no expertise, whereas Collingwood himself had acquired some.

Our age is obsessed with utilitarianism, which compels us to assign a purpose to everything we do. Yet a great deal of what we do in our everyday lives is simply the expression of emotions, and magic may be defined as "the systematic and organized expression of emotion" (PE, 207). Why, Collingwood asks, does he wash his hands before going to lunch? The utilitarian answer is, of course, to rid himself of germs. But Collingwood admits to having no idea whether washing his hands actually accomplishes this. A more plausible explanation is that he is expressing his feeling of a separateness between work and lunch: "For the meal is not a mere taking of food. It is also a social ceremony for which one prepares oneself with a ceremonial ablution symbolizing the dismissal from one's mind of work and its preoccupations" (PE, 209). Similarly, wearing a hat gives a feeling of assurance and safety, which is why a man is supposed to take his hat off indoors, where he presumably is safe (PE, 210–11). We wear clothes even in temperatures where we could comfortably go naked, because being naked in public feels undignified (PE, 213). Collingwood shaves every morning, because otherwise he would not feel prepared for work. And so on.

Similarly, "the savage" performs sowing dances to put himself in the right frame of mind for sowing, war dances to generate courage and hostility toward the enemy. It does not occur to the savage that these rituals will cause the grain to grow, or the enemy to be defeated. And we can understand this because we routinely do similar things for similar reasons. The conclusion appears to be that, already in 1936, Collingwood was broadening the concept of re-enactment to include emotions, although this certainly appears to have been ruled out in *The Idea of History*.

Further Reading

Peter Johnson, *R.G. Collingwood: An Introduction*, Chapter Six.

William Dray, *History as Re-enactment: R.G. Collingwood's Idea of History*.

Peter Skagestad, *Making Sense of History: The Philosophies of Popper and Collingwood*, Chapters Five to Six, Ten.

W.H. Walsh, *Philosophy of History: An Introduction*, Chapters Three to Five.

5

The Principles of Art

Second only to his work in the philosophy of history, Collingwood's most widely known and influential work has been in the philosophy of art. Like many of his contemporaries—but undoubtedly more than most—Collingwood was keenly aware that European civilization was under siege. It had received a catastrophic blow in the form of what was known as the Great War, now known as the First World War; yet worse was brewing in the form, first, of Italian fascism, then of German Nazism. (Like Karl Popper in *The Open Society and Its Enemies* (1945), Collingwood was relatively unconcerned about Soviet communism; communism was rarely included within the scope of totalitarianism until Hannah Arendt famously included it after the Second World War, more of which in Chapter 8.[1]) History, as we have seen, was one antidote to modern irrationalism; art was another. Collingwood believed art to have a vital role in preserving civilization; thus, a clear understanding of what art is, what role it plays, and how it plays that role was essential to combating irrationalism.

To this task Collingwood brought with him an aesthetic education dating from early childhood. He was homeschooled by his parents till the age of thirteen. Both parents and his paternal grandfather were professional painters. His mother was also an accomplished pianist, while his father was a novelist, folklorist, and archaeologist, and unpaid secretary to John Ruskin. Visitors to the Collingwood home included the family friend and pre-Raphaelite painter Edward Burne-Jones.[2]

In his early years Collingwood followed Benedetto Croce, whose study of Vico he had translated into English from the Italian, and Samuel Taylor Coleridge in holding that art is pure imagination, a view expressed, as we have seen, in *Speculum Mentis*, and developed in greater detail in a short book called *Outlines of a Philosophy of Art* in 1925. Later, in the wake of *An Essay on*

Philosophical Method, he developed a more nuanced philosophy of art set forth in *The Principles of Art*, published in 1938. This work is divided into three books: "Art and Not Art," "The Theory of the Imagination," and "The Theory of Art."

1. What Art Is and Is Not

a. The Technical Theory of Art

Collingwood opens the book by posing its central question, what is art? One might think that the way to approach this question would be first to come up with a definition of "art" and then use this definition to determine what does and does not count as art. Collingwood's approach is the opposite; first, he maintains, we need to get clear about what does and does not count as art, and only then are we ready to define the concept of art. The presumption, of course, is that the reader is sufficiently educated to have an informed opinion of what is and is not art, and throughout this part of the book Collingwood repeatedly emphasizes that he is not saying anything the reader does not already know, but only *reminding* the reader of what we all know (PA, 45, 105). This of course is a consequence of Collingwood's Socratic/Aristotelian insistence, in *An Essay on Philosophical Method*—that in philosophy we only come to know better what in a sense we knew already. This preliminary exercise will in fact occupy more than one-third of the book and thus must be considered integral to Collingwood's theory of art, although it is presented as a mere prolegomenon to such a theory.

The first, and most important, step is to rid our minds of an obsolete meaning of the word "art," namely, that art is a type of craft. This meaning, which is responsible for what Collingwood calls the technical theory of art, goes back to Plato and Aristotle, for whom there was no distinction between arts and crafts. Both τεχνη in ancient Greek and *ars* in classical Latin simply meant craft; neither language had a word for art in our sense. This is a distinctly modern concept. Only in the seventeenth century did artists begin to realize that what they were doing was something different from crafts, leading to the distinction between the fine and the useful arts, sometimes called "practical," and finally in the nineteenth century the qualifier "fine" was dropped and "art" in the singular replaced "arts" in the plural.

Why is art not a type of craft? Collingwood lists six characteristics of crafts:

1) "Craft always involves a distinction between means and end, each clearly conceived as something distinct from the other but related to it" (PA, 15). The means are the actions taken to realize a particular, end, to be distinguished from the relationship of part to whole or of material to product.
2) "It involves a distinction between planning and execution" (PA, 15). The craftsman always sets out with a precise and detailed foreknowledge of what he means to achieve.
3) "Means and end are related in one way in the process of planning; in the opposite way in the process of execution" (PA, 16). In the process of planning I first have the end in mind, then work my way backward to the steps I have to take; in the process of execution I begin with the first step and ultimately arrive at the end.
4) "There is a distinction between raw material and finished product or artifact" (PA, 16).
5) "There is a distinction between form and matter" (PA, 16).
6) "There is a hierarchical relation between various crafts, one supplying what another needs, one using what another provides" (PA, 16). Thus, for instance, the silviculturist provides raw material—trees—for the loggers, who provide raw material—timber—for the sawmills, which provide raw material—planks—for the carpenter.

In what we recognize as art none of the six need be present. First, there need not be a distinction between means and end. What are the means to composing a poem? The poet might sit down at his desk, place paper on his desk, and fill his fountain pen, but these actions are preliminary to *writing*, and a short poem could be composed entirely in the poet's head. There are other things the poet might do as means to composing—consulting a rhyming dictionary, pounding his foot on the floor, getting drunk—but the poet *need* not do any of these things (PA, 20). So, the point is not that there never is a means-end relation, but only that there *need* not be one in art, whereas in craft it is essential.

But might not the poem be a means to an end, say, to arouse certain emotions in the mind or heart or soul of the audience? Perhaps. But if the reading of a poem failed to arouse the intended emotions in a particular audience, would that prove it a bad poem? Collingwood grants that this is open to discussion. But if poetry were a craft, there would be no room for disagreement about it.

Secondly, the distinction between plan and execution *may* be present in art, and as Collingwood grants an overlap between art and crafts, it obviously is present in arts that are also crafts, such as painting and sculpture. But again, it need not be present, as in the composition of a brief tune or poem: "But suppose a poet were making up verses as he walked; suddenly finding a line in his head, and then another, and then dissatisfied with them and altering them until he got them to his liking: what is the plan which he is executing?" (PA, 21). Collingwood grants the possibility that only trifling works of art can be unplanned and that really great works of art always require planning, but *all* craft requires planning and if *some* art does not, art is not craft.

Thirdly, if there is no means-end distinction, there can be no reversal of the order of means and end.

Fourthly, what could be the raw materials out of which a poem, say, is made? Perhaps words. But it is not as if the words out of which a poem is made first appeared in a different order in the poet's mind, and then were shuffled into the order of the final poem. The words and the order appeared simultaneously (PA, 23). Perhaps the raw material is emotions, which the poet converts into a poem. No doubt that happens, but the blacksmith is also motivated by an emotion, say, the desire to pay the rent, but this emotion alone cannot be converted into a horseshoe. So, to a craftsman, there has to be some raw material other than his or her emotions.

Fifthly, every work of art has a particular form, but, just as there is no raw material, so there is nothing in the work of art corresponding to matter. "[W]hen the poem is written, there is nothing in it of which we can say, 'this is a matter which might have taken a different form'" (PA, 24). There are certain important analogous distinctions, such as the distinction between that which is expressed and that which expresses it, but this is not the distinction between matter and form.

Sixthly, and finally, in art there is nothing corresponding to the hierarchy of crafts. A poet may write words for a composer to set to music. But these words are not means to an end, as they are incorporated into the song. Nor are the words raw material, as the composer does not convert them into music (PA, 25).

The technical theory of art having been thus refuted, it follows, among other things, that art is not representation, as has often been thought. Representation is a skill, or craft of a particular kind. There is a preconceived end, to which the drawing, painting, or sculpting is the means. The work of the representational artist is the execution of a preconceived plan. Since art and crafts overlap, a representation may also be a work of art, but in that case it is not its representative aspect that makes it art (PA, 43). Collingwood here echoes John Dewey and anticipates Mark Rothko in their insistence that technique is not artistry.[3] This leaves it an open question in my mind whether John James Audubon, for instance, counts as an artist or simply as a superb craftsman.

My late teacher Morris Weitz once objected that there is no a priori reason "art" should be definable at all. Following Ludwig Wittgenstein's famous observation that there is no set of necessary and sufficient conditions that all games have in common, Weitz argues that the same may be true of all the activities we call "art," in other words that art is, in his terminology, an "open" concept, one for which we cannot anticipate all the things to which it may be applied. Alan Donagan has responded, however, that it has not been shown that no "open" concept can be defined; the most that can be claimed is that the definition must also be open in texture.[4]

b. Art as Magic

One version of the technical theory of art holds that art is the craft of arousing emotions on the part of its audience. These emotions may be of two kinds. They may be emotions that are discharged in the experience of the arousal; they may be emotions that require some action on part of the audience for their discharge. In the former case what the theory identifies is the pseudo-art called *amusement*; in the latter case the pseudo-art known as *magic*.

What, then, is magic? We already noted, in the last chapter, Collingwood's dismissal of the theory that magic is a kind of pseudoscience. To enlarge a bit on what we said there, one example used by anthropologists—Collingwood does not name them, but cites Sir Edward Tyler and Sir James Frazer as the most prominent representatives of the anthropology of his day—was the practice, among certain "savages," to burn their own nail clippings so as to prevent them from falling into the hands of one's enemies. The reason for this, according to standard anthropological theory, was that the savages perceived a causal connection between any part of one's body and the whole body, so that the destruction of the nail clippings would kill the owner of the clippings. Collingwood finds a couple of things wrong with this explanation. First, it attributes to savages an incredible lack of understanding of causal connections—incredible, given the savages' mastery of mining, metallurgy, animal husbandry, and agriculture (PA, 59).

Secondly, if the savage believed that the destruction of the clippings would kill him, then his own burning of the clippings would be suicide (PA, 60). Clearly, what the savage fears is not the destruction of the clippings, but their falling into hostile hands. The hostility, not the destruction, is what must be warded off. Similarly, we today may form attachments to prized possessions so that it would hurt us to see them treated disrespectfully. We may form such an attachment, for example, to an old, well-worn coat. In the "Folktales" manuscript Collingwood also instances the scuttling of King George V's yacht after his death, to prevent it from being sold into commercial uses and thus demeaned; the esteem in which the late king was held in this case extended to his property, such as the yacht (PE, 198). I am personally struck by a vivid recent example in the movie *Phantom Thread*, where the master dressmaker and his model and lover, seeing a customer carelessly spill wine on her brand new dress, spontaneously pull the dress off her and repossess it. The mistreatment of their labor of love does not hurt them physically, but it does hurt them emotionally to the point where they are prepared to commit assault and robbery.

So, magic is actions designed to instill emotions, for the sake of motivating action. Magic, Collingwood tells us, essentially incorporates art, such as singing, dancing, or drawing, but since, in magic, these are means to a preconceived end, they function, not as art, but as craft, or quasi-art (PA, 65). And the preconceived end is the arousal of emotions for the further purpose of stimulating action, a purpose for which magic is absolutely essential:

> Magical activity is a kind of dynamo supplying the mechanism of practical life with the emotional current that drives it. Hence magic is a necessity for every sort and condition of man, and is actually found in every healthy society. (PA, 68–9)

Examples from Collingwood's own society include patriotic songs, school songs, military music, war memorials, sports such as fox-hunting and amateur soccer, and of course weddings. The pageantry of marriage, Collingwood notes, has nothing to do with any love that may exist between the parties and is therefore often resented as an irrelevancy by young couples in love:

> Its purpose is to create an emotional motive for maintaining a partnership of a certain kind, not the partnership of lovers but the partnership of married people, recognized as such by the world, whether love is present or no. (PA, 75)

Weddings of course include processional music, songs, incantations as in the wedding vows, and dance, and these elements of art play an essential role in the wedding. Generally art, in one form or another, enters into every example of magic, but in these cases it is not the magical function that makes it art; magic *as such* is craft, not art.

c. Art as Amusement

Whereas Collingwood regards magic as essential to the health of society, he regards amusement rather as a disease. Every emotion goes through two stages: charge, or excitation, and discharge, in which the emotion plays itself out. Amusement is emotion whose discharge does not affect practical life, although strictly speaking that is a circular statement since practical life may be defined as that aspect of life which is not affected by amusement (PA, 78). This discharge is achieved by creating make-believe situations which represent real situations, up to a point. A prominent example is the use of sex in popular media, such as movies, love stories, and above all magazine covers:

> [P]ictures of pretty girls variously dressed or undressed, or (for the female reader) of attractive young men: pornography homoeopathically administered in doses too small to shock the desire for respectability, but quite large enough to produce the intended effect. (PA, 84–5)

Collingwood's quarrel here is of course not with the use of eroticism in art, but with titillation that becomes a substitute for the real thing. The constant exposure to explicitly sexual material in his view actually reduced the spectator's ability to enjoy healthy, real-life sex.

Another example of amusement art is the detective story, which produces pleasure by inducing fear, the delight in power, "the intellectual excitement of solving a puzzle; a fourth, the desire for adventure, ..." (PA, 86).

That amusement art is not real art is clear enough; like magic, it is a craft, which aims at producing a preconceived end. But what is wrong with amusement? Nothing, unless and until the quantity of amusement art reaches a critical mass, where it places an unbearable strain on practical life. There is fun that, as Collingwood puts it, is "paid for" in the very experience of it; for instance, the fun he gets out of writing *The Principles of Art* is paid for by the frustration experienced when the writing is going badly. But when he spends a day relaxing in the garden with a detective story by Dorothy L. Sayers, there is no payment in that experience, only a "bill run up," which comes due with the "Monday-morning" feeling when he returns to work (PA, 95). Now the danger is that, with the proliferation of amusement art in the modern world, the Monday-morning feeling will spread and intensify to the point where practical life becomes mere drudgery, in which people take less and less enjoyment.

As an aficionado of crime fiction, I personally cannot forbear to observe that Collingwood wrote this at a time when the apex of the genre was represented by the amusing but lightweight novels of Agatha Christie and Dorothy L. Sayers, of which Sayers's novels are no doubt more carefully crafted than Christie's. Had he lived to see the psychologically complex novels of P. D. James, Patricia Cornwell, Elizabeth George, or Louise Penny, he might have been moved to accept a blurrier line between amusement and art. In fairness, however, Collingwood did not deny that one and the same work can be *both* amusement *and* art, although in that case what makes it art must be something different from its amusement value.

Be that as it may, Collingwood lays the decline and fall of the Roman Empire at the feet of the practice of showering bread and circus on an urban proletariat "whose only function was to eat free bread and watch the shows" (PA, 99). His fear is that Great Britain in the 1930s stands at the threshold of a similar disaster, as urbanization and the mass production of amusement art have replaced the folk art that was traditionally the life blood of rural communities (PA, 101–02). A similar alarm, we may note, was sounded in the posthumously published "Art and the Machine," tentatively dated to 1926, where Collingwood blames photography, movies, and gramophone records for undermining art appreciation among the modern public by representing inferior reproductions as the real thing (PE, 285–304). While this may sound extreme, we shall note that it was written before the advent of either color photography or stereo sound. The far better known 1936 essay "The Work of

Art in the Age of Mechanical Reproducibility" by the German Critical Theorist Walter Benjamin presents a more nuanced view of mechanical reproduction of art, admitting the reproduction's lack of "aura," while emphasizing the accessibility of reproduced art to the masses.[5] Significantly, this essay was written a decade after Collingwood's, and it focuses primarily on motion pictures, a technology which Collingwood only mentioned in passing in 1926, and which was to be dramatically transformed over the following decade, for example, through the introduction of sound and colors.[6] But Collingwood's underlying concern about passively received pop culture replacing collectively created and continually re-created folk art in no way sounds dated. Indeed, the current proliferation of online games renders this concern as urgent as ever.

d. Expression

While the technical theory of art has been definitively refuted, we can take some clues from where it went wrong. There are three main lessons from our discussion of the technical theory:

(1) "[T]here is in art proper a distinction resembling that between means and ends, but not identical with it."
(2) "Art has something to do with emotion; what it does with it has a certain resemblance to arousing it, but is not arousing it."
(3) "Art has something to do with making things, but these things are not material things, made by imposing form on matter, and they are not made by skill" (PA, 108).

The first two lessons will be addressed in this section, the third lesson in the section that follows.

What has art got to do with emotions? It *expresses* them, and it does this in order to gain consciousness of them. When a person has an emotion, she is initially conscious of having an emotion, but not of what the emotion is. That consciousness comes to her in and through expressing the emotion. Since consciousness of the emotion is the purpose of expression, she expresses it primarily to herself and only secondarily to an audience. Expressing an emotion is a purposive process, that is, it is something at which we may succeed or fail. I may mistake one emotion for another, or find no expression of the emotion at all. (I may also *disown* my emotion; more of this in Section 2.)

In being purposive and directed, the expression of emotions bears some resemblance to the means-ends distinction, but they are not identical. Since I do not know what emotion I am trying to express until I have expressed it, there is no preconceived end toward which I am adopting appropriate means (PA, 111).

Expressing emotions must be distinguished from *describing* emotions. Saying "I am angry" describes an emotion, but does not really express it. "Angry" is a general term that refers to a class of emotions; *my* anger at *this* particular moment is a unique individual emotion, which is distorted by the use of a generalizing term, which is why a poet, when expressing a particular emotion, never uses the name of that emotion (PA, 112). This is another example of how art differs from craft; the true poet, when expressing an emotion, tries to express it in its unique individuality, how it differs from all other emotions. The amusement artist, who is really a craftsperson, tries to arouse emotions generally understood—lust, say, or thrill—only so can he or she reach a mass audience (PA, 113).

Expressing an emotion is also different from *betraying* an emotion. When I am afraid I may turn pale and stammer, but I do not do this purposively, and these symptoms of my fear do not necessarily bring me to consciousness of my fear (PA, 122).

We have spoken so far of the expression of emotions in general; what is the special role of the artist in this context? Collingwood will return to this question when formulating his final theory; we are still at the pre-theoretic stage of nailing down the generally known facts, and at this point he is concerned to emphasize what *unites* the artist and her audience. When reading a poem and understanding it as the poet intended it, I am expressing my emotions in the poet's words, and I am to that extent a poet. Collingwood approvingly quotes Coleridge as saying that "we know a man for a poet by the fact that he makes us poets" (PA, 118). There is, in this view, no distinction *in kind* between artist and audience, but there is an important division of labor: "[T]he poet is a man who can solve for himself the problem of expressing [an emotion], whereas the audience can express it only when the poet has shown them how" (PA, 119).

We shall pause here to note that the above account recognizably foreshadows the philosophy that was to animate the American Abstract Expressionist movement, a philosophy most explicitly articulated by Mark Rothko, as follows: "A picture is not its color, its form, or its anecdote, but an intent entity idea";[7] more succinctly yet: "A painting is not a picture of an experience, but is the experience."[8] Somewhat less explicitly Clyfford Still, a lesser known figure but a major influence on Rothko's later work, as well as on Robert Motherwell and other representatives of the movement, was to remove the titles from all his works, presumably lest spectators would be tempted to divine the artist's experience, rather than identify their own experience. Differing somewhat from Rothko, Still once observed that communication "'is what the comic strip does.' And when he was asked whether he painted solely for himself, the answer was yes."[9] As Collingwood had put it in 1924, the painter paints in order to see (OPA, 129). So, in Collingwoodian terms, the artist strives to express and thereby come to know her own emotions, not specifically to communicate those emotions to the spectators; but she will succeed as an artist to the extent that the spectators independently recognize the work of art as expressing *their* emotions. This, I take it, is what Still was driving at.

Abstract Expressionism appeared in the 1940s, well after the publication of *The Principles of Art*, and I do not mean to suggest that its practitioners were in any way influenced by Collingwood. Rather, my contention is that both Collingwood and the practitioners had captured the same *Zeitgeist*, presumably through absorption of the European predecessors of Abstract Expressionism, such as, for example, German Expressionism, Cubism, and Surrealism, all known to be early influences on Rothko, at least. The main point, however, is that this striking echo of Collingwood's theory in the self-understanding of a major artistic movement apparently uninfluenced by Collingwood speaks volumes for that theory, as we have considered it so far.

e. Imagination

The technical theory is also correct that art has to do with making things, but what is it that is being made? And how is it being made? What the artist does is not technical making, or *fabrication*, but rather something called *creation*, which differs significantly from fabrication, as when one creates a disturbance, or a demand, or a political system:

> The person who makes these things is acting voluntarily; he is acting responsibly; but he need not be acting in order to achieve any ulterior end; he need not be following a preconceived plan; and he is certainly not transforming anything that can properly be called raw material. (PA, 129)

So, artistic creation is voluntary and deliberate; yet the artist does not know in advance what is going to come of it. Secondly, a work of art differs from a disturbance or a political system in that it can be completely created in the artist's mind. We may say that the work of art is imagined or imaginary, but not in the sense in which "imaginary" is distinct from and contrasted with "real." A bridge that exists only in an engineer's head is an imaginary bridge; the bridge becomes real only when it is actually constructed in the physical world (PA, 131). But there is nothing corresponding to this distinction in the composition of a tune. In the process of composing the tune the composer may hum it, play it on an instrument, or write down notes on paper. But she may do none of these things and yet the tune, if sufficiently simple, may be completely composed in her mind. And even if she does write the notes down on paper, what is on the paper is not the tune, but only musical notation which enables readers to construct the tune in their own heads (PA, 135).

Imagination, so understood, is different from make-believe, which implies a distinction between the make-believe situation and a real situation which it simulates. Imagination, unlike make-believe, is simply indifferent to the distinction between real and unreal (PA, 136). By calling a tune, a painting, or any work of art imaginary, we are abstracting from any physical properties that may accompany it. The symphony we listen to is not a succession of sounds; it is what listening to those sounds enables us to imagine. In that process of imagination we, the listeners, supply sounds that are not actually heard, while screening out other sounds that are not part of the symphony (PA, 143). Painters do not paint what they see; in fact, Cézanne "began to paint like a blind man" (PA, 144). What Collingwood has in mind is Cézanne's use of multiple perspectives in his paintings, which was to form the basis for Picasso and Braque's Cubism. Collingwood instances specifically Cézanne's paintings of *Mont Saint-Victoire*, but the point may be more evident in his still lives, where we see the table top from above while the apples and the wine bottle on the table are—impossibly—at eye level. And the enjoyment of a painting, as Cézanne exemplified, and the art historian Bernard Berenson made explicit, is not a specifically visual experience; it may equally be a tactile experience, in which one experiences, say, certain muscular movements (PA, 147). So, though a tune is a work of the imagination, it is not sounds that we imagine; in a painting, it is not color patterns that we imagine; in all forms of art what is imagined is a total experience (PA, 151).

Once again, Collingwood echoes Dewey, who observed that, just because we read poetry with our eyes, we do not therefore think of the experience as a visual experience. Similarly, the fact that we view a painting with our eyes does not make the aesthetic experience a specifically visual one.[10] But there are other ways of looking at the matter. Yes, as Collingwood observes, a blind person utilizes multiple perspectives to glean the shape of an object, but so do seeing people. As noted by the philosopher Nelson Goodman, we do not determine the shape of an unfamiliar object by standing stock still staring straight at it; instead we move around, or at least move our head, to gain depth perception.[11] Such considerations led the celebrated artist David Hockney to comment that Cézanne "was the first artist to paint using two eyes," a conclusion basically opposite to Collingwood's.[12] This does not, however, undermine Dewey's and Collingwood's recognition that the aesthetic experience may be tactile, *as well as* visual. And Goodman concurs that painters do not paint what they see; they paint what, under normal gallery conditions, will convey the same experience as what they see.[13]

This point was forcefully driven home to me personally by recently encountering Joseph Raffael's 1974 painting *Paper Mill*.[14] There was nothing in the painting that "resembled" a paper mill; if I were pressured to specify what the painting looked like I would say either a stormy sea or the eye of a hurricane. Yet to one who has worked in paper mills, as I have, the painting vividly evokes the experience of watching the paper web rolling at high speed through a machine the length of a football field. And the experience is not a visual one, but rather a visceral one: I could close my eyes and hear the rhythmic beat of the machine and smell the hot, moist scent of paper. So the painting, without actually representing a paper mill, evoked the experience, in a suitably prepared viewer, of actually being in a paper mill.

To return to the concept of imagination: In discussing Collingwood's theory, Richard Wollheim has distinguished a stronger and a weaker sense of "imaginary"; something can be imaginary in a sense incompatible with its being real, like gods or heroes, or fictitious characters, or it can be imaginary in the weaker sense of simply being imagined, like the bridge in the engineer's head, which may later be built. Wollheim finds it unclear which sense Collingwood intends when he calls a work of art "imaginary"— Wollheim is not the only one to complain of carelessness in Collingwood's writing—but he holds that only in the stronger sense does it say anything about the nature of art.[15] And in this sense he finds it clearly false to say that a work of art is imaginary.

Alan Donagan has also found problems with Collingwood's use of the term "imaginary" as interchangeable with "in the artist's head." A work of art is imaginary, Donagan grants, in the sense of being expressive or linguistic, but it does not follow that it exists in anybody's head.[16]

Finally, imagination, as understood by Collingwood, forms a bridge between feeling and intellect, a point noted by David Boucher in the previous chapter (PA, 215).

2. Consciousness and Its Corruption

Collingwood's psychology occupies a substantial portion of *The Principles of Art*. There are three levels of emotion: "psychical emotions," which are preconscious (PA, 230), "emotions of consciousness" (PA, 232), and intellectual emotions (PA, 266). The first level combines sensation and an "emotional charge" which, though conceptually distinct, are yet not separate experiences:

> When an infant is terrified at the sight of a scarlet curtain blazing in the sunlight, there are not two distinct experiences in his mind, one sensation of red and the other an emotion of fear; there is only one experience, a terrifying red. (PA, 161)

The sensation takes precedence over the emotion, not temporally, but in the sense that the sensation is a precondition for the emotion.

At the second level we find emotions which arise only through the consciousness of self, such as hatred, love, anger, and shame (PA, 231). Here we are aware both of ourselves and of some object that we are attracted to or that opposes or resists us. Unlike psychical emotions, the emotions of consciousness are expressible in language as well as in bodily expressions, such as blushing, tensing of muscles, and the like.

The intellectual emotions are emotional charges on thought experiences, and these are expressible in language.

The concept of emotion is thus analyzable as a scale of overlapping forms, as discussed in Chapter 3.

It has been pointed out by Donagan that later, in *The New Leviathan*, Collingwood was to introduce a more nuanced—and, in Donagan's view, more adequate—distinction between appetite, passion, desire, self-liberation, and reason.[17] We shall return to this in Chapter 8.

Feeling, the psychical level, differs from thinking, the intellectual level, in several respects. First, in thinking there is what Collingwood calls "bipolarity": thinking can be done well or badly, successfully or unsuccessfully; there is nothing corresponding in feeling. Secondly, there is a certain privacy about feeling: I cannot share my feeling of cold, unlike the thought that there are ten degrees of frost. Thirdly, and following from the preceding two distinctions, feelings, unlike thoughts, cannot contradict each other: from my feeling cold, nothing follows about anyone else feeling either cold or hot (PA, 157–8).

However, the expression of a feeling brings that feeling into consciousness, and in consciousness there is bipolarity; the statement "This is how I feel" has as its opposite "This is not how I feel": "A true consciousness is the confession to ourselves of our feelings; a false consciousness would be disowning them, i.e. thinking about one of them 'That feeling is not mine'" (PA, 216). How might that happen? As a particular feeling comes into my consciousness, I find myself frightened or ashamed of it; then instead of expressing it and dealing with it, I turn my attention away from it, as if it were not my feeling, perhaps projecting it on to someone else. Collingwood gives the example—a somewhat trivial one—of coming to breakfast in ill humor but, not wishing to admit this feeling, accusing the others at breakfast of ill humor (PA, 218). More serious examples are easy to come by: a feeling of superiority toward those thought to belong to a different race, or toward the lower classes, enjoyment of someone else's misfortune, sexual desire for a close relative, intense dislike of a close relative, and so on. We do not want to recognize these feelings in ourselves, so we repress them. In a recent book on political philosophy Howard DeLong—a long-time student of Collingwood's philosophy—instances the American Founding Fathers' toleration of slavery as an example of corruption of consciousness.[18]

The problem with corruption of consciousness is not just that the disowned feelings do not get confronted, which is bad enough, but the corruption also infects those feelings that are brought into consciousness; their expression becomes a false expression: "But whenever some element in experience is disowned by consciousness, that other element upon which attention is fixed, and which consciousness claims as its own, becomes a sham" (PA, 218). Thus the corruption of consciousness may poison a person's mind to an incalculable extent. To hark back to our examples, if I disown racial prejudice, my feeling of being open minded is a false one even if it does not reference race; if I disown class prejudice, my professed universalism is false even if it does not reference class and so on.

Collingwood notes that this phenomenon has already been recognized and described by psychologists:

> The disowning of experiences they call repression; the ascription of these to other persons, projection; their consolidation into a mass of experience, homogeneous in itself (as it well may be, if the disowning is systematically done), dissociation; and the building up of a bowdlerized experience which we will admit to be our own, fantasy-building. (PA, 218–19)

We ordinarily divide untruth into two kinds: errors and lies. But at the level of mere consciousness this distinction is not yet made, so the corruption of consciousness is neither error nor lie:

> The untruthful consciousness, in disowning certain features of its own experience, is not making a bona fide mistake, for its faith is not good; it is shirking something which its business is to face. But it is not concealing the truth, for there is no truth which it knows and is concealing. (PA, 219)

"Self-deception," Collingwood aptly notes, is an inappropriate term which attempts to explain what takes place in one mind by analogy with something taking place between two minds. Corruption of consciousness, he concludes, is "sheer or undifferentiated evil, evil in itself, as yet undifferentiated into evil suffered or misfortune and evil done or wickedness" (PA, 220). We may add that there is also a striking parallel to Jean-Paul Sartre's later articulation of "bad faith," where the agent disowns her own agency as a way of escaping responsibility for her actions. Finally, while corruption of consciousness is a form of denial, Collingwood is not saying or implying that *all* denial is bad. If there is absolutely nothing I can do about an unfortunate circumstance, being in denial may be a good thing.

3. Art as Language

Art, we have seen so far, is expression and imagination. Art, Collingwood finally tells us, is also language. But what is language? First of all, language is both imaginative and expressive: "to call it imaginative is to describe what it is, to call it expressive is to describe what it does" (PA, 225). The primary, most fundamental function of language is the expression of emotions; the use of language to make statements is a secondary development; in its primary function language is not something that is there to be used, it comes into being through its use. The artist does not express preexisting emotions which hitherto lay unexpressed; since her expression is a conscious activity the expressed emotions must be appropriate to the conscious level of experience (PA, 238).

> [T]he expression of emotion is not, as it were, a dress made to fit an emotion already existing, but is an activity without which the experience of that emotion cannot exist. Take away the language, and you take away that which is expressed; there is nothing left but crude feeling at the merely psychic level. (PA, 244)

As has been noted, for example, by Louis Mink, while Collingwood was apparently unaware of the linguistic philosophy being developed by Ludwig Wittgenstein, but published only after Collingwood's death, nonetheless there are notable parallels to Wittgenstein's conception of a language game that we inhabit rather than use.[19] Similarly, when Collingwood says, "one does not first acquire a language and then use it. To possess it and to use it are the same" (PA, 225). David Boucher has noted the parallel to Wittgenstein's observation that "the meaning of a word is its use in language."[20]

Language, Collingwood holds, originates in gesture, from which speech gradually evolves. When hunger drives a baby to cry, the cry is not speech, but it is already language. But when the baby learns that crying causes it to be fed, and cries deliberately so as to be fed, this cry is a primitive form of speech (PA, 236).

Art, as we have seen, is expression. It takes mere psychic feeling and converts it into something else, an emotion, or total imaginative experience, which is a conscious state, and which the artist is conscious of only in so far as she expresses it. It differs from craft in that the latter aims at inducing certain states of mind in other people. Now, although the end of the artistic activity is not preconceived—the artist cannot describe the end in advance since, if she could, she would already have expressed it and the artistic activity would have been completed—nonetheless it is a purposive activity, and the artist knows what she is trying to do, in the specific sense that in the process of doing it she can tell whether she is doing it successfully or unsuccessfully. Or rather, she knows it in so far as her consciousness is uncorrupted; of this, more later. While this may sound paradoxical—and it has been suggested that this view is inconsistent as I cannot know that I have fallen short without knowing precisely what I have fallen short of[21]—Collingwood is really saying something fairly commonplace. As noted by Aaron Ridley, if art is *trying to say something*, then as an artist of course I cannot say in advance what I am trying to say—that would amount to saying it—and yet, as I am saying it, I know what I am doing and I can tell whether the words come out right or not.[22] There is no doubt in my mind when I say, "Oh no, that is not what I meant to say," even though I could not—logically could not—have specified in advance what I meant to say, since that would amount to saying it:

> The watching of his own work with a vigilant and discriminating eye, which decides at every moment of the process whether it is being successful or not, is not a critical activity subsequent to, and reflective upon, the artist's work, it is an integral part of that work itself. (PA, 281)

To try to do something is to try to do it well; to succeed in expressing something is to express it well; therefore the definition of art is at the same time a definition of *good* art (PA, 282). What then is bad art? It is not magic or amusement; these, we have seen, are activities falsely believed to be art. Bad art happens when a consciousness fails to grasp its own emotion. This failure, the corruption of consciousness, is not sheer inaction; it is doing something, but doing something other than expressing it:

> What he has done is either to shirk it or dodge it: to disguise it from itself by pretending either that the emotion he feels is not that one but a different one, or that the person who feels it is not himself but someone else: two alternatives which are so far from being mutually exclusive that in fact they are always concurrent and correlative. (PA, 282)

Bad art is the corruption of consciousness. "Art is not a luxury, and bad art is not something we can afford to tolerate" (PA, 284). We need art in order to know ourselves, and we need self-knowledge in order to rise above the merely psychical level of experience. "Bad art, the corrupt consciousness, is the true *radix malorum*" (PA, 285). That is, the root of all evil.

4. The Artist and the Community

As we have seen, art is the expression of emotions which do not exist until brought into consciousness. It is thus not a matter of externalizing an experience that already exists in the artist's mind. A painter may paint what she sees, but it is not a matter of first seeing and then painting; she paints the subject in order to see it (PA, 304). The work of art is not a physical object, but something that exists in the artist's imagination and in the audience's imagination in so far as she has an audience. Here again, Collingwood is at one with Dewey.[23] However, the conscious experience presupposes a sensuous experience, not in the sense that the sensuous experience comes first and is succeeded and superseded by the conscious experience, but rather in the sense that imagination is a sensuous experience raised to the level of consciousness (PA, 306). There is thus a necessary connection between the aesthetic experience and the bodily work of art, although the art is strictly speaking not, as we have seen, the bodily work. Now, the sensuous experience of seeing a painting produces in the spectator's mind the same imaginative experience as the sensuous experience of painting produced in the painter's mind—as was also noted by Dewey.[24]

How do we know that it is *the same* experience? Collingwood admits that we can never know for certain, and the greater an artist is, the more likely it is that we have only understood him partially and imperfectly (PA, 309). But understanding someone else is always an uncertain business. In a conversation, how do I know that my interlocutor attaches the same meaning to his words that I do? I don't know, but the longer the conversation goes on without generating blank stares, the more likely it is that we understand each other. Similarly, the increased sense of understanding—subjective as it is— that comes with prolonged acquaintance with a work of art—or the works of an artist—is a pretty good indicator of actual understanding.

Collingwood uses the example of T. S. Eliot's *Sweeney among the Nightingales*, which he read and enjoyed for many years before it finally hit him what the poem was actually about; that is, that Rachel and "the lady in the cape" were both Clytemnestra (PA, 310). In my personal experience I was for many years puzzled by Degas's nudes. Why were they posed so awkwardly? Why did the same painter who painted such graceful dancers also paint such ugly nudes?

The hypothesis of misogyny could not quite account for it. It was not until I saw a special exhibit of dozens of Degas's nudes together that it finally struck me that he was deliberately subverting the classic conception of the nude as a sex object. By painting his nudes not as things to be looked at, but as people *doing* things, he was humanizing the nude in an almost unprecedented way. (I say "almost," since Goya's *The Naked Maja* subverted the nude in its own way by turning her from a sexual object into a sexual agent, as did Manet later, but that is a different story.) Am I *certain* that this is what was in Degas's mind? Of course not, and the next time I see one of Degas's nudes I may see something else in it. There is no finality possible.

(To be clear, the fact that Degas and Goya each had a preconceived goal in mind does not preclude their *also* expressing emotions that came to them only in the act of painting. It is arguable, for instance, that while Goya intended Maja as a sexual agent, he may not have preconceived the subtle ambiguity—either challenging or inviting—of her facial expression.)

The audience is in this way the artist's collaborator; by interpreting the artist's work the audience recreates in their own minds the emotions expressed by the artist, a point later also made at length by the art historian Ernst Gombrich.[25] The converse of this observation is that the artist's business is to express emotions that she shares with the audience. To live fully above the merely sensuous level we need to become conscious of our emotions, and it is the special skill and the special responsibility of the artist to enable us to do this. The artist also collaborates with performers; no amount of notation can specify exactly how a piece of music is to be played or sung, and no amount of stage direction can specify exactly how a play is to be performed (PA, 320). Again, examples readily come to mind. Does Shakespeare's *Henry V* glorify war, as in Sir Lawrence Olivier's version, or is it an antiwar play, as in Kenneth Branagh's version? Is *The Merchant of Venice* Shylock's play, as played, for example, by F. Murray Abraham, or Portia's play, as played by Lili Rabe? There is no answer. Thus, while the author collaborates with the performers, the performers collaborate with their audience: "The company is not acting a play at all; it is performing certain actions which will become a play when there is an audience present to act as a sounding-board" (PA, 322).

Finally, the artist collaborates with his or her predecessors—a collaboration which, in the twentieth century, is seriously hampered by the institution of copyright, from which Shakespeare and Bach were free (PA, 325). There are echoes here of T. S. Eliot's 1919 essay "Tradition and the Individual Talent," which Collingwood does not explicitly cite, although he cites with approval Eliot's 1923 essay "The Function of Criticism."

Collingwood saw Western civilization of the 1930s decaying around him, largely through the promiscuous proliferation of mass-produced amusement art, which dramatically eroded audience participation in real art. He saw this decay most vividly recounted in T. S. Eliot's *The Waste Land*, with its stark depiction of the modern human condition. By holding up this completely depressing mirror in front of us, Eliot brings us to a vital awareness of our condition:

> The reason why they need [the artist] is that no community altogether knows its own heart; and by failing in this knowledge a community deceives itself on the one subject concerning which ignorance means death. (PA, 336)

Art, Collingwood concludes, is "the community's medicine for the worst disease of the mind, the corruption of consciousness" (PA, 336).

We have noted along the way several parallels with Dewey's *Art as Experience*, which was published in 1934, although I know of no evidence that Collingwood was familiar with this work. We may now summarize their points of agreement as follows: (i) Art is not technique and therefore not representation. (ii) Art is expression of an experience that comes into being *through* the act of expression. (iii) The artistic experience and the aesthetic experience are one and the same. (iv) The work of art is the experience, not the physical object enabling the experience. (v) Aesthetic experience involves multiple senses; the experience of a painting is not specifically visual. Finally, both recognized their aesthetics as part of a critique of industrial capitalism; this critique is muted in *The Principles of Art*, but explicit in the two essays, unpublished in Collingwood's lifetime, "Art and the Machine" (c. 1926, PE, 291–304) and "Man Goes Mad" (c. 1936, PE, 305–5).[26]

Collingwood's biographer Fred Inglis has called *The Principles of Art* an "undoubted masterpiece," and I would concur.[27] In the same vein the philosopher Aaron Ridley has claimed that Collingwood "was one of the twentieth century's few outstanding philosophers of art."[28] It is nonetheless hard to disagree with Donagan's conclusion that *The Principles of Art* "is at bottom the most desperate of all of Collingwood's books," a sentiment echoed by Ridley, who finds Collingwood's final conclusion "a rather bleak claim."[29]

The corruption of consciousness was pervasively at work in the Continental acceptance of fascist and Nazi irrationalism, and in the willful obtuseness of the British public and its leaders vis-à-vis the totalitarian danger. Collingwood is holding up art as civilization's hope for survival, but it is a faint hope. Unlike Collingwood in 1938, we of course know what was to happen next, the descent of European civilization into the depths of barbarism, but there are durable lessons here for our own time, which may not be as different from the 1930s as we might like to think, a theme to which we will return in Chapter 8.

Further Reading

Aaron Ridley, *R.G. Collingwood, A Philosophy of Art*.
Peter Johnson, *R.G. Collingwood: An Introduction*, Chapter Seven.
Alan Donagan, *The Later Philosophy of R.G. Collingwood*, Chapter Five.
Louis Mink, *Mind, History, and Dialectic: The Philosophy of R.G. Collingwood*, Chapter Seven.

6

Questions and Answers

In 1938, at the age of forty-nine, Collingwood wrote what may be both his most celebrated and his most controversial work, *An Autobiography*. The literary qualities of this work are universally acknowledged to be superb, but the philosophical doctrines set forth in it have sparked intense controversy, and the veracity of Collingwood's account of his philosophical development has come into question. Both concerns will be addressed in this chapter.

Although forty-nine is a rather young age for an autobiographer, Collingwood was in ill health and aware that he might not live to complete several major works in progress. Hence the purpose of the autobiography was, in Collingwood's words, "to put on record some brief account of the work I have not yet been able to publish, in case I am not able to publish it in full" (A, 118). This purpose explains the often noted selectivity of the autobiography: Collingwood's major published works—such as *Religion and Philosophy*, *Speculum Mentis*, *An Essay on Philosophical Method*, and *The Principles of Art*—are all mentioned in passing, but nothing is said about their contents. It is Collingwood's *unpublished* work that he is concerned to explain, primarily *An Essay on Metaphysics*, *The Idea of History*, and *The Principles of History*. And this, to Collingwood, was a matter of urgency—an urgency reflected in the often intemperate tone of the book. Collingwood was alarmed by the rise of fascism and Nazism in Europe and by his own government's apparent indifference to the totalitarian threat. Combating this threat, he held, required a philosophical understanding of the relationship of thought to action, and this in turn required an understanding of history. The autobiography thus has a clear and openly avowed political purpose, as well as a polemical, often hectoring, tone.

1. Critique of the Realists

An Autobiography is in large part a frontal attack on the Oxbridge Realists: primarily Collingwood's teacher John Cook Wilson and H. A. Prichard, both at Oxford, secondarily Bertrand Russell and G. E. Moore at Cambridge. The vehemence of the criticism reflects Collingwood's conviction that the Realists by virtue of their doctrine deprived their students of the ability and inclination to think critically about morals and politics. For instance Prichard, in his famous paper "Does Moral Philosophy Rest on a Mistake?," argued that moral philosophy should be pursued as a purely theoretical science, with no implications for practice, while Russell proposed eliminating ethics from philosophy altogether (A, 47).[1] As an undergraduate at Oxford, Collingwood initially accepted the Realism of his teachers, while at the same time growing increasingly doubtful of both the positive doctrine and the critical methods of the Realists. Their central positive doctrine he characterizes as the doctrine that knowledge is a single act of intuition, what Cook Wilson at Oxford called "apprehending," what Moore at Cambridge referred to as "transparency," and what Alexander at Manchester called "compresence." Their chief method, according to Collingwood, consisted in simply criticizing and refuting an isolated philosophical doctrine or proposition without raising the historical question of whether anybody had actually held it in the precise form in which it was "refuted." So Moore, in his "Refutation of Idealism," attacked Berkeley for a position which was almost the exact opposite of Berkeley's, while Cook Wilson, in his lectures on Bradley, "constantly criticized Bradley for views which were not Bradley's" (A, 22).

This complaint against the Realists may strike a familiar note: it is, in part, Collingwood's case against "Critical Philosophy" in *An Essay on Philosophical Method*. Now Collingwood tells us that, from the point of view of his own preoccupation with history, he grew dissatisfied with the ahistorical methods of the Realists, and that, from his personal experience of archaeological research, he came to doubt their doctrine that knowledge consists in some sort of simple and direct intuition. By degrees he came to suspect that his dissatisfaction with both the methods and the doctrine of the Realists was not coincidental; that there was, in fact, an intimate connection between the two.

This connection Collingwood found in the Realists' neglect of the role played by the questioning activity in the act of knowing. The importance of the questioning activity was disclosed to Collingwood in the course of archaeological excavations, where he found himself in what he termed a "laboratory of knowledge":

> Experience soon taught me that under these laboratory conditions one found out nothing at all except in answer to a question; and not a vague question either, but a definite one. That when one dug saying merely, "let us see what there is here," one learnt nothing, except casually in so far as casual questions arose in one's mind while digging: "Is that black stuff peat or occupation soil? Is that a potsherd under your foot? Are those loose stones a ruined wall?" (A, 24)

This firsthand experience of archaeological research struck Collingwood by its contrast to the classroom account of knowledge handed down by his professors; his experience seemed both a refutation of Realist epistemology and a corroboration of a very different approach which Collingwood repeatedly associated with the names of Bacon and Descartes: "Each of them had said very plainly that knowledge comes only by asking questions, and that these questions must be the right questions and asked in the right order" (A, 25). The reference to Bacon, of course, is to his injunction that nature be "put to the question"; the reference to Descartes is presumably to his methodological injunction that complex questions be broken down into simpler ones, to be dealt with in a piecemeal and orderly fashion. Combining these two ideas, as he had rediscovered them in his own archaeological work, Collingwood arrived at his proposal for a new, revolutionary logic, which he named "the logic of question and answer."

2. The Logic of Question and Answer

During the First World War Collingwood was working at the Admiralty in London and daily walked past the Albert Memorial on his way to and from his office. At first, he found the memorial so ugly that he could not bear to look at it, but averted his eyes, but then he forced himself to look and was confronted with the question, why had the architect Scott created something that ugly? That question prompted the second one, what had Scott tried to achieve?

> Had he tried to produce a beautiful thing; a thing, I meant, which we should have thought beautiful? If so, he had of course failed. But had he perhaps

been trying to produce something different? If so, he might possibly have succeeded. (A, 29)

(Though Collingwood did not pursue the question of Scott's intentions, it seems reasonably clear that the Albert Memorial was intended as "magic," as that concept is elucidated in both the "Folktales" manuscript and *The Principles of Art*.)

This observation reinforced the lessons already derived from Collingwood's archaeological work and led him to propose what he envisioned as a revolution in logic. The new logic he proposed was founded on a principle derived from Bacon and Descartes:

> ... the principle that a body of knowledge consists not of "propositions," "statements," "judgements," ... but of these together with the questions they are meant to answer; and that a logic in which the answers are attended to and the questions neglected is a false logic. (A, 30–1)

The idea of the logic of question and answer is this: you cannot find out what someone means by a written or spoken statement without knowing what question that statement was meant to answer. The *specific* question, not a general one. If, in Collingwood's example, my car will not start, and after checking number one plug, I were to say "number one plug is all right," this is not an answer to the question "Why won't my car go?" but to the more specific question "Is it because number one plug is not sparking that my car won't go?" (A, 32). Someone who takes my statement to be an answer to the former question simply does not get the meaning of my statement. So the unit of meaning is not the statement, or proposition, but the question-and-answer complex of which the statement or proposition is a part. (In his earlier works, we saw Collingwood write of "judgements"; in *An Autobiography* he replaces this with "propositions.")

Already in *Speculum Mentis* Collingwood had noted that "assertions are only answers to questions," and he added that "the same truth has lately dawned on the astonished gaze of the pragmatists" (SM, 77–8). Collingwood does not elaborate, nor tell us which pragmatists he has in mind, but the most famous pragmatist of the day was presumably William James, whose work Collingwood was familiar with and whose psychology of religion had come under fire in Collingwood's *Religion and Philosophy*. James's famous squirrel example may therefore further illustrate Collingwood's point. On a field trip

2. The Logic of Question and Answer 119

James once found his companions in a heated discussion over this question: Suppose a hunter faces a tree and there is a squirrel on the opposite side. As the hunter walks around the tree, the squirrel moves with him, so that it is always out of sight of the hunter. Now the question is, does the hunter go around the squirrel, or not? James's answer:

> depends on what you *practically mean* by "going round" the squirrel. If you mean passing from the north of him to the east, then to the south, then to the west, and then to the north of him again, obviously the man does go round him. . . . But if on the contrary you mean being first in front of him, then on the right of him, then behind him, then on his left, and finally in front again, it is quite as obvious that the man fails to go round him.[2]

James's purpose, clearly stated, was to illustrate *practical* meaning, but the example can equally be taken to illustrate the need for *specificity* in questioning. The statement "The man goes around the squirrel" is clearly not understood so long as you take it to be an answer to "Does the man go around the squirrel?" To understand the statement we need to take it as an answer to a more specific question. This is precisely Collingwood's point in the sparkplug example; whether he so interpreted James must remain a matter for speculation.

In *An Autobiography*, Collingwood goes on to argue that contradiction does not belong to propositions but to question-and-answer complexes. In Collingwood's example, the propositions "the content of this box is one" and "the content of this box is many" do not contradict each other if the first is an answer to the question "are there one or many chess sets in this box?" and the second is the answer to the question "are there one or many chessmen in this box?" (A, 41). In general, Collingwood concludes, no two propositions can contradict each other unless they are answers to the same question.

The same applies to truth. A proposition is not per se either true or false; it is true or false only relatively to some particular question.

Propositional logic, under which rubric Collingwood includes both traditional logic and modern symbolic logic (without distinguishing between propositional and predicate logic), takes the proposition to be the unit of meaning, truth, and contradiction, and so must be rejected in favor of a logic of question and answer.

Collingwood claims to have spelled out the logic of question and answer in detail in 1917, in a manuscript called *Truth and Contradiction*, which he destroyed after it was rejected by a publisher. (A fragment of the manuscript has actually survived.) In *An Autobiography* he offers only a few suggestions as to what this logic would consist in. First, every question and answer has to be relevant or appropriate to the context in which it appears. Secondly, each question has to "arise." Later, in *An Essay on Metaphysics*, Collingwood gave this example: the question "Have you stopped beating your wife yet?" arises only on the presupposition that the person addressed has been in the habit of beating his wife (EM, 26). Thirdly, each answer must be "the right" answer to the question it seeks to answer (A, 37). By "right," Collingwood tells us, he does not mean "true," but his explanation of the distinction has been widely regarded as unhelpful. When Socrates asks, in Plato's *Republic*, whether you would prefer a just man or a man who knows how to play draughts, as your partner in draughts, Polemarchus's answer "a man who knows how to play draughts," is "false" because it falsely supposes justice and the ability to play draughts are comparable skills. Yet it is the "right" answer "because it constitutes a link, and a sound one, in the chain of questions and answers by which the falseness of that presupposition is made manifest" (A, 38). This could be clearer: Alan Donagan has clarified it by explaining that if a thinker is following a false scent, inadvertently or in the course of a reductio ad absurdum, the "right" answer—the one that allows the question-and-answer process to go forward, will be "false" in the ordinary sense of the word.[3]

Collingwood distinguishes the ordinary sense of the word "true" from what he considers the proper sense, as follows:

> What is ordinarily meant when a proposition is called "true," I thought, was this: (a) the proposition belongs to a question-and-answer complex which as a whole is "true" in the proper sense of the word; (b) within this complex it is an answer to a certain question; (c) the question is what we ordinarily call a sensible or intelligent question, not a silly one, or in my terminology it "arises"; (d) the proposition is the "right" answer to that question. (A, 38)

Collingwood's reflections on the Albert Memorial further led him to ponder issues in the history of philosophy. Specifically, he came to question whether, as the Realists maintained, there are "eternal" problems in philosophy. Plato's *Republic* and Hobbes's *Leviathan* are both about "the state," but is there really some one thing that they are both about? Plato wrote about the Greek polis of the fourth century BCE, whereas Hobbes wrote about the absolutist state of the seventeenth century. The problems confronting Plato were thus obviously very different from those confronting Hobbes (A, 61). Yet there is a reason why we use the same word "state" to refer to their respective political entities:

> The sameness is the sameness of an historical process . . . Plato's πολις and Hobbes's absolutist State are related by a traceable historical process, whereby one has turned into the other; any one who ignores that process, denies the difference between them, and argues that here Plato's theory contradicts Hobbes's one of them must be wrong. (A, 62)

Listening to the Realists, Collingwood tells us, was like having a nightmare in which someone has got it into his head that the word τριηρης is the Greek word for "steamship," and when shown that Greek descriptions of triremes did not sound anything like steamships, would say, "'That is just what I say. These Greek philosophers … were terribly muddle-headed, and their theory of steamers is all wrong'" (A, 64).

One implication of the logic of question and answer for the history of philosophy is that there is a special problem with understanding what the philosophical "classics" were saying. If they answered their question successfully, that question would no longer be asked, and so would need to be reconstructed by the historian (A, 39). But what this means is that we can only understand past philosophers (and other historical actors; cf. Chapter 4) to the extent that they successfully solved their problems. For the passage stating the solution is our chief and often sole evidence of what the problem was; so, if it was not the right solution, it would be impossible to infer what the problem was (A, 69–70).

In this context, Collingwood makes one of his most controversial claims:

> Naval historians think it worth while to argue about Nelson's tactical plan at Trafalgar because he won the battle. It is not worth while arguing about Villeneuve's plan. He did not succeed in carrying it out, and therefore no one will ever know what it was. We can only guess. And guessing is not history. (A, 70)

Disclaimer: I am not personally familiar with the literature about the Battle of Trafalgar, so Collingwood may very well be right about this particular case. But to the extent that he is making a more general point, it is surely exaggerated. Even when an agent is unsuccessful, we can frequently infer their intentions from their actions and the situation in which they found themselves. As I am more familiar with the American Civil War than with the Napoleonic Wars, the example of Ulysses Grant comes to mind. At the siege of Vicksburg, Grant made numerous unsuccessful attempts at invading the city before finally succeeding. In each case it is perfectly clear to historians what Grant was trying to do, and why he failed. The same is true of the Wilderness Campaign in which, time and time again, Grant tried to outflank and ambush Lee's army, but was every time thwarted by Lee. Again, historians have no problem discerning Grant's intentions, without any written record left by Grant.

This caveat having been noted, in Collingwood's view, with regard to any passage from a past philosopher, there is not an historical question of what the author meant and the philosophical question of whether he or she was right, but only one question, historical. But Collingwood hastens to add that this does not mean that we cannot judge past philosophers; the question of whether a given philosopher solved his problem or not can and ought to be raised, but this, too, is an *historical* question (A, 72).

To illustrate this latter point Collingwood considers a passage from the Greek historian Thucydides describing how Phormio rowed around the Corinthians' circle, the Corinthians being the enemy. The question "was Plato right to think what he did?" is perfectly analogous to the question "was Phormio right to row round the Corinthians' circle?" To deny that the former question is an historical one, one is committed to denying that the latter question is historical, with the "lunatic" implication that "it is history that Phormio rowed round the Corinthians, but not that he beat the Corinthians by doing it?" (A, 72). This point is reinforced by Collingwood's claim, cited above, that we can know what an historical agent's problem was—be that agent the philosopher Leibniz or Admiral Nelson—only to the extent that he solved the problem, because the solution is the sole evidence of what the problem was (A, 69–70).

We have examined Collingwood's conception of history in detail in an earlier chapter; for now, let us pause to take stock of the preceding.

3. Some Critical Observations

a. The Question of Logic

Not surprisingly, Collingwood's logic of question and answer has proven controversial. First of all, Collingwood's call for a revolution in logic is puzzling. Whether it is true or not that you can only determine the meaning of a proposition by finding what question it is an answer to, this is irrelevant to logic as usually understood. Certainly logic was understood more broadly in Collingwood's time than it is today. But Collingwood explicitly includes modern symbolic logic in the propositional logic that needs to be abandoned and specifically instances the logic of Russell and Whitehead (A, 35, n 52). And modern symbolic logic—the logic that was formulated in the nineteenth century by Charles Peirce and Gottlob Frege, restated by Russell and Whitehead, and that has been taught in American colleges at least since the 1960s—has no interest in determining either the meaning or the truth of propositions; it is a purely formal science, which studies simply implication, or truth transmission. In that sense Collingwood's logic of question and answer is not a logic and certainly not a rival to formal logic.

This criticism was made already in 1962 by Alan Donagan, in a monograph that is in many respects quite critical of Collingwood. "The task of logic," Donagan wrote, "is not to investigate whether or not a given conclusion is in fact true, but only whether or not it is logically necessary that it be true, given that this or that premiss or set of premisses be true."[4] Collingwood also errs by attributing to the propositional logicians what he calls "the central doctrine of propositional logic":

> that there is, or ought to be, or in a well-constructed and well-used language would be, a one-one correspondence between propositions and indicative sentences, every indicative sentence expressing a proposition, and a proposition being defined as ... that which is true or false. (A, 35–6)[5]

This principle, Donagan notes, was never presupposed by propositional logic, although it was at one point believed by Russell.

Collingwood is also plainly mistaken in claiming that two statements cannot contradict each other unless they are the answers to the same question. Donagan offers this counterexample: Suppose someone asks you, "Which of those is the Bodleian?" and you point to a building and say, "That building is the Bodleian." Now later, this person points to the same building and asks me, "What is that building?" and I reply, "Not the Bodleian, at any rate." In that case, Collingwood would have to say that the two answers do not contradict each other, which Donagan rightly concludes is absurd.[6] Other counterexamples are easy enough to think of. "It is raining" and "It is not raining" contradict each other even if the first is the answer to "Why are you taking your umbrella?" and the second is the answer to "Why are you not taking your umbrella?" Since the same person cannot both take and not take his umbrella, we have to suppose these questions posed to two different people, but at the same time, a time at which it either is raining or it is not.

Donagan goes on to note that Collingwood's claim that truth and falsity belong to question-and-answer complexes, rather than to propositions, was tacitly abandoned two years later, in *An Essay on Metaphysics*, where truth and falsity are explicitly attributed to propositions.[7] The problematic relationship between the logic of question and answer and the doctrine of presuppositions expounded in the later work continues to be a subject of discussion and will be addressed in the next chapter.

Donagan is, as noted, quite critical of Collingwood. But essentially the same points about the logic of question and answer have been made by the largely sympathetic commentator Louis Mink: "The Logic of Question and Answer is not a theory of logic at all, in the ordinary sense of that term."[8] In Mink's view, Collingwood's "logic" is actually a hermeneutic, that is, a method of interpretation, a view later also defended by Peter Johnson, who does not use that exact term, but describes Collingwood's logic as "a fascinating method for throwing light on those kinds of thinking, in history for example, which propositional logic cannot capture."[9]

It is also questionable whether Collingwood is entirely fair in opposing this logic to that of the Oxbridge Realists. For instance, Michael Beaney has recently argued convincingly that Collingwood's logic of question and answer itself has its roots in Oxbridge Realism. Specifically, Cook Wilson argued, in his posthumously published *Statement and Inference* (1926), that to analyze a sentence into logical subject and predicate, we need to know what question it is an answer to.[10] In Cook Wilson's example, in the sentence "That building is the Bodleian," "that building" is the subject if the sentence is an answer to the question "What is that building?" But if the question is, "Which building is the Bodleian?" "the Bodleian" is the subject. And Cook Wilson was preceded, in 1896, by the Realist G. F. Stout, who offered a similar analysis of statements as answers to questions. It is thus likely that Collingwood absorbed this idea from the Realists whom he then turned it against.[11] Furthermore, already in 1962 it was pointed out by Alan Donagan, in the passage considered above, that Collingwood cited Cook Wilson's analysis favorably in 1937, so he was certainly aware of it.

Beaney also argues, with Donagan, that the "principle of propositional logic" is in no way presupposed by propositional logic and goes on to identify a more basic principle which is presupposed: "every sentence, as used on a given occasion to express a thought, has a content that can be expressed by a different sentence on a different occasion."[12] And this principle, which Beaney calls "the principle of logic," is actually presupposed by Collingwood's own "Socratic principle," the very cornerstone of *An Essay on Philosophical Method*. According to that principle, in philosophy we come to know better something which in a sense we knew already; but for that to be possible there must be some content that our initial knowledge and our subsequent knowledge have in common.[13] Again, Collingwood cannot escape the presuppositions of logic, and his "logic" of question and answer cannot serve as a substitute for logic as ordinarily understood.

b. The Question of Meaning

Nobody disputes that meaning is contextual, or that the required context is *often* a question. But it cannot be generally true that I cannot understand a proposition without knowing what question it is an answer to. As, for example, Mink has pointed out, if I do not understand the proposition at some level, however minimal, I would not know how to go about looking for the question, nor, should I find the question, would I be able to tell that this is the question the proposition is the answer to unless I already had sufficient grasp of the meaning of the proposition to match it up with the question.[14] The most that can be claimed, it appears, is that my understanding of the proposition *improves* by finding the relevant question: once I know the question to which the proposition is an answer I understand the proposition *better*. It might perhaps be argued that, once I know the question I understand the proposition *completely*; that up until then I have only a partial understanding of the proposition. What must at any rate be granted is the context dependence of meaning; certain terms, especially scientific terms, have a meaning only within certain thought complexes; thus "cause" in Aristotelian physics does not mean what it means in Newtonian physics, and we do not understand a proposition about causes unless we know which theory the proposition belongs in.

Equally, it has been argued—though this is more controversial—that individual propositions are not the proper candidates for truth or falsity; when a thought complex encounters recalcitrant experience, we may *choose* which proposition to drop as "false" and which to retain as "true." This is known as the Duhem-Quine Hypothesis, although it was also argued by William James. In his *Pragmatism* (1907), James argued that, as existing beliefs come into conflict with novel experience, the "true" propositions are those which will best integrate the new experience into our system of beliefs, and he approvingly quotes J. C. S. Schiller and John Dewey to the effect that *"ideas . . . become true just in so far as they help us get into satisfactory relation with other parts of our experience."*[15] In the same vein Willard Quine, citing Pierre Duhem, proposes "that our statements about the external world face the tribunal of sense experience not individually but only as a corporate body."[16] As noted, this view is controversial, but it is at least arguable.

4. The Radical Conversion Hypothesis

In his Preface to Collingwood's posthumously published *The Idea of History* (a Preface significantly not reprinted in the 1993 Revised Edition), Collingwood's editor T. M. Knox propounded the view that, in the years between 1936 and 1938, immediately prior to writing *An Autobiography*, Collingwood underwent a fundamental change in his philosophical outlook, from idealism to historicism, meaning thereby an historical relativism that entailed philosophical skepticism. Knox notes that no such change is recorded in the autobiography, some of the central doctrines of which are traced, as we have seen, to between 1916 and 1918. Collingwood's own chronology, therefore, cannot be accepted.

Knox offers the following evidence for his interpretation:

First, in a series of notes written in 1939, Collingwood wrote: "philosophy as a separate discipline is liquidated by being converted into history." [17]

Secondly, in the *Autobiography*, as well as in *An Essay on Metaphysics*, begun while Collingwood was writing the former book, and published in 1940, Collingwood affirms the view of metaphysics as the purely historical study of the absolute presuppositions of the thought of a certain age. In the *Autobiography*, by presenting this doctrine in conjunction with the logic of questions and answer, Collingwood implies that this doctrine was formulated well before the publication of *An Essay on Philosophical Method*, which cannot have been the case, given the definitive rejection of both skepticism and dogmatism in that work.[18]

Thirdly, Knox references the thesis, discussed above, that once we have answered the historical question, "What did Plato think?" there is not a second philosophical question, "Was he right?" Knox takes this as evidence that philosophy has been absorbed into history.[19]

Fourthly, Knox cites a 1936 manuscript in which Collingwood notes that St. Augustine, Tillemont, Gibbon, and Mommsen looked at Roman history from their different points of view, adding, "There is no point in asking which was the right point of view. Each was the only one possible for the man who adopted it." This, to Knox, is an expression of extreme historical relativism.[20]

Fifthly, in *An Essay on Metaphysics*, Collingwood, as noted, describes metaphysics as the historical study of the absolute presuppositions of successive ages. But the philosophically important question of exactly how the absolute presuppositions change from one age to the next is addressed only in a footnote, added in proof at the last moment.[21]

Sixthly, why did Collingwood never finish *The Principles of History*, which he was working on in 1939, and left unfinished after completing one-third? Declining strength is one explanation; also, work on *The New Leviathan* may have taken priority. But the real reason, in Knox's view, is that a philosophical treatise on the principles of history was no longer possible, once philosophy had been absorbed into history.[22]

How could Collingwood have so radically changed his philosophical outlook without anywhere acknowledging it? Knox's answer is that Collingwood's declining health in these years worked a complete transformation of his personality.

This is heavy artillery. Knox's interpretation was accepted, with modifications, by Leo Strauss in 1952 and by Alan Donagan in 1962, in the first major monograph on Collingwood's philosophy.[23] It was, however, rejected by Louis Mink in 1969, by Lionel Rubinoff, who coined the term "Radical Conversion Hypothesis," in 1970; by myself in 1973; by Tariq Modood in 1989; and, more recently, by Giuseppina D'Oro in 2002 and by James Connelly in 2013. Thus, Mink considered *Speculum Mentis* "in certain ways the most illuminating" of Collingwood's books because "it is his first attempt to give content to an emerging idea of the formal characteristics of dialectical patterns and is necessary to an understanding of his later and more subtle dialectic."[24] Rubinoff has pointed out that the very same 1936 lecture cited by Knox as evidence of Collingwood's historicism itself contains an explicit repudiation of radical historicism. Moreover, in this lecture Collingwood rejected the idea of history as purely descriptive and non-judgmental, and claimed that "by understanding [the past] historically we incorporate it into our present thought,"—hardly an historicist idea.[25] In my unpublished doctoral dissertation I myself argued, among other things, that the appearance of inconsistencies between *An Essay on Philosophical Method* and *An Autobiography* is misleading. When Collingwood says in the former work that the history of thought is the history of "one single sustained attempt to solve a single permanent problem," this may *appear* to be contradicted by the statement in the latter work, that there are no permanent philosophical problems. But this appearance, I argued, is illusory: the one single problem is that of rendering our historical experience intelligible, but this experience is, of course, constantly changing.[26]

Arguing specifically against Donagan and N. Rotenstreich, Giuseppina D'Oro has advanced four arguments for the essential continuity of the later *An Essay on Metaphysics* (1940) with the earlier *Essay on Philosophical Method*. First, in both essays the goal of philosophy is that of clarifying; philosophy "elucidates, explains, makes explicit what is implicit." Secondly, in the earlier essay it is argued that philosophy does not proceed deductively from self-evident first principles; similarly, in the later essay, absolute presuppositions are not first principles from which philosophers make deductions. Thirdly, both essays take philosophy to be a second-order study whose subject matter is the basic principles of the first-order sciences. And fourthly, Collingwood does not deny the possibility of rational comparisons of knowledge claims across time, as a radical historicist would be obliged to do; indeed, Collingwood himself makes such comparisons.[27]

The most comprehensive refutation of Knox's hypothesis that I have encountered is that originally set forth in 2003 and more recently restated in greater detail by James Connelly in 2013.[28]

To Knox's first argument, to the extent that philosophy as a separate discipline is liquidated by being converted into history, Connelly responds that the emphasis here should be on the word "separate." It is not philosophy as such that is liquidated, but its separateness from history is denied. The attempt to maintain the two as separate disciplines would be to commit the "fallacy of precarious margins" denounced in *An Essay on Philosophical Method*.[29] The question is whether Collingwood, by simply conflating the two, is committing the opposite fallacy of "identified coincidents." As against this, Connelly quotes the following a 1938 letter from Collingwood to de Ruggiero: "The absorption is mutual: the product is not philosophy based on history nor history based on philosophy, it is both these things at once, ..."[30] So by being, in Collingwood's sense, absorbed into history, philosophy does not cease to be philosophy.

Knox's second and third arguments are thus also disposed of. To the fourth argument, that Collingwood's relativism is revealed in the claim that each historian's point of view is the only one possible for that historian, the question is how to take the phrase "point of view." It could, no doubt, be understood relativistically. However, if all that is meant is that "every historian works within an inherited framework of problems and solutions," no relativism is implied, but only what Stephen Toulmin has called "relationalism." Moreover, the inescapability of the historian's own point of view was emphasized by Collingwood already in 1930, and so is hardly evidence of a radical conversion six years later.[31]

I see no discussion in Connelly's essay, of Knox's fifth and sixth objections. To the fifth, that Collingwood only as an afterthought in *An Essay on Metaphysics*, addressed the question of how absolute presuppositions change, it may be replied that Knox's objection is not quite accurate: Collingwood did address presuppositional change in the text of the *Essay*, then added a footnote *clarifying* what was said in the text, with page references included. Of this, more in the next chapter. To the question of why Collingwood did not finish *The Principles of History*, Knox ignores the fact that the book was *begun* only after Collingwood had completed the *Autobiography*. If a radical conversion to historicism had already rendered the project unfeasible, why start it? And Knox himself offers the plausible explanations of ill health and the priority of finishing *The New Leviathan* as Collingwood's contribution to the war effort.

Connelly also finds unpersuasive Knox's explanation of Collingwood's "conversion" as a result of declining health. *An Essay on Philosophical Method*, which Knox thought very highly of, was written after a period of serious illness. Collingwood's first stroke took place in 1938, *after* his conversion was supposed to have taken place. And Knox also praises Collingwood's last book,

The New Leviathan, which was the one most affected by his strokes.[32] So, the effect of declining health on Collingwood's thinking is implausible.

Many of the central themes of *An Autobiography* are developed further in *An Essay on Metaphysics*, to which we turn next.

Further Reading

Peter Johnson, *R.G. Collingwood: An Introduction*, Chapter Five.
Alan Donagan, *The Later Philosophy of R.G. Collingwood*, Chapter Four.
Louis Mink, *Mind, History, and Dialectic: The Philosophy of R.G. Collingwood*, Chapter Five.

7

The Doctrine of Absolute Presuppositions

Toward the end of Chapter 3 we considered Collingwood's account of philosophical development, as formulated in the idea of a dialectical scale of forms, and we saw how this account in important respects breaks down when applied to the history of cosmology. In terms of the logic of question and answer, this matter may now be reformulated as follows. The account of the history of philosophy given in *An Essay on Philosophical Method* is the account of a continuous chain of questions and answers; new questions are constantly arising, but each new question arises from a presupposition which formed the answer to an earlier question. The questions we ask today presuppose, mediately and indirectly, the entire chain of answers given to all questions previously asked; this is another way of stating what, in the first *Essay*, was expressed by saying that each term on the scale sums up the entire scale to that point. It is implicit in this account that the chain of questions and answers terminates in one set of absolute presuppositions; presuppositions, that is, that are not themselves answers to further questions. The idea that there is one set of constant and unchanging absolute presuppositions is at variance with some of Collingwood's earlier writings, notably the lecture "Ruskin's Philosophy," but it nonetheless appears to be presupposed by the claim made for the essential continuity of the history of thought.

This claim was seen to break down in *The Idea of Nature*. Greek, Renaissance, and Modern science each rests on its own set of absolute presuppositions. The presuppositions on which the questions of Renaissance science arise are not themselves answers to questions arising out of Greek science, and the same discontinuity obtains between Renaissance and Modern science. One question which Collingwood addresses in *An Essay on Metaphysics*, as well as in *The Idea of History*, is whether the historical change from one set of absolute presuppositions to another can itself be made amenable to rational explanation. In *An Autobiography* this question was not directly addressed, but in the *Essay* there is an attempt made, which it is part of the purpose of the present chapter to explore. We shall note that *An Essay on Metaphysics* is titled "Volume II" of "Philosophical Essays," signaling an intended continuity with the earlier *Essay*. Is this intention fulfilled?

1. "Absolute Presuppositions" Defined

At a department meeting once one professor, in some exasperation, exclaimed, "I have always assumed that there is no one in this room who is smarter than Einstein." What did he mean by that? He had not necessarily had this thought in his head until he uttered it, nor had any of his colleagues, but once it was uttered they all agreed that they too had always assumed this. However, once you make this assumption explicit, you may start to notice what else this assumption commits you to, namely that there is such a thing as measurable general intelligence. And as soon as you articulate this assumption, you are struck by the oddity of it, given that you are surrounded in daily life by people who are smart each in his or her own way, be they artists, salespeople, plumbers, or carpenters, while no generally intelligent person ever came your way. So, why make such an odd assumption? Probably because quantitative intelligence tests have long been routinely administered in government, industry, and academia. And this answer reveals a further assumption, namely, that our institutionalized culture is by and large and for the most part based on facts—infected with various biases, of course, but mostly in touch with reality—an assumption which nobody thought of questioning or even stating until it recently was rejected outright by climate-change deniers and fake-news denouncers.

This is so far quite informal. Collingwood's doctrine of absolute presuppositions provides a tool for analyzing the structure and function of the kind of assumptions instanced above.

It is time to inquire what Collingwood means by "absolute presuppositions." The skeleton of Collingwood's doctrine of presuppositions is set out in five Propositions and six Definitions, as follows.

1. "Absolute Presuppositions" Defined

Prop. 1. *Every statement that anybody ever makes is made in answer to a question.* (EM, 23)

By a "statement," Collingwood explains, he does not mean merely a statement uttered out loud from one person to another, but also unspoken thoughts, statements that I make tacitly to myself. I may not know that my statements are answers; to the extent that I am thinking scientifically—that is, methodically—I know this; to the extent that I do not think scientifically, I do not know this. While a question is logically prior to its answer, temporally they overlap; I have to continue asking the question while trying to formulate the answer; otherwise, I have lost interest in trying to answer it.

Def. 1. *Let that which is stated (i.e. that which can be true or false) be called a proposition, and let stating it be called propounding it.* (EM, 25)

Collingwood admits that this usage is arbitrary, but adopts it because it is customary among logicians.

Prop. 2. *Every question involves a presupposition.* (EM, 25)

Indirectly, a question may no doubt involve many presuppositions, but directly a question involves one and only one presupposition, the one from which the question "arises"; that is, the one that makes it logically possible for the question to be asked. For instance, the question, "Have you stopped beating your wife?" arises from the presupposition that the person addressed has been in the habit of beating his wife.

Def. 2. *To say that a question "does not arise" is the ordinary English way of saying that it involves a presupposition which is not in fact being made.* (EM, 26)

To ask a question that in this sense does not arise is to speak nonsense, not intrinsic nonsense, but nonsense in this context. "Have you stopped beating your wife yet?" is not nonsense when asked of a notorious wife-beater, although it is nonsense when asked of a presumed indulgent husband. Collingwood notes in this context that we may not be aware of the presuppositions we make, or even of the fact that we are making a presupposition. Thus I may ask, "What is that thing for?" without realizing that I am making the presupposition that the thing is for *something*.

Def. 3. *The fact that something causes a certain question to arise I call the "logical efficacy" of that thing.* (EM, 27)
The statement "This mark means something" has the logical efficacy of causing the question, "What does that mark mean?" to arise. But I may not know that the mark means something; I may simply suppose it for the sake of argument, and this supposition will then have the same logical efficacy.

Def. 4. *To assume is to suppose by an act of free choice.* (EM, 27)
All assumptions are suppositions, but not all suppositions are assumptions. Many suppositions are made unconsciously; also, among the suppositions I consciously make many are made without awareness that I could have made a different supposition. I need not believe all my assumptions to be true; I may knowingly make a false assumption in order to insult, as in "What do you mean by stepping on my toe," when I know perfectly well that it was not intentional.

Prop. 3. *The logical efficacy of a supposition does not depend upon the truth of what is supposed, or even on its being thought true, but only on its being supposed.* (EM, 28)
For instance, when someone is asked for a receipt for a sum of money or a prenuptial agreement prior to marriage, the assumption is that he may someday act dishonorably, but this does not mean that anybody actually believes that he will.

Prop. 4. *A presupposition is either relative or absolute.* (EM, 29)
"Presupposition" here means that which is presupposed.

Def. 5. *By a relative presupposition I mean one which stands relatively to one question as its presupposition and relatively to another question as its answer.* (EM, 29)
Whenever I use a tape to measure a distance and ask what the distance is between two points, I presuppose that the reading on the tape will give the right answer. This is a relative presupposition, because the tape may have stretched and so give an inaccurate reading. It may not occur to me to wonder whether the tape has stretched, but I am nonetheless presupposing that it has not. To verify a presupposition is to ask a question that admits of alternate

answers, in this case "the tape is accurate" or "the tape is not accurate." So, only relative presuppositions are candidates for verification.

Def. 6. *An absolute presupposition is one which stands, relatively to all questions to which it is related, as a presupposition, never as an answer.* (EM, 31)
Thus, when a pathologist seeks the cause of a particular disease, he assumes that there is a cause because everything that happens has a cause. If you ask him how he knows this, and he keeps his temper, the answer will be something like this: "That is a thing we take for granted in my job. We don't question it. We don't try to verify it. It isn't a thing anybody has discovered, like microbes or the circulation of the blood. It is a thing we just take for granted" (EM, 31). Absolute presuppositions are not verifiable because they are not answers to any questions.

Prop. 5. *Absolute presuppositions are not propositions.* (EM, 32)
Because an absolute presupposition is not the answer to a question, the notions of truth and falsity do not apply to it, and since, by Def. 1, a proposition is that which is capable of being true or false, absolute presuppositions are not propositions. Hence, it is nonsense to ask about the truth of an absolute presupposition, or about the evidence for it, or our reasons for believing it.

Absolute presuppositions, then, are characteristically tacitly presupposed; when they are stated at all, they are usually stated with reluctance, and they are stated as something taken for granted, something which it makes no sense to question, or to give reasons for. Nor does it make sense to subject them to verification, because they are presupposed prior to the questions to which the procedures of verification are offered as answers. In other words, absolute presuppositions make up the entire framework within which it makes sense to propose procedures of verification.

The doctrine of absolute presuppositions is not explicitly articulated until *An Autobiography* in 1938, but it is tacitly implied in much of Collingwood's earlier thought, and, as has been noticed, strongly hinted at in one of his earliest publications, "Ruskin's Philosophy" in 1919.[1] In that lecture, while noting that Ruskin was not a philosopher as ordinarily understood, nonetheless:

> There are certain principles which the man takes as fundamental and incontrovertible, which he assumes as true in all his thinking and acting. These principles form, as it were, the nucleus of his whole mental life; they are the centre from which all his activities radiate. (RUP, 10)

So far, we have simply recapitulated Collingwood's account of absolute presuppositions. There is obviously an overlap with the logic of question and answer examined in the previous chapter. But there are also differences. As noted by Donagan, truth and falsity are now attributed to propositions, not to question-and-answer complexes. More importantly, although Collingwood says that every statement is the answer to a question (Prop. 1), he is not now saying, as in *An Autobiography*, that you have to know the question in order to know the meaning of the statement. This is important because, as Rex Martin has pointed out in his Introduction to the new edition of the *Essay*, according to the logic of question and answer, absolute presuppositions would be meaningless since they are not answers to any questions.[2] Hence, to make sense of the doctrine of absolute presuppositions, we have to abandon the logic of question and answer, at least as literally formulated by Collingwood.

However, Collingwood has still retained too much of the logic of question and answer. As Martin has also pointed out, to presuppose something is to presuppose it *as true*, so it cannot be the case that absolute presuppositions are neither true nor false. What makes more sense is to say that, while they are in fact propositions, they may, however, be held immune to verification because they are not *asserted*. Rather, they are simply taken for granted, as basic conceptions and standards embedded in the practices of any particular science or branch of inquiry. In Collingwood's words, "An absolute presupposition cannot be undermined by the verdict of 'experience', because it is the yard-stick by which 'experience' is judged" (EM, 193–4). Tariq Modood has emphasized that this does not mean, and that Collingwood did not think, that absolute presuppositions cannot be challenged or criticized: "*Within a particular conceptual scheme* some concepts cannot be questioned, but there is nothing to prevent us from getting outside those conceptual schemes or transforming them."[3] Similarly, Giuseppina D'Oro has argued that, while absolute presuppositions are not verifiable by the methods appropriate to empirical propositions, it does not follow that they are not verifiable by other means, an idea developed, as we have seen, in the earlier *Essay on Philosophical Method*.[4] Martin has noted the similarity to Ludwig Wittgenstein's concept of a "language game," the rules of which are not open to question or justification within the game itself.[5] More surprisingly, but quite plausibly, D'Oro has likened Collingwood's distinction between propositions and presuppositions to Rudolph Carnap's internal/external distinction.[6] Finally, Kenneth Ketner has drawn attention to parallels with Charles Peirce's concept of inquiry which, in Peirce's view, has to begin from doubts that we actually have and which always presuppose certain "indubitables" which we cannot doubt, largely because we are not normally aware of them.[7] In this sense, absolute presuppositions are not "absolute" in the sense of being a priori or self-evident or unchangeable; they are absolute or unquestionable only *relatively* to a particular stage of inquiry.

So, Collingwood's distinction between absolute and relative presuppositions can be upheld without accepting Collingwood's extreme view that absolute presuppositions are not propositions and are therefore not capable of being true or false.

2. Metaphysics as the Analysis of Absolute Presuppositions

Metaphysics, in Collingwood's view, is the science of absolute presuppositions. Collingwood traces this conception back to Aristotle who, however, *also* held that metaphysics is ontology, that is, a science of pure being. (To avoid misunderstanding, Collingwood makes it clear that Aristotle did not use the word "metaphysics," which was introduced posthumously by his editors.) Pure being is being from which everything has been abstracted; that is, it is nothing, and there can be no science of it. So ontology, in this sense, does not exist (EM, 15). But metaphysics exists; it is "the attempt to find out what absolute presuppositions have been made by this or that group of persons, on this or that occasion or group of occasions" (EM, 47). There is also something called pseudo-metaphysics, which attempts to study absolute presuppositions (AP) as if they were relative presuppositions. Pseudo-metaphysicians will ask such unanswerable questions as: "Is AP true? Upon what evidence is AP accepted? How can we demonstrate AP?" (EM, 47). To ask such questions about a presupposition is, as we have seen, to treat it as a relative presupposition.

Metaphysics, as defined above, is in Collingwood's view, an historical science: "All metaphysical questions are historical questions, and all metaphysical propositions are historical propositions" (EM, 49). As examples Collingwood cites three absolute presuppositions about causation. Newtonian science presupposes that some events have causes, Kantian science that all events have causes, and Einsteinian science that no events have causes. Scientists make these presuppositions and metaphysicians discover what they are (EM, 54). Collingwood does not think he is saying anything novel here; this is what metaphysicians have always been doing, although they have not always been aware of it. True, the propositions found in the works of Aristotle, Leibniz, or Kant do not *look* like historical propositions. That is because they tacitly presuppose the following "metaphysical rubric": "*in such and such a phase of scientific thought it is (or was) absolutely presupposed that . . .*" (EM, 55, emphasis in the original). It would be tiresome to constantly repeat this rubric, so metaphysicians don't; instead they take it as understood. Similarly, historians do not bother to preface each statement with "the evidence at our disposal obliges us to conclude that," this rubric being presumed to be understood by the reader (EM, 56).

Rex Martin has noted that, although metaphysical propositions are "historical" in that they are accounts of particular cases, several scholars, including David Boucher, Bruce Haddock, and Lorraine Code, have argued that they are not historical in the specifically Collingwoodian sense that was examined in Chapter 4. Historical knowledge, in this view, is attained by the historian re-enacting the thoughts of historical agents. Since absolute presuppositions are adopted unconsciously, there is in this case no past thought to be re-enacted.[8] Martin goes on to argue, however, that the correct way to read Collingwood's claim is to understand metaphysics as historical, not in that it exemplifies historical knowledge, but in that it exhibits a process of development, a process he names a "modified scale of forms," more of which below.[9]

While Martin cites an unpublished manuscript by Boucher, Boucher has later, in his Introduction to *The New Leviathan*, argued that absolute presuppositions *can* be re-enacted. Specifically, it is by re-enacting reflective thought that we recover the normally unconscious presuppositions that are logically implied by our reflective thought (NL, xxviii).

All work of analysis consists of disentangling and arranging presuppositions; it is the special task of metaphysical analysis to disentangle the absolute presuppositions of science, where "science" is taken to mean all orderly and methodical thought of a determinate subject matter. It is not the task of metaphysics to assert, justify, or criticize absolute presuppositions, these operations being applicable only to propositions. Attempts to justify or criticize absolute presuppositions involve the error of mistaking absolute presuppositions for propositions, an error that has been responsible for

2. Metaphysics as the Analysis of Absolute Presuppositions   139

generating a great deal of pseudo-metaphysics. This does not, however, mean that metaphysics itself is immune to criticism, or that the metaphysician is not faced with the task of criticism. The body of metaphysical work does consist of propositions which metaphysics asserts and attempts to justify, and which are, consequently, open to criticism and refutation. These are, as noted, historical propositions to the effect that, at such-and-such a time, and by such-and-such person(s), such-and-such absolute presupposition was made (EM, 49).

Although metaphysicians down through the ages have been practicing history, they have not always—or even normally—been aware that this is what they were doing. There is a need, therefore, for a reform of metaphysics—a reform that consists in raising the consciousness of metaphysicians about the historical nature of their task. There are several advantages to be gained from such a reform. First, this reform will do away with the idea of "schools" and "doctrines" in metaphysics (EM, 68). Secondly, it will free metaphysicians from a certain parochialism: not realizing that their task is an historical one, metaphysicians tend to focus only on the presuppositions of what they take to be the present, which in practice normally is the recent past. A recognition of the historical nature of metaphysics will vastly enlarge the scope of metaphysical inquiry (EM, 70–1). Thirdly, the reform will disabuse metaphysicians of the anachronism of studying the philosophers of the past as if they were trying to solve certain "unchanging," "crucial," or "central" problems of philosophy; an historical approach will show them that there are no such problems (EM, 72).

Science, at every stage of its development, rests on not one absolute presupposition, but several of them. These presuppositions form a complex, which Collingwood names a "constellation." There is an interdependence between these presuppositions; you cannot simply drop one and leave the others unchanged. None of them implies any of the others, which in that case would be relative presuppositions. Also, they cannot be literally consistent, since consistency is the capability of them all to be true, and truth belongs only to propositions. But they must be capable of being supposed together; they must be "consuponible." Collingwood illustrates this concept by saying that "they are not like a set of carpenter's tools, of which the carpenter uses one at a time; they are like a suit of clothes, of which every part is worn simultaneously with all the rest" (EM, 66). Collingwood comes perilously close to equating consupponibility with consistency when he adds: "It must be logically possible for a person who supposes one of them to suppose concurrently all the rest" (EM, 66). Since we have already argued that absolute presuppositions must have truth value, although they are not asserted and are not candidates for verification, we can safely substitute consistency for consupponibility, acknowledging that this is a departure from what Collingwood himself said.

In actual practice, every constellation of absolute presuppositions is under internal strain. This explains how and why one set of absolute presuppositions gives way to another: "One phase changes into another because the first phase was in unstable equilibrium and had in itself the seeds of change" (EM, 74). Civilization, Collingwood goes on, "works itself out by a dynamic logic in which different and at first sight incompatible formulae somehow contrive a precarious coexistence ..." (EM, 75)

I am not alone in finding one of the most interesting parts of the *Essay* to be that contained in a long footnote, added in proofs as an afterthought. Collingwood is here responding to a question from a friend, later identified as A. D. Lindsay, of how absolute presuppositions change. They are not propositions, so they cannot be refuted. Might not readers suppose, then, that the changes are simply changes of fashion? After establishing that absolute presuppositions, unlike changes, cannot be chosen because we are not normally conscious of them, Collingwood goes on:

> Why, asks my friend, do such changes happen? Briefly, because the absolute presuppositions of any given society, at any given phase of its history, form a structure which is subject to "strains" (pp. 74, 76) of greater or lesser intensity, which are "taken up" (p. 74) in various ways, but never annihilated. If the strains are too great, the structure collapses and is replaced by another which will be a modification of the old with the destructive strain removed; a modification not consciously devised but created by a process of unconscious thought. (EM, 48 n)

The philosopher of science Stephen Toulmin, who was in the main highly respectful of Collingwood and in fact contributed a preface to the second edition of *An Autobiography*, has complained that the above is too metaphorical, and that Collingwood sidesteps a crucial question: "Do we make the change from one constellation of absolute presuppositions to another because we have reasons for doing so; or do we do so only because certain causes compel us to?"[10] If the former, the distinction between absolute and relative presuppositions is seriously weakened; if the latter, Collingwood cannot avoid a relativism similar to Thomas Kuhn's.[11] Toulmin concluded that Collingwood landed on the second horn of the dilemma; in my earlier book on Collingwood I myself, without specific reference to Toulmin, suggested that Collingwood ended up on the first horn of the dilemma, effectively relativizing absolute presuppositions.[12] That is no longer my view, except in so far as I agree with Rex Martin's view, spelled out above, that absolute presuppositions are propositions. Collingwood's view was that this amounts to treating them as relative presuppositions, but we have seen reasons to disagree with: while they are propositions they are absolute in that they are not asserted, questioned, or defended.

An interpretation that at least appears to avoid Toulmin's dilemma is offered by Martin:

> Neither the scientist nor the metaphysician can occupy a standpoint outside the practice. And they cannot just *will* changes into being there, changes that will then redound on the practice (rather than the reverse). Instead, they must stay within the practice; it is the only standpoint they, the scientist or the metaphysician, can occupy. And changes that occur there, in the practice, can become—usually in time they will amount to—fundamental changes in the very groundform, in the governing assumptions of the practice.[13]

In the case of the history of science, this means that conflicting absolute presuppositions—presuppositions that are jointly under excessive strain—give rise to practices which are mutually incompatible, or which are seen not to yield the best possible results. Scientists do not as a rule examine their absolute presuppositions and reject one or more of them; rather, they change their scientific practices and *thereby* make new absolute presuppositions, thus eliminating the particular strain in question. Seen this way, science progresses rationally, not in the sense that there is a vantage point outside science—a "God's eye view" in Hilary Putnam's famous phrase—from which to judge the progress in science—that there is not was made clear, as we have seen, at the end of *The Idea of Nature*—but in the sense that, at each stage of the development of science, this stage can be justly seen as progress over the previous one, whereas the reverse is not the case. We cannot absolutely say that monotheism is superior to polytheism, but the monotheistic cosmologist can see monotheism as superior to its predecessor.[14]

So understood, the *Essay on Metaphysics* solves the problem posed in *The Idea of Nature* and restated at the opening of this chapter. The history of science progresses rationally because each change of absolute presupposition can be understood, not from an absolute vantage point but from the vantage point of each subsequent stage of scientific development, as the removal of strains vitiating the earlier stage. The doctrine of absolute presuppositions can now be seen as a reformulation of the scale of forms developed in *An Essay on Philosophical Method*, or at least, as Martin has argued, a modified scale of forms.[15] It is modified in the sense of being temporalized; the forms now succeed each other in time, rather than coexisting simultaneously, as in the earlier *Essay*. This conclusion thus finds a continuity between the two *Essays*, and reinforces our rejection, at the end of Chapter 6, of the "radical conversion hypothesis."

Collingwood's doctrine now appears less like Kuhn's and more similar to that of Kuhn's critic Imre Lakatos. Whereas Kuhn famously described, in great detail, *how* scientific revolutions happen, he nowhere explained *why* they happen *when* they do. Lakatos filled this lacuna with his distinction between progressive and degenerating research programs. A degenerating research program—one which increasingly solves problems generated within the program itself, rather than expanding the scope of its problem-solving capacity—is not thereby automatically rejected. It is rationally rejected when a new, progressive research program emerges, one which can explain everything the old program explained, and more.[16] This seems reasonably close to what Martin formulated as a modified scale of forms. We should note that, while Lakatos explicitly presented his methodology as an emendation of the falsificationism of Karl Popper, it can be equally seen as a complement to Kuhn's work, which Lakatos also engaged with. Also, while the mature Lakatos indignantly disavowed any Hegelian influence on his thought, he was in fact thoroughly trained in Hegel's philosophy in his native Hungary.

3. A Case Study: Isaiah Berlin's Critique of the Enlightenment

I have elsewhere illustrated Collingwood's account of the change of absolute presuppositions with Isaiah Berlin's critique of the European Enlightenment.[17]

3. A Case Study: Isaiah Berlin's Critique of the Enlightenment

Berlin was Collingwood's student and, as I have argued, strongly influenced by him. An excellent case study in how the structure of absolute presuppositions of the Enlightenment collapses from the pressure of its internal strains is provided in Berlin's most famous lecture, "Two Concepts of Liberty" from 1958, a lecture which brings exceptionally clearly into focus a theme found in a number of Berlin's writings. To be clear, Berlin does not in this specific context refer to Collingwood, but he has elsewhere cited the doctrine of absolute presuppositions approvingly.[18] In his 1958 lecture Berlin argued that, at the very heart of the liberal tradition dating from the Enlightenment, there was a profound, and profoundly destructive, ambiguity in the concept of liberty, an ambiguity which in the end turned the liberal tradition itself into an ideological justification of totalitarian coercion. Central to this argument is the famous distinction between negative and positive liberty, which Berlin formulated as follows:

> The first of these political senses of freedom or liberty (I shall use both words to mean the same), which (following much precedent) I shall call the "negative" sense, is involved in the answer to the question "What is the area within which the subject—a person or group of persons—is or should be left to do or be what he is able to do or be, without interference from other persons?" The second, which I shall call the positive sense, is involved in the answer to the question "What, or who, is the source of control or interference that can determine someone to do, or be, this rather than that?"[19]

Now, there is obviously no inconsistency, or self-contradiction, in using the words liberty or freedom in both the negative and the positive sense. But a dangerous confusion arises when the two concepts are taken to be one and the same, as they are in Kant's claim that freedom is obedience to a self-imposed law, as well as in John Stuart Mill's claim that liberty consists in the fullest possible development of the individual self.[20] And such confusion is encouraged by the central tenet of classical liberalism, to wit, that liberty is limited only by liberty itself, and that coercion can be justified only by the imperative to protect everyone's liberty.[21] Once one refuses to acknowledge other goods besides liberty, which pose rival claims on the body politic, the temptation becomes irresistible to include all sorts of other goods within the compass of positive liberty—full self-development is not possible without relative equality, universal education, national self-determination, ownership of the means of production, or what have you—thus opening the door to re-describing the coercion necessary to attain these possibly worthy goals as not coercion at all, but as a type of "liberation" or "emancipation."[22] The role of external factors, such as, for example, urbanization and industrialization, in forcing these goals to the foreground may not have been explicitly explored by Berlin, but is by no means precluded by his (or Collingwood's) analysis of presuppositions.

We have here two crucial—albeit relative—presuppositions of the creed of the European Enlightenment. One is "Liberty is the absence of coercion"; the other is "Liberty is self-determination," that is, the absence of external obstructions. These two presuppositions are similar, their respective contents overlap to a large extent, and they are certainly not logically inconsistent with each other. Both are necessary presuppositions of the liberal belief that liberty is limited only by the requirements inherent in liberty itself. Yet there is an inherent tension between them, in that the second presupposition promotes thinking and behavior which undermine the first presupposition, and it is this tension or strain which, in Berlin's account, finally causes the demise of Enlightenment liberalism, albeit not of the positive concept of liberty, which he believes continues to exert a strong appeal. And the way the tension does its work is by forcing an underlying, absolute presupposition to be brought to light and abandoned, and to wit the presupposition that there is one universal human good, to which all other goods are subordinate, thus guaranteeing that genuine goods will never conflict with one another. The only element of Collingwood's account of presuppositional change that is missing from Berlin's story is the emergence of a new system purged of this particular strain. But after all, since we are not normally aware of our own absolute presuppositions, we should expect to have to wait for a future generation to supply that part of the story.

4. Anti-metaphysics

Collingwood notes that the nineteenth and early twentieth centuries have been characterized by a pervasive prejudice against metaphysics, a prejudice he labels "anti-metaphysics." By this term he means "a kind of thought that regards metaphysics as a delusion and an impediment to the progress of knowledge, and demands its abolition" (EM, 81). There are three different kinds of anti-metaphysics: progressive, reactionary, and irrationalist.

Progressive anti-metaphysics may arise when professional metaphysicians—those who get paid to do metaphysics—fail to do their job and do not keep up with the progress of thought. In that case their metaphysics becomes out of date, and scientists will come to regard metaphysics itself as essentially obscurantist and an impediment to the progress of science (EM, 82).

This situation gets exacerbated when scientists stand in need of a particular contribution from metaphysics, as when there is a need to determine whether a newly discovered presupposition is absolute or relative. Since the metaphysicians are not doing their job, the scientists now have to do the job for them; since they are not qualified for the task, the result is amateur metaphysics, and scientists become amateur metaphysicians. Uncomfortable with their amateur status, scientists come to resent the metaphysicians for placing them in this position; thereby "amateur metaphysicians become anti-metaphysicians, and amateur metaphysics becomes anti-metaphysics" (EM, 88).

Reactionary anti-metaphysics is the opposite case. People engaged in "ordinary" (Collingwood's scare quotes) thought may not keep up with the science of their day and may treat as absolute presuppositions which current science treats as relative, and which current metaphysics has declared to be relative. Such a person may develop a bad metaphysical conscience and demand the abolition of metaphysics out of fear (EM, 83).

Collingwood gives two examples. Between 1820 and 1880 engineers did practically nothing other than build ever bigger steam engines on the principles discovered by James Watt in the eighteenth century. These engines were incredibly inefficient, wasting 94 to 95 percent of the coal consumed. Late in the nineteenth century, with the emergence of both the gasoline engine and the new physics, those with a vested interest in the status quo attempted to arrest the new developments with the calls "Back to Kant" and "No More Metaphysics" (EM, 94–5). The second example is the Lockean system of government, which was formulated in the seventeenth century and which absolutely presupposed nationality as its foundation. This system, which had become the British political system, was threatened by the growth of historical thought in the nineteenth century; to modern historians, nationality was a relative presupposition, not an absolute one. Those with a vested interest in the political system saw this interest threatened and again took recourse to the demand "No More Metaphysics" (EM, 99).

Irrationalist anti-metaphysics may arise when a movement sets out to abolish science itself, but needs to conceal its true intent because of the high respect in which science is generally held. In such a case, an assault on systematic and orderly thinking may be portrayed as an attack on metaphysics rather than on science (EM, 83–4).

Collingwood devotes five chapters to denouncing irrationalist antimetaphysics, exemplified by contemporary psychology understood as the science of thought. We need not follow him into the details of this critique, but its basis is noteworthy. In every act of thought, Collingwood argued, the mind judges itself. In thinking a thought I at the same time judge my own success in thinking that thought. I cannot think the thought, for instance, "the Earth is round" without at the same time judging myself to be *right* in thinking that the Earth is round. The Greeks expressed this by saying that thought is normative, a term which Collingwood wants to avoid because of its judgmental overtones. The word appears to imply only that thought is capable of being judged by other people, whereas it is essential that I constantly judge my own thoughts. So for the term "normative" Collingwood substitutes "criteriological" (EM, 109). Collingwood concludes: "The business of thinking includes the discovery and correction of its own errors" (EM, 110). And this central function is, deliberately and as a matter of principle, ignored by psychology: "Psychology has always approached the study of thought with a perfectly clear and conscious determination to ignore one whole department of thought, namely to ignore the self-critical function of thought and the criteria which that function implied" (EM, 115–16). The true science of thought, Collingwood repeatedly claimed, is history, as we saw in Chapter 4. To Collingwood's conclusion that the psychologists of his day donned the mantle of scientific respectability for the specific purpose of undermining science and civilization, it may be sufficient to note that our civilization has survived so far, and that one can certainly imagine more serious threats to civilization than any posed by psychologists. It should also be emphasized, as in previous chapters, that Collingwood's quarrel was not with psychology per se, but with what he perceived as an illegitimate trespass of psychology into other areas of thought.

5. Collingwood's Disagreement with Ayer

Perhaps the most widely noted feature of *An Essay on Metaphysics* is Collingwood's critique of the logical positivism of A. J. Ayer's conspicuous bestseller *Language, Truth, and Logic*, published in 1936. My own personal interest in Collingwood as a graduate student was in fact kindled by his critique of Ayer, whose book was in the 1970s assigned in virtually every Philosophy 101 course in the country. Despite his profound disagreement with Ayer, Collingwood thought highly of the book; Gilbert Ryle once overheard him prophetically telling the Realists H. W. B. Joseph and H. A. Prichard, "Gentlemen, his book will be read when your names are forgotten."[23] Like his Viennese predecessors and contemporaries, Ayer contended that all sentences fall into one of the three categories synthetic a posteriori, analytical a priori, and meaningless pseudo-sentences. According to this tripartite schema, all sentences which assert the existence of states of affairs are verifiable by experience and belong properly to one or another of the empirical sciences. Any sentence which is not so verifiable is either in the nature of a tautology, and belongs to mathematics or logic, or else it is sheer gibberish. Ayer applies this analysis to the body of philosophical assertions with the following results: (i) a great many sentences traditionally belonging to philosophy are actually verifiable and should be allotted to the various empirical sciences; for instance a great deal of moral and religious philosophy speaks of how people in fact feel or act and should be allotted to psychology or sociology; (ii) a great deal of philosophy is tautological, but useful, in so far as it provides definitions which elucidate the language of science; Ayer's chief example is our old friend Russell's Theory of Descriptions, discussed in Chapter 3; (iii) the bulk of what is known as metaphysics is neither verifiable nor tautological, but is sheer gibberish, entirely devoid of intellectual value; among Ayer's examples are the metaphysics of Descartes, Hegel, and Bradley.[24] Clearly the verifiability principle, at least as understood by Ayer, is another version of Hume's Fork discussed in Chapter 3, in the context of Gilbert Ryle's critique of Collingwood.

Central to this position is, evidently, the division of all propositions into analytical a priori and synthetic a posteriori propositions—the same dichotomy which we have previously seen Collingwood attack as against Ryle and, indirectly, against Russell. Now, however, Collingwood does not confront the dichotomy directly, but argues instead that it has restricted applicability, and that Ayer's application of it exceeds its proper boundaries. Even though it is granted that the realm of propositions is subject to such a dichotomy, that realm itself is bounded by that of "absolute presuppositions." So Collingwood accepts both the analytic-synthetic dichotomy and the principle of the verifiability of synthetic propositions, but argues that Ayer's application of this schema to metaphysical sentences misses the point. According to Collingwood, in so far as metaphysical sentences are unverifiable, they do not purport to be propositions; hence they are not pseudo-propositions. In so far as they do purport to be propositions, they are in fact verifiable. Metaphysics, Collingwood holds, is the science of "absolute presuppositions"; these are not propositions; they are neither true nor false, so the principle of verifiability does not apply to them. But metaphysics does, all the same, consist of propositions: historical propositions to the effect that such-and-such absolute presuppositions were made at such-and-such a time. And these propositions are neither more nor less verifiable than any other historical propositions. Hence Ayer's attack on "metaphysics" is in fact an attack on pseudo-metaphysics, the kind that mistakes absolute presuppositions for relative ones (EM, p. 163).

The weakest point in Collingwood's argument—and its oddest feature—is his acceptance of the verifiability criterion of meaning, which appears to be at variance with the central argument of *An Essay on Philosophical Method*, to the effect that philosophy rests on universal categorical judgments that are not verifiable by experience. Heikki Saari has observed that Collingwood felt "uncomfortable" with this position, since it made it difficult for him to assign meaning to absolute presuppositions.[25] In his Introduction, Martin suggests that we should not take Collingwood to be endorsing Ayer's view: "rather, we could better regard *An Essay on Metaphysics* as a clever and well-devised attempt to get around Ayer's strictures."[26] Whether he quite gets around them is open to dispute. As we have seen, Collingwood's claim that absolute presuppositions are immune to verification because they are not propositions will not do, according to the interpretation here set forth. But Collingwood also held, as we have also seen, that absolute presuppositions are presupposed by our very methods of verification and therefore exempt from verification, and this may constitute a successful rebuttal of Ayer.[27] But of course the verifiability criterion has long been discredited, and I know of no one who would defend it today. A very basic criticism is that, apart from failing to assign meaning to certain important statements in science, the verifiability principle is *itself* neither analytic nor empirically verifiable.

When *An Essay on Metaphysics* was published, Ayer was busy fighting the Second World War, and by the time the war ended, Collingwood had died, so Ayer had no real opportunity to respond to Collingwood's criticisms. But some decades later, in his *Philosophy in the Twentieth Century*, Ayer devoted an entire chapter to Collingwood, the only philosopher who was thus honored.[28] Ayer here accepts "some responsibility" for Collingwood's essay and proceeds to raise some critical points. He does not think it is true either that every statement is the answer to a question or that every question arises from some presupposition.[29] He has more serious reservations about absolute presuppositions. If "God exists" is an absolute presupposition of Christianity, then presumably Christians believe that God exists without holding it to be true, which is distinctly odd. The question of truth or falsity may simply not arise, which sounds less odd. But why shouldn't nonbelievers treat "God exists" as a proposition and judge it to be false?[30] We turn next to Collingwood's discussion of the existence of God as an absolute presupposition.

6. Illustration: The Existence of God

Collingwood offers three extended examples of metaphysics: the existence of God, Kant's metaphysics, and the concept of causation; we shall only look at the first of these. Collingwood begins by attributing to Ayer the view that "God exists" means "that there is a being more or less like human beings in respect of his mental powers and dispositions, but having the mental powers and dispositions greatly, perhaps infinitely, magnified" (EM, 185). If that were simply the private meaning Ayer ascribed to those words, that would be well and good; however, Collingwood takes Ayer to be attributing this meaning to Christians, and Collingwood is quite certain that no Christian theologian has ever interpreted "God exists" in this way. Rather, for the Patristic writers— that is, the Church Fathers—"God exists" was a metaphysical proposition, carrying with it the metaphysical rubric; that is, it is absolutely presupposed that God exists. This is why Christians typically confess their faith, not by the words "God exists" alone, but by the words "I believe" or "We believe in God"

(EM, 187). The metaphysical proposition, being a historical proposition, is either true or false and is capable of being proven true by a historical proof.

We saw in Chapter 3 that Collingwood accepted St. Anselm's Ontological Proof as valid, while denying that it proved the existence of any *particular* god. He now returns to this proof, arguing that it proves the metaphysical proposition "God exists," thus establishing God's existence as an absolute presupposition. The evidence is found, not in Anselm's treatise *Proslogion*, where the proof was originally formulated, but in his subsequent correspondence with his critic Gaunilo. Gaunilo argued that Anselm proved the existence of God only to someone who already believed it; instead of challenging that assertion, Anselm responded that he did not care. Thereby Anselm was treating God's existence as an absolute presupposition: "For it follows not only that Anselm's proof assumed the metaphysical rubric but that Anselm personally endorsed the assumption when it was pointed out to him whether he had meant to make it from the first or no" (EM, 189). Clearly, Ayer's later objection—that a nonbeliever can deny the existence of God—is not an objection to anything Collingwood actually said.

So, God's existence is an absolute presupposition, but what is it a presupposition of? Collingwood's answer is: of natural science. Ancient Greek science, going back to Thales, was monotheistic—or at least monomorphic in supposing the unity of nature—amidst a polytheistic religion. Aristotle spelled out the monotheistic presuppositions of natural science, but erred in denying that God created the natural world. So, to Aristotle, nature is not absolutely presupposed, but something to be discovered by the senses. Modern science, by contrasts, absolutely presupposes the existence of one natural world, which is studied by all the natural sciences (EM, 206). Only on that assumption can a discovery made in one science affect work in the other sciences. The Church Fathers first remedied Aristotle's error by adopting the Hebrew doctrine of God as the creator of the world; this adoption amounts to a presupposition of nature as something given, not something to be discovered. But modern science, while needing to absolutely presuppose the unity of science, actually studies the manifold of nature and natural processes. This need for differentiation, too, was recognized by the Church Fathers, and their recognition found expression in the doctrine of the trinity of the Father, the Son, and the Holy Ghost:

> By believing in the Father they meant (always with reference solely to the procedure of natural science) absolutely presupposing that there is a

world of nature which is always and indivisibly one world. By believing in
the Son they meant absolutely presupposing that this one natural world is
nevertheless a multiplicity of natural realms. By believing in the Holy Ghost
they meant absolutely presupposing that the world of nature, throughout
its entire fabric, is a world not merely of things but of events or movements.
(EM, 225–6)

The last line is eerily reminiscent of the opening page of Ludwig Wittgenstein's *Tractatus Logico-Philosophicus*: "The world is the totality of facts, not of things."[31] It may be no coincidence that the *Essay* was written while Collingwood served as the outside elector for the Cambridge University chair for which Wittgenstein was then a candidate; in that capacity Collingwood presumably would have read the *Tractatus*, Wittgenstein's only published book at that time. It may also be no coincidence that, for his next book, *The New Leviathan*, Collingwood adopts the numbered paragraph structure of the *Tractatus*.

I am not qualified to pass judgment on Collingwood's interpretation of the Church Fathers. I want, in conclusion, to raise the question whether "God" is an example of what W. B. Gallie has later labeled "essentially contested concepts," concepts that are given different meanings by different groups, where each group insists that its meaning is the correct one, and which thereby give rise to endless disputes over who has given the concept its "true" meaning.[32] There are, of course, numerous cases of simple confusion, where the disputing parties just use the same word to express different concepts, but Gallie holds that, under certain complex conditions, the parties can be truly said to embrace the "same" concept, even if they attach rival meanings to it. The conditions are as follows: (i) The concept is "appraisive" in that it signifies an important achievement. (ii) The achievement is complex. (iii) An explanation of its worth must include reference to the contributions of its various features. (iv) The concept must be "open" in a specified sense. (v) The concept is used both aggressively and defensively.[33] Gallie's examples are "the Christian way of life," "art," "democracy," and "justice." If we can add "God" to the list, we need not conclude that either the Anglican Collingwood or the atheist Ayer was in error about the meaning of "God"; it may simply be that each was immersed in a way of life and a web of belief that necessitated his attaching his particular meaning to the concept.

Further Reading

Peter Johnson, *R.G. Collingwood: An Introduction*, Chapter Nine.

Louis Mink, *Mind, History, and Dialectic: The Philosophy of R.G. Collingwood*, Chapter Five.

James Connelly, *Metaphysics, Method, and Politics: The Political Philosophy of R.G. Collingwood*, Chapter Three.

Peter Skagestad, *Making Sense of History: The Philosophies of Popper and Collingwood*, Chapters Eight and Nine.

8

Politics, Society, and Civilization

Long after Collingwood ceased to be referred to as an unjustly neglected philosopher, his social and political philosophy remained largely unnoticed. It has been noted by David Boucher, in his Introduction to the revised edition of *The New Leviathan*, that although the book was well received upon publication, it fell into obscurity after the end of the Second World War. Boucher cites several reasons for this neglect, including the fact that political theory in general remained in "suspended animation" for a generation until the appearance of the works by John Rawls and Robert Nozick in the 1970s (NL, xiv–xv).

In 1961 Collingwood's one-time student Isaiah Berlin could ask in all seriousness, "Does Political Theory Still Exist?", a question that had in effect been answered in the negative the previous year in Daniel Bell's *The End of Ideology*. Today, thanks largely to Rawls and Nozick, as well as their numerous critics, political theory is alive and as healthy as ever, and recent decades have seen a renewed interest in Collingwood's contribution to the field.

1. Collingwood's Politics

a. Collingwood's Supposed Radicalization

As we saw in Chapter 6, Collingwood's *Autobiography* was believed by many, including his friend and editor T. M. Knox, to signal a radical turn from his earlier idealism to a relativistic historicism. It has been noted by David Boucher that the *Autobiography* was also taken by many, including Knox, to signal a political radicalization and an embrace of Marxism.[1] Collingwood had, in that book, expressed considerable admiration for Karl

Marx, as well as sympathy for the socialist Spanish Republic. Furthermore, in the 1938 parliamentary election, he supported the candidacy of A. D. Lindsay who was running as an independent against Chamberlain's appeasement policy, earning him the support of the communists. Finally, in 1939 he returned from a voyage to the Dutch East Indies sporting a beard! However, as Boucher notes, opposition to appeasement cut across party lines, and Lindsay also had the support of the future Conservative prime ministers Winston Churchill, Harold McMillan, and Edward Heath.[2] And Collingwood's admiration for Marx did not entail an embrace of Marx's materialistic theory of history as class struggle, a theory clearly at variance with Collingwood's conception of history examined in Chapter 4. What Collingwood admired was Marx's "gloves-off" philosophy, his commitment to use philosophy to change the world, not merely interpret it, as well as his insistence on understanding economics historically. Finally, Collingwood's defense of Spain's popularly elected republican government against the overthrow by Franco's fascists is best understood simply as a defense of democracy and does not necessarily imply approval of any particular *policies* pursued by that government.

As Boucher and also James Connelly have made clear, Collingwood was a lifelong liberal in the Continental, though not the British, sense of the word, which denoted the Liberal Party.[3] Liberalism, in the continental sense, is a belief in representative democracy with free elections, freedom of the press, and freedom of speech and of religion. This sense also differs from the two senses in which "liberal" and "liberalism" are used in today's United States. In American *politics* liberalism refers to a commitment to public—and more specifically federal—spending on domestic human programs such as health, education, and reduction of poverty. Since it is widely thought that the stagflation of the 1970s demonstrated the failure of liberalism so understood, the term is today mostly used as a pejorative term, and proponents of domestic spending generally prefer to call themselves progressives. In American, and British, *philosophy* liberalism more often refers to the conception of the state as a morally neutral arbiter of conflicting claims by individuals and interest groups. Neither of these senses corresponds to the Continental sense of liberalism embraced by Collingwood.

b. Continental Liberalism

Continental liberalism finds its most complete expression in *The History of European Liberalism* by Collingwood's friend Guido de Ruggiero, a book which Collingwood personally translated from the Italian and persuaded Oxford University Press to publish. According to de Ruggiero, humans are not born free; we become free by degrees as we attain degrees of self-control. In the eighteenth century freedom was mostly understood negatively, as the absence of external coercion. But in the course of the nineteenth century, freedom came to mean the ability to control one's actions, to be free from caprice, to be *autonomous* in the Kantian sense.[4] To be free in this sense is also to recognize freedom in others; thus freedom implies sociality. While earlier adherents of negative liberty regarded the state as their enemy, liberals now recognize the state as "the highest expression of liberty."[5] The primary function of the liberal state is to protect individuals from the enslavement of caprice, for instance, by prescribing compulsory elementary education or restricting the sale of alcoholic beverages.[6]

It is of interest that de Ruggiero recognized the risk that a Liberal party might easily become complacent and intolerant, and attempt to impose its program on an unwilling population; to guard against this, liberals need to recognize that they and the conservatives are not simply adversaries but are also united in a shared pursuit of the common good:

> A more comprehensive Liberalism would recognize the dialectical ground of the antithesis and would see resistance and movement, conservation and progress, justified and validated in a higher synthesis which is political life in its concreteness.[7]

De Ruggiero considers democracy an obvious offshoot of liberalism, but, as with Liberal parties, democracy carries the seed of illiberalism, in that it may come to promote the interest of a numerical majority, rather than the common good. The only defense is the education of the public in the liberal conception of political opposition as a form of creative cooperation.[8]

Socialism is similarly an offshoot of democracy. To be sure, its insistence on the interests of a particular class runs counter to liberalism's commitment to the common good. However, socialism has proven an advance over earlier individualism, and trade unions inculcate a spirit of sociality internally, among its members, and thus may serve as an education in sociality more broadly understood.⁹

Thus far we have followed de Ruggiero. We return to Collingwood.

c. Political Action

Writing in 1928, Collingwood takes political action, rather than the state, as the fundamental concept of political theory. And by political action he meant action which seeks to promote orderliness, of which he gives four examples. First, clearing away slums and providing better housing for the poor might not make the poor happier, healthier, or more virtuous, but slums are an example of disorder, and that alone is a sufficient reason for clearing them away. Secondly, why do Englishmen (unlike Frenchmen) stand in line to buy tickets for the train or the theatre? Keeping your place in the line does not get you your ticket any faster than cutting in line. But keeping your place is obviously orderly behavior. Thirdly, I may make a promise and later find that neither I nor anyone else stands to gain by my keeping my promise. In that case, why should I keep it? Because the keeping of promises is an instance of orderly conduct. Fourthly, if I see two strangers, one of whom is about to shoot the other, I may or may not consider it my duty to interfere. But suppose I consider it my duty; what would be the basis for that duty? "[O]ne possible motive for this would be the feeling that one can't have this sort of thing going on . . . shooting people like that . . ." (EPP, 98). Again, the motive is to prevent disorderly conduct.

As the last three examples make clear, political action is not specifically the domain of the state; individuals can act politically, as can associations, such as families. The modern state is "an almost fortuitous collection of functions left over from other bodies . . ." (EPP, 106). The division of labor between the state and, say, the family is a matter of mutual convenience: "The family does not want to hang its own criminals, and the state does not want to fix the hour of Sunday dinner" (EPP, 107). So, like de Ruggiero's, Collingwood's liberalism allows state intervention in economic affairs. As we have seen, the state may take action to clear away slums. In his 1925 essay "Economics as a Philosophical Science," Collingwood also allowed that the state may require a legal minimum wage to prevent the poor from having to accept inadequate pay for their work (EPP, 69). A. J. M. Milne has criticized Collingwood for failing to distinguish between a "public" and a "private" sphere: "The role of government is to be the custodian of the public life of the nation."[10] Collingwood's answer, given in 1925, is that there are no such two spheres to be distinguished: "[The argument for the gold standard] is based on the fallacious assumption that governments can be kept out of mischief by denying them certain powers, as one denies firearms to a child" (EPP, 76). If the government cannot be trusted to exercise its powers for the good of society, the people need to remove the government and replace it with one they trust. What Milne considers a bug in Collingwood's theory is, from Collingwood's perspective, a feature.

d. Liberalism under Siege

In his essay "Fascism and Nazism" from 1940 Collingwood analyzed the totalitarian threat to civilization with an argument that in part harks back to *Speculum Mentis*. The vital inspiration of any civilization is its religion; thus modern European civilization depends on Christianity as its source of inspiration. Yet something curious has happened over the past two centuries, starting with the French Enlightenment. Everything in Christianity that is capable of logical formulation has been gradually detached from Christianity, while everything that is not so capable—"whatever is in the nature of religious emotion, passion, faith" (EPP, 188)—has been gradually eliminated and rejected by enlightened people as mere superstition. The consequence for liberalism is that liberals have lost their passion for freedom. "The real ground for the 'liberal' or 'democratic' devotion to freedom was religious love of a God who set an absolute value on every individual human being" (EPP, 190). Without this "irrational" love of God, one may of course still believe that freedom is, on the whole, a good thing, but the passion required for an effective defense of freedom against a totalitarian threat will be absent. It has been significantly weakened in England, France, and the United States, and it is an open question how much longer these democracies can survive.

Fascism and Nazism do not recommend themselves to the intellect the way liberalism and democracy do, but they are able to tap into the emotional energy of their respective populations as defenders of liberal democracy are not. "Fascism and Nazism have succeeded in evoking for their own service stores of emotional energy in their devotees which in their opponents are either latent or non-existent" (EPP, 191). How do they do this? Have Italy and

Germany not gone through the Enlightenment process of being drained of religious passion as much as France or England has? Yes, but both countries have been able to fall back on a pre-Christian paganism capable of supplying the required religious fervor. In Italy the worship of pagan idols has been tolerated throughout the Christian era; in Germany paganism has been officially suppressed, but has nonetheless survived beneath the surface, and has now re-emerged with full vitality in the Nazi ideology. This resuscitated paganism provides the principal motivation for totalitarianism and the principal threat to liberal democracy. Relics of pre-Christian paganism survive in all European countries and may quite possibly erupt to the surface in England as they have in Italy and Germany. The only remedy is a renewed and forceful commitment to Christianity by England's philosophers and other thinking people.

Written in 1940 during the Blitz when England stood alone in the fight against Nazism, "Fascism and Nazism" is not an optimistic document. But, as Collingwood notes in an endnote, it is vital for England's philosophers to understand the enemy that its soldiers, sailors, and airmen are fighting (EPP, 196, n2). This project of promoting understanding was to be advanced, at length, in *The New Leviathan*, Collingwood's last book.

2. Collingwood's Moral Philosophy

Collingwood's moral philosophy was developed in lectures and articles over a period of more than twenty years, but finds its most complete and mature expression in his 1940 Lectures on Moral Philosophy, now published as an Addendum to the revised edition of *The New Leviathan*. Collingwood here develops his views in the form of a critique of the Realists G. E. Moore, H. A. Prichard, E. F. Carritt, and W. D. Ross. As Ross is singled out for especially detailed and trenchant criticism, it is to the point to remember Collingwood's rule, announced in the preface to his *Autobiography*, never to mention a person by name except honoris causa. And Collingwood's grudging admiration for Ross is evident in these lectures, although he also indulges in a certain mock reverence by repeatedly referring to Ross by his title the Provost of Oriel College.

Collingwood's point of departure, however, is to take exception to Moore's famous claim, in his *Principia Ethica*, that "good" is a simple notion, like "yellow," which Collingwood considers "a monstrous falsehood" (GRU, 407). First of all, goodness or badness admits of degrees: "A person who calls anything good or bad is stating that it does or does not satisfy a standard arising out of the purpose which, as a practical agent, he entertains towards it" (GRU, 407). But secondly, this difference in degree is not measurable. If a doctor asks a patient, "Does this hurt?" and then, "Does this hurt more?" and the patient answers "Yes," the doctor may go on to ask how much more, to which the patient may answer "Much more!" But if the doctor now asks, But tell me *exactly* how much more it hurts, the patient will not have an answer, or even attach any meaning to the question (GRU, 408). Similarly, I may like one painting much more than another, but may be quite unable to say *exactly* how much more I like it.

Collingwood is here explicitly disputing Ross's statement, in *The Right and the Good*: "if anything is greater than another thing, it must be greater by some definite amount" (GRU, 408).[11] Ross goes on to claim that we are sometimes able to say that one pleasure is at least twice as intense as another, but he draws the line at our ability to get more precise and say that one pleasure is exactly twice or three times as intense as another. The reason:

> The pleasures have precise intensities, which in principle makes them commensurable. But they have not the characteristics that make material objects comparatively easy to measure, the characteristics of being fairly permanent and of being easily compared with standards of measurement which can be applied to each in turn. (GRU, 413)[12]

In other words, Collingwood sarcastically observes, when Ross calls pleasures measurable he does not mean that anybody can actually measure them. Collingwood concludes that Ross uses the word "measuring" simply to mean "guessing" (GRU, 415).

The heart of the lectures is Collingwood's analysis of goodness into utility, rightness, and duty. When we act without knowing the reason for our action, we are acting capriciously, and each of the three forms of goodness provides a reason for action which reduces the amount of caprice, thus increasing the rationality of our action. (Not that all caprice is bad; Collingwood explicitly allows for healthy forms of caprice [GRU, 431].) The three thus form a hierarchy; in fact, a scale of forms as that idea was explained in *An Essay on Philosophical Method*. Utility aims at determination of action that only a rule can actually provide; rightness, or regularianism, aims for a determination that only duty can provide. And the three are not mutually exclusive: an action done in obedience to a rule may also be expedient, and an action done for the sake of duty may also conform to a rule.

The progression is this. In utility I choose an action as a means to an end; that is, I analyze my action into two components: means and end. Of the two, the end is logically prior, the mean is temporally prior. The means are chosen as useful or expedient to reach the end, but the end must be chosen as good in itself. To be sure, the end of one action may be another action, or a better condition for performing some further action, and so on. But if utility is to serve as a reason for action, the series of actions must at some point reach an end point, which can only be chosen as good in itself (GRU, 435). Thus, utility cannot provide a reason for choosing ends, leaving a large residue of caprice. The same point was made in *The First Mate's Log* when considering the social utility of the life of the monks at the monastery of the Prophet Elijah in Pyrgos, Greece (FML, 150).

Later, in *The New Leviathan*, Collingwood instances a second element of caprice in utilitarianism, namely the need to choose which of several possible means to adopt to reach a particular end. If I want to buy a pound of tobacco I have to hand over a specific sum made up out of the coins in my pocket. But it is up to me to choose which *particular* combination of coins to use to make up this sum (NL, 15.63).

These elements of caprice are reduced by regularianism, by doing the "right" action in the sense of conformity to a rule. In ancient and medieval times, rules were universally regarded as given; they were just there. In recent centuries, however, with the emergence of legislative bodies, people have come to regard themselves as rule-makers as well as rule followers. It was Kant's great discovery that, by obeying rules which I have accepted as rules, I am in effect obeying my own will; I am legislator as well as law abiding, and so *autonomous* in Kant's terminology (GRU, 458). But elements of caprice remain. A rule is general; it tells me to perform a certain *kind* of action, not a particular action. The rule that obliges me to return a library book I have borrowed does not tell me how to return it—by mail, for instance, or in person (GRU, 466). Also, depending on how I perceive the situation I am in, I may have a choice among several possible rules, which may easily conflict with each other. Obeying the rule that obliges me to tell the truth may easily violate the rule of not causing unnecessary harm to others (GRU, 458).

One is reminded here of Jean-Paul Sartre's famous anecdote about the young student torn between the alternatives of joining Free France to fight the Germans or stay home to take care of his mother. The Bible told him to be charitable, but charitable toward whom? His mother, or the resistance fighters? Kant told him not to use other people as merely a means, but again, whom? His mother, or the resistance? Utilitarianism told him to promote the greatest good, but how could he know which course that was? Running off to join Free France might land him in detention in Spain or at a desk job somewhere, whereas his mother was certain to suffer from his desertion. Finally, some told him to follow his instincts, but which one? The filial one, or the patriotic one? Lacking the concept of duty, Sartre concluded that his student was thrown back on pure, ungrounded choice—caprice, in Collingwood's terminology.[13]

To Collingwood, by contrast, the elements of caprice inherent in regularianism are eliminated in an ethics of duty. My duty is the individual action which I am now obliged to perform. Collingwood praises both Kant and F. H. Bradley for recognizing duty as the highest form of goodness, but also takes them both to task for equating duty with right, or rule-following (GRU, 462–3). An action and its omission may both be right, but if the action is my duty, its omission is a violation of my duty:

> Thus, if it is only right for me to spend the evening working on my new book, it does not follow that it is wrong for me to spend that same evening in a different and incompatible way. But if it is my duty to spend the evening working at my book it follows that it is my duty not to spend it in a different and incompatible way. (GRU, 464)

Obviously, Collingwood's dialectic owes a debt to Bradley's in his *Ethical Studies*, which Collingwood cites approvingly. In that work Bradley passes in review "Pleasure for Pleasure's Sake," "Duty for Duty's Sake," "My Station and Its Duties," and finally "Ideal Morality." But there are differences. As we have just seen, Collingwood distinguishes right and duty in a way that Bradley did not. Also, as my station is a function of a social order which itself may be morally questionable, Bradley could not rest with its duties, but needed to progress to ideal morality, where Collingwood does not follow him. As was made clear in *An Essay on Philosophical Method*, *The Idea of Nature*, and *An Essay on Metaphysics*, the philosopher does not have an independent vantage point to stand on outside his own time and place. Toward the end of *The Idea of Nature*, Collingwood quotes Hegel to this effect: "*Bis hierher ist das Bewusstseyn gekommen.* 'That is as far as consciousness has reached'" (IN, 174).

3. *The New Leviathan* I: Collingwood's Psychology Revisited

The New Leviathan, Collingwood's last book, has given rise to several puzzles, beginning with the title. In his preface Collingwood refers to Hobbes's *Leviathan* as "the world's greatest store of political wisdom" (NL, lx), but he does not pay special attention to Hobbes in the book itself, and Boucher has pointed out that Collingwood did not pay particular attention to Hobbes over more than twenty years of writing and lecturing on moral and political philosophy.[14] As Louis Mink has noted, the four parts of the book mirror the structure of Hobbes's book, but Boucher notes that this was not intentional, as Collingwood planned a fifth part that was never written due to ill health.[15] Boucher concludes that the significance Collingwood attributes to *Leviathan* is its ushering in the era of classical political theory, whereas it is now time for a new era to begin.[16]

A second puzzle is Collingwood's abandonment of his usual mellifluous prose style in favor of epigrammatic numbered paragraphs with decimals in the style of Wittgenstein's *Tractatus*, which he had presumably quite recently read, as the outside elector for the Cambridge professorship for which Wittgenstein was chosen. Unlike, for example, Spinoza's *Ethics*, the book does not have a deductive structure that would indicate this style. Boucher hypothesizes that King James's Bible, rather than the *Tractatus*, was Collingwood's model, and that Collingwood was painfully aware of how little time he had left and therefore chose the most economical mode of expression available to him.[17] Even so, as noted, the book was not completed as planned.

Collingwood begins *The New Leviathan* by reformulating and refining the psychology originally articulated in *The Principles of Art*. Consciousness is now analyzed into four levels, distinguished by Boucher.

First, simple feeling, for example, fear aroused by a sound, delight aroused by a different sound, or disgust caused by a smell.[18] This is what, in *The Principles of Art*, was called "psychical experience." Feelings do not have objects, although they themselves are objects of consciousness, and in fact one cannot have feelings of which one is unconscious (NL, 5.39, 5.82). Freud's concept of "repression" can therefore not be understood as unconscious feeling, since I cannot repress something of which I am not conscious (NL, 5.87). Feelings are *evanescent*; as soon as I become aware of a particular feeling, it starts to disappear (NL, 5.5). Feelings cannot be remembered; people who believe they remember a feeling in fact remember a proposition about the feeling. Thus I can remember having been afraid, although I cannot remember my fear (NL, 5.54). It is not clear what Collingwood would have said about either the experience of torture or post-traumatic stress syndrome, both of which appear problematic for this account of feeling.

The second level is where consciousness takes an attitude toward its feelings; at this level, something called *appetite* emerges. An appetite, such as hunger, is not a simple feeling, because it involves a comparison of two states: the state of emptiness and the state of repletion (NL, 7.15). A person does not want a simple feeling, such as pleasure; what one wants is satisfaction of one's appetites, that is, an escape from one feeling state to another (NL, 7.52). So, what is desired is simply an escape from one's present state; the state one wants to escape to is contrasted with one's present state, but is otherwise perfectly indeterminate (NL, 7.52).

Hunger, we have seen, is one appetite; another that is discussed by Collingwood is love. In love I am conscious of a distinction between my actual self, which is a lonely self, and an ideal self: "The ideal self of love has achieved a relation with something other than itself (I will call it a *not-self*) of such a kind that the dissatisfaction is removed" (NL, 8.16). Thus hunger is simply the consciousness of a defect, not of a self in which this defect inheres, while in love there is a consciousness both of the self in which the defect inheres and of the not-self that constitutes the removal of the defect (NL, 8.51, 8.57).

The third level of consciousness is that of desire and happiness. Desire differs from appetite, in that appetite is mere wanting without knowing what one wants; in desire, one also knows what one wants (NL, 11.1). One can also be mistaken about the object of one's desire, so there is a distinction between true desires and false desires, whereas there is no corresponding distinction in the case of appetite (NL, 11.3). Desire is made possible by *propositional* thinking, which is never about a first-order object, in which case no mistake would be possible, but always about a concept, which may or may not correspond to its intended object (NL, 11.34). Hobbes is faulted for failing to distinguish between appetite and desire, while Spinoza conflated desire with four different things: conation, volition, appetite, and desire (NL, 11.42).

The one thing everybody desires, as Aristotle was the first to note, is happiness. But by happiness Aristotle did not mean pleasure, or a collection of pleasures, but rather well-being, a concept which he unwrapped in great detail. Collingwood notes two aspects of well-being:

> 12.21. Internal well-being, or well-being in relation to oneself is *virtue*.
>
> 12.22. External well-being, or well-being to what is other than oneself is *power*.
>
> 12.23. Virtue and power, which together make up happiness, are so far from being incompatible that it may be doubted whether they are separable. (NL, 12.21–3)

Happiness so understood is not a feeling, as Bentham and Mill thought, but a state of being, as Spinoza understood. Happiness is freedom from passion and the force of circumstances; however, unhappiness is subjection to these things (NL, 12.33–4).

The fourth and highest level of consciousness is reason. Reason, or rational thinking, is "thinking one thing, x, because you think another thing, y; where y is your 'reason' or, as it is sometimes called, your 'ground' for thinking x" (NL, 14.1). Rational thinking presupposes propositional thinking, and hence language, but is not implicit in propositional thinking per se; it emerges when the thinker makes the distinction between "the that" and "the why" (NL, 14.2). With rational thinking we arrive at knowledge, along with the realization that all knowledge is fallible and may turn out to be mistaken (NL, 14.25). Collingwood makes an important distinction between *practical* reason and *theoretical* reason. Practical reason takes place when one forms an intention and reflects on it, asking whether one really means it. We are confirmed in our intention only by discovering another intention that may serve as a ground for the first intention. For instance, I decide to get up and hammer in a tent peg *because* I do not want the tent to blow down. Theoretical reason come into being when, through propositional reasoning, I come to believe that something is so, and then seek a reason why I should believe that it is so (NL, 14.35).

Boucher and James Connelly, among others, have noted that the four levels are ranged on a scale of overlapping forms, as that idea was explained in *An Essay on Philosophical Method*, but also that Collingwood now has introduced a new element, called the "Law of Primitive Survivals."[19] This law states: "*When A is modified into B there survives in any example of B, side by side with the function B which is the modified form of A, an element of A in its primitive or unmodified state*" (NL, 9.51, emphasis in the original). Now, according to the *Essay*, *only* the modified form of A survives in B, so this law would require a reworking of the scale-of-forms theory, a reworking which Collingwood did not live to carry out.

4. *The New Leviathan* II: Society

a. "Society" and Society

Collingwood opens the discussion of society by distinguishing between a *society* and a *class*. Both are wholes composed of parts, but the parts of a class belong to the class by virtue of *resemblance*, while the parts of a society belong to that society by virtue of *participation* (NL, 19.61). Next, Collingwood distinguishes between "society," in quotes, and society, without quotes. In each, there is something shared among the members and assigned to each member in equal proportion. Collingwood calls this something a suum cuique, "that is, a one-one relation between sharers or participants and shares"(NL, 19.64). The Latin phrase really means something like "to each his or her due," but Collingwood uses this phrase as a noun. A society—without quotes—differs from a "society" in that, in the former "the establishment and maintenance of the *suum cuique* is effected by *their joint activity as free agents*" (NL, 19.8). Again, "A society is a 'society' constituted by free activity on the part of its members" (NL, 19.81).

Karl Marx, Collingwood notes, denied the existence of societies in this sense. To this effect he quotes the famous line from Marx's *Critique of Political Economy*: "It is not men's consciousness that determines their existence; on the contrary, it is their social existence that determines their consciousness" (NL, 19.9). Nineteenth-century capitalism claimed to be a society, based on the voluntary cooperation of free agents, but it was, in Marx's view, a slave society. If Marx was right, if consciousness does not determine existence, then there simply are no societies, Collingwood concludes. But Marx could not have been right since, if there are no societies, there is no social existence and so social existence cannot determine consciousness (NL, 19.94). The later Collingwood evidently was very far from embracing Marxism!

b. Community and Society

Having made these initial distinctions Collingwood proceeds to replace the word "society," in quotes, with the narrower term "community." It is distinguished from "society" in that a community consists of human beings: "By a community I shall mean a state of affairs in which something is divided or shared by a number of human beings" (NL, 20.12). A society, then, is a kind of community; it is a community in which what the members share is *social consciousness* (NL, 20.2). Social consciousness is a practical consciousness, not a theoretical consciousness; it is the act of "deciding to become a member and to go on being a member" (NL, 20.21). Social consciousness thus involves an awareness of choice and hence of freedom: "A society consists of persons who are free and know themselves to be free. Each knows the others to be free as well as himself" (NL, 20.23). There is here a recognizable echo of de Ruggiero's views noted earlier. (We shall note that Collingwood's usage here is somewhat idiosyncratic, as "community" is more commonly used to denote a subgroup within a society.)

A society, or social community, rules itself; a nonsocial community, which Collingwood also calls a "nursery," a community whose members are not free and socially conscious, needs to be ruled by something other than itself. A society is "*self-originating* and *self-maintaining*; it comes into existence by the act of this joint will, and is kept in existence by the same joint will" (NL, 20.43). A self-ruling society may *appear* to be ruled by something other than itself, because its members may authorize some part of society to execute some of the society's functions on behalf of the whole society: "*Authority is a relation between a society and a part of that society to which the society assigns the execution of a part of its joint enterprise*" (NL, 20.48, emphasis in the original). This may involve the use of force against some members of society, as in arresting and punishing criminals, but this authority does not amount to ruling the society, which remains self-ruling. By "rulers," then, Collingwood intends participants in the political process, as distinct from the state, to which the citizens have delegated authority over themselves.

What constitutes self-rule is articulated by Collingwood in a modified social contract theory, derived from Hobbes, Locke, and Rousseau. In place of a contract Collingwood substitutes a declaration to enter into society: "this declaration to be made or subscribed to by every party in joining the society, in any terms that make his decision clear to the other or others" (NL, 20.63). In making such a declaration, each member undertakes certain obligations, which are limited by what Collingwood calls the *Principle of Limited Liability*: "It is in the nature of a society that the obligations of membership should be limited to obligations involved in the pursuit of the common aim" (NL, 20.66). The details of the obligations will depend on the details of that aim. Agreeing to go for a walk with someone may oblige me to risk my life to save my companion's life; agreeing to play a game of chess obliges me to keep my temper when losing. So, self-rule depends on a contract, in the sense of a shared consciousness of adopting a certain aim, which imposes on each member certain obligations. So long as this consciousness is there, the members are free and self-ruling, even though certain functions—including coercive functions—may be delegated to some part of the society.

Most communities are mixed communities, that is, both social and nonsocial. Collingwood's principal example of a mixed community is the family, in which the parents, having consented to marry and produce children, form a social community, while the children, being too young to consent to anything, form a nonsocial community ruled by the parents (NL, 22.13). The role of the parents is, of course, to take care of the children, feed, clothe, and house them, and so forth, but also to educate them to the point where they can be incorporated into a social community, either the parent-society or, upon marrying, their own family-society, or both (NL, 23.6). More generally, in any mixed community, an important function of the rulers is to educate the ruled to the point where they can become self-ruled.

c. The Body Politic

A community that is of special interest to political theory is that called the body politic. This was thought of by the Greeks and Romans as a social community. The Greek πόλις and the Roman res publica were regarded as associations where free male citizens voluntarily cooperated to advance a shared purpose. In the Middle Ages, by contrast, the body politic came to be regarded more as a nonsocial collection of human animals. It was Hobbes's discovery that it is both: The body politic is a nonsocial community in the process of changing into a society (NL, 24.52). To the possible objection that it has to be one or the other, but not both, Collingwood responds by invoking Plato's dialectic and, more specifically, Plato's distinction between "eristic" and "dialectical" discussions:

> **24.58**. What Plato calls an eristic discussion is one in which each party tries to prove that he was right and the other wrong.
>
> **24.59**. In a dialectical discussion you aim at showing that your own view is one with which your opponent really agrees, even if at one time he denied it; or conversely that it was yourself and not your opponent who began by denying a view with which you really agree. (NL, 24.58–9)

It is through a process of dialectical discussion that nonsociality, the negative element, is by degrees driven out by the positive element of sociality. Conversely, it is through eristic discussion that the sociality of the body politic is undermined. As an example Collingwood instances the recognition, in Britain, of the need for both a party of progress and a party of reaction and blames the decline of the Liberal party on its failure to recognize the need for a party of reaction (NL, 27.95). Again, we are reminded of de Ruggiero's warning against complacent liberalism. Collingwood's words are also eerily prophetic about current American politics, whose discourse is today more eristic than at any time since the end of the Vietnam War. Examples would include the announcement by the Senate majority leader, in the midst of the worst recession since the Great Depression, that his party's first priority was to ensure that Barack Obama would be a one-term president; in other words, to ensure that there would be no recovery prior to the 2012 election, thereby ushering in a decade of unbridled partisanship.

So, the body politic is a nonsocial community in a perpetual process of transformation into a social community—a transformation which it never quite completes. It is composed of two communities: the rulers and the ruled. Ruling is *immanent* when that which rules, rules itself; *transeunt* when that which rules, rules something other than itself (NL, 20.37–9). The rulers are a social community, which is self-ruled; the ruled are a nonsocial community.

While the rulers are continually educating the ruled, bringing them up to the level of consciousness and self-control where they are ready to join the rulers, the population of the ruled is continually replenished, as new babies are born. Evidently, by "rulers" Collingwood does not intend simply the government, but rather all the participants in the political process.

Collingwood summarizes his discussion of the body politic in what he calls the "Three Laws of Politics":

"The First Law of Politics is that *a body politic is divided into a ruling class and a ruled class*" (NL, 25.7). We have just seen what this means.

"The Second Law of Politics is that *the barrier between the two classes is permeable in an upward sense*" (NL, 25.8). The ruling class needs to be continually replenished by recruiting into it members of the ruled class. It does this by educating the ruled to the point where they have sufficient self-control to be said to have a *free will* and thus be capable of ruling themselves and also others.

"This brings us to the Third Law of Politics: namely that *there is a correspondence between the ruler and the ruled*, whereby the former become adapted to ruling these as distinct from other persons, and the latter to being ruled by these as distinct from other persons" (NL, 25.9). What can this mean? It is not, on its face, as straightforward as the first two laws. Collingwood notes that the third law may operate in an "inverse" form, "in the mere blind, unpolitical stupidity of the ruled, imposing limits on what the rulers can do with them" (NL, 25.93). Boucher notes that "there is a tendency, in any body politic, for the ruled, whether consciously or not, to imitate the rulers."[20] Thus an ineffectual ruler may instill habits in the ruled that make them virtually ungovernable. An effective ruler will foster cooperation between the classes by relying, whenever possible, on peaceful resolution of conflicts.[21] James Connelly adds that it is "Through the operation of this third law the ruled class receive a training for political action which enables them to succeed their rulers."[22] The rulers, then, need to conduct themselves in a manner that the ruled will want to imitate and that, if they imitate it, will promote increased self-control and freedom of the will.

A society thus understood is neither purely democratic nor purely aristocratic; rather democracy and aristocracy coexist in a dialectical relationship: "But democracy and aristocracy, properly understood, are not hostile to each other. They are mutually complementary" (NL, 26.12). Society is aristocratic in that the stronger—those with the most developed consciousness and self-control—rule over the weaker—those in whom consciousness and self-control is less developed (unlike the United States today). But it is democratic to the extent that the boundary between the ruler and the ruled, by the Second Law of Politics, is permeable, and it is one of the functions of the rulers to convert the ruled into rulers. The process is dialectical in that this conversion by degrees reduces the aristocratic element, which democracy yet needs for its survival. Where the attempt is made to eliminate the aristocratic element from democracy, a tyrannical reaction is likely to occur, as in the post–First World War Italy and Germany. Democracy remains alive in Britain because the British still understand the dialectical relationship between democracy and aristocracy (NL, 27.64).

While peaceful conflict resolution is the preferred modus operandi in governing, the use of force cannot be altogether avoided, but "force" in politics does not mean physical force, but "moral" or "mental" force: "When A is said to exercise force over B, what is meant is that A is strong relatively to B, and uses this superiority to make B do what he wants" (NL, 20.51).

Collingwood does not specify criteria by which the rulers may decide which of the ruled are ready for self-rule and hence for inclusion in the ruling class. This may seem a serious omission. In the 1960s I personally had occasion to attend a college in the American South, at a time when I encountered African Americans almost exclusively in menial positions, as cafeteria workers, laundry workers, or janitors. I say "almost" only because there were a total of four African American students in my college. In an environment such as that, even intelligent, educated Southern whites generally deemed African Americans insufficiently mature for responsible positions and so did not entrust African Americans with high degrees of responsibility. (By recalling the 1960s I do not mean to minimize the racial problems that exist today, but I believe them to be in important respects different from what I observed then.) So, even if the rulers acknowledge the upward permeability of the boundary between rulers and ruled, their judgment of who is or is not ready to cross the boundary is subject to a variety of biases which need to be counteracted by a set of rules.

Collingwood's perhaps not completely satisfactory answer is that this is a problem for *politics*, not for political *philosophy*. Specifically, the three problems of determining the way of life for the ruling class (the "council"), the way of life for the ruled (the "nursery"), and the relation between the two make up what Collingwood calls "the *constitutional* problem." So, each society needs a constitution, but a society's constitution cannot be written once and for all: "Because the composition of a body politic is always changing the constitutional problem can never be solved once for all; there must always be a 'state' ready to solve it" (NL, 25.28). It follows that it is not the political philosopher's task to write a constitution, but rather to specify the requirements any constitution has to meet. As Collingwood put it in his 1929 Lectures on Moral Philosophy: "It is not the business of moral philosophy to give a list of rules which the philosopher advises his disciples to follow, any more than it is the task of political philosophy to draw up civil or criminal, or even constitutional, codes" (EPP, 117). So, racism is a serious problem, but it is not Collingwood's problem in his capacity as political philosopher. It is a problem for legislators and the writers of constitutions, and Collingwood's advice to them is that it is their task to maximize freedom, as elucidated above.

5. *The New Leviathan* III: Civilization and Barbarism

Part IV of *The New Leviathan*, on "Barbarism," is the briefest of the book's four parts, and it was completed under considerable time pressure, as Collingwood found his powers declining. However, much of what he had to say about barbarism is said by implication in his discussion of civilization, so it makes sense to treat the two topics as one.

No part of *The New Leviathan* has greater contemporary relevance than the discussion of civilization, now that Western civilization again faces the threat of authoritarian nationalism, a threat felt perhaps most acutely in Hungary, Poland, Israel, and the United States, but neither Great Britain nor the Scandinavian countries are quite immune. Ironically, it is Germany that today appears as the bastion of democracy!

a. What "Civilization" Means

By "civilization" Collingwood does not mean a state of affairs that has been finally arrived at, but rather a process of transition; it is "*something which happens to a community*" (NL, 34.4). It is a process of approximation toward an ideal state called "civility" and away from an ideal state called "barbarity." By calling these states "ideal" Collingwood means that neither of them ever is or can be completely realized. There never was a completely barbarous community, and there never will be a completely civilized community: "The process of civilization would thus be one of *asymptotic approximation to the ideal condition of civility*" (NL, 34.56).

Well and good; but what is civility? It is, as Collingwood initially puts it, an x, which consists of the two components (a) and (b), of which (b) in turn consists of the two components (b_1) and (b_2). The first component (a) is "concerned with the relation of a community to itself; the relation of its members to one another" (NL, 35.3). The second component (b) concerns "the relation of the community to what is outside the community" (NL, 35.31). Now, there are two such relations: the relation of any member of the community to the natural world and the relation of any member of the community to members of another community.

Beginning with (a), civilization means "*coming to obey rules of civil intercourse*" (NL, 35.35). More specifically:

> Behaving civilly to a man means respecting his feelings: abstaining from shocking him, annoying him, frightening him, or (briefly) arousing in him any passion or desire which might diminish his self-respect (13.31); that is, threaten his consciousness of freedom by making him feel that his power of choice is in danger of breaking down and the passion or desire likely to take charge (13.67). (NL, 35.41)

To arouse uncontrollable passions or desires in someone is, in Collingwood's view, one way of exercising force over another, and so the ideal of civility in one's dealings with others "is the ideal of *refraining from the use of force towards them*" (NL, 35.44). As noted before, no community can dispense with the use of force altogether, so the ideal is to treat others as civilly *as possible*.

In the community's dealing with the natural world, dealt with only briefly, civilization consists in the ability to get what the community needs and wants out of nature, by its own efforts, and by the use of intelligent labor governed by a scientific understanding of nature.

A more complex question, in Collingwood's view, is whether civilization requires an increase in civility toward members of other communities. We are required to show civility toward those who themselves possess civility, so the question comes down to that of whether foreigners are human or not. This question is not as silly as it sounds, as many communities in the past have regarded foreigners as nonhumans, who can be murdered with total impunity (NL, 35.66). And, of course, we have recently (2019) heard a president of the United States refer to foreign asylum seekers as "animals" and proceed to lock them up in cages. The consciousness of foreigners as humans like us arises through interactions that require cooperation, through which a shared social consciousness emerges. A prominent type of such interaction is commercial action: "A community accustomed to trading with strangers is commonly accustomed to treat strangers with civility" (NL, 35.69).

It may be apposite to note here, though Collingwood does not, that the Torah—also known as the Pentateuch or the Five Books of Moses—no less than fourteen times admonishes the Israelites to protect the strangers among them, because "you know the heart of a stranger, for you were strangers in the land of Egypt" (Exod. 23:9). To the best of my knowledge, this is the earliest known example of purely ethical reasoning; the appeal is not to either prudence or the will of God, but simply to human empathy.

Collingwood summarizes the above by noting that civilization consists of three processes:

> The first is the process whereby the members of that community become less addicted to force in their dealings with one another. (35.4)
>
> The second is one whereby they become more able to get what necessaries or luxuries they demand … by the intelligent or scientific exploitation of the natural world. (35.5)
>
> The third is one whereby … they come to considers [foreigners] under the first head as human beings and thereby as much entitled to civility as if they had been members of the community. (NL, 36.12–14)

I know of no evidence that Collingwood was familiar with the writings of John Dewey, but there is a striking parallel here to a famous saying by Dewey: "[I]t is no exaggeration to say that the measure of civilization is the degree to which the method of cooperative intelligence replaces the method of brute conflict."[23] This theme is further illuminated by Collingwood's inquiry into exactly what the first two processes have in common. As an example of the intelligent control of nature Collingwood instances knot-tying, a craft from which every sailor knows a variety of knots. (Collingwood, we recall, was an expert sailor.) This craft as it now exists has come into being through a gradual building up of knowledge over centuries, a building up in which the sharing of knowledge is essential. There has to be a dialectic of knowledge, in which practical knowledge is not hoarded, but progresses through agreement and cooperation. Thus, what the first two civilizing processes have in common is quite simply *civility*. This is what enables both peaceful coexistence in a community and the intelligent exploitation of nature (NL, 36.51).

This concludes our overview over Collingwood's general conception of civilization. We turn next to some specific aspects of civilization.

b. Education

As we have seen, a paramount function of the rulers is to educate the ruled. Interestingly, however, Collingwood did not think it was the business of the state to educate *children*, or even that the education of children should be entrusted to professional educators at all. Ideally, children should be educated by their parents. (Collingwood himself, we recall, was homeschooled for several years before spending some miserable years at Rugby.) There are two reasons why childhood education is best left to parents:

First, the parents have greater power over the child than any professional educator can attain; in fact parents are omnipotent vis-à-vis the child.
Secondly, the parents have greater versatility. A professional educator is bound, by the terms of his or her employment, to teach a particular subject matter, usually by a particular method. Parents are under no such constraint; they can teach whatever they choose, or even leave the child free to do whatever he or she chooses (NL, 37.36).

It is hard to disagree with Boucher's observation that this view of childhood education is rather naïve and insensitive to the needs of children born to uneducated or uncaring parents.[24] In fact, Collingwood's advice to ignorant parents is to just read to their children, or leave the children to their own devises, and they'll be fine; most modern children are over-taught as it is (NL, 37.94).

c. Wealth

As a community grows more civilized, its ability to exploit natural resources increases, and so it grows wealthier. But what does "wealth" mean? It cannot mean the ability to extract enough from nature to satisfy its needs. In that sense *every* community is wealthy in that every community adapts to its power; what it cannot get, it learns to do without. Even a community where large numbers of families cannot feed their children adapts by exposing its newborn. So, extreme poverty would count as wealth by this definition (NL, 38.16). But at the same time, *no* community is wealthy in this sense, because needs grow with powers. As soon as a new commodity is produced, there immediately arises a need for it (NL, 38.25). Nobody needed cars before they existed. Now everybody does.

A community is wealthy only in relation to some other community: "the community A, owing to its superiority in 'natural science' and 'industry' combined, *demands more of the natural world than B and is able to get more*" (NL, 38.27). However, "wealthy," which belongs to communities, is a *comparative* term, as distinct from "rich," which belongs to individuals and is a *relative* term. A comparative term is one that has a reference to a standard; for instance, when I say "This is a good book" I am not necessarily thinking of it as better than certain other books (although I may), but "I am thinking simply that *it comes up to my standard of goodness*" (NL, 38.4). If, by contrast, I say, "This is a fast car," I am thinking of it by contrast with other, slower cars; there is no standard of speed applicable to automobiles. So, a community is wealthy to the degree that its ability to extract from nature what its members want comes up to the standard of wealth that its members then have. The standard will of course change over time.

A person is rich relative to other individuals. Riches amount to economic power, whereby the rich may be able to force the poorer to enter into transactions which do not leave them better off, for example, by buying labor for less than what may be considered its just price (NL, 38.67). Earlier, in 1925, Collingwood had opined that the state could intervene and prohibit unjust transactions; now he has become skeptical: "if once the contrast between riches and poverty is allowed to exist a force is set up which henceforth it is idle to resist" (NL, 38.7). So, rather than try to curb the exercise of economic power, a civilized community will take measures to prevent the emergence of a significant contrast between rich and poor, such contrast being "an offence against the idea of civility" (NL, 38.74). Allowing such a contrast to arise undermines civilization: "To accumulate wealth in order to create by its means a contrast between rich and poor is to use it for the destruction of civilization, or the pursuit of barbarism" (NL, 38.53). The relevance of this insight for the United States today need not be labored; there is also a clear echo of the eighteenth-century poet Oliver Goldsmith:

> Ill fares the land, to hastening ills a prey,
> Where wealth accumulates, and men decay;[25]

d. The Rule of Law

We have established that civilization is the process of making people more civil, where that means substituting, wherever possible, dialectical relations for eristical ones. Collingwood summarizes this conclusion as follows: "*Being civilized* means *living, so far as possible, dialectically*, that is, in constant endeavour to convert every occasion of non-agreement into an occasion of agreement" (NL, 39.15). A central aspect of civilization so understood is the rule of law.

The rule of law comprises four elements:

First, that there is a law. There may or may not be a legislature; the law may be customary, or the edict of a tyrant.
Second, that the law is publicly promulgated so that those who are under the law can find out what it is.
Third, that there are courts that enforce the law.
Fourth, that there is equality before the law (NL, 39.31–4).

The rule of law is intrinsic to civilization in that it implies "the substitution, in every quarrel which the law can handle, of dialectical for eristical methods" (NL, 39.52).

As an example of law enforcement Collingwood instances the concept of *wergild* in medieval Anglo-Saxon law, the *wergild* being the compensation that an injured party could be forced by the court to accept for its injury. First, the *wergild* involves the use of force and not against a criminal, but against an innocent, injured party. But this force is applied to prevent the greater use of force found in the vendetta that would ensue should the injured party not accept the compensation. "The lawgiver uses force; but he uses it for the sake of agreement" (NL, 39.72). Secondly, the *wergild* exemplifies equality before the law, albeit in an inegalitarian society. The life of a nobleman was worth more than the life of a peasant, so not everybody's *wergild* was the same. But "whatever a man's wergild was, it was the same for anyone who might happen to kill him" (NL, 39.83). The rank of the offender was irrelevant to the amount of the punishment.

Lastly, living under the rule of law is a discipline that builds strength of character. "*Law and order means strength*" (NL, 39.92). This, Collingwood tells us, is the most important thing in his book.

e. Barbarism

Collingwood distinguishes between savagery and barbarism. By savagery he means simply the absence of civilization—a relative absence since there can never be a complete absence of civilization. By barbarism he means hostility to civilization, the effort to destroy civilization. A civilized person is subject to social sentiments, which may control one's conduct and direct it toward greater sociality without one being conscious of it. It is thus possible to promote civilization without being conscious of doing so. The "barbarist," by contrast, needs to have a clear idea of what he is doing, of what civilization is, and what constitutes the destruction of civilization (NL, 41.53). The barbarist can succeed only when civilized people are unprepared and can be taken by surprise. Moreover, the barbarist must, throughout the project of barbarization, keep the element of surprise, so his enemies never know what he is going to do next:

> The rules for success in barbarism, therefore, urge the barbarist above all else to keep the ice moving and to reproduce every day, so far as possible, the fluid conditions that prevailed at the beginning of his career. (NL, 41.64)

Collingwood is here noting a phenomenon that Hannah Arendt was later, in 1950, to document in great detail in her celebrated work on totalitarianism. Both Hitler and Stalin, she noted, governed—and could only govern—by "creating a state of permanent instability."[26] One example cited by Arendt is Hitler's deliberate refusal to draw a clear line between the state and the Nazi Party.[27] The Weimar division of the nation into states and provinces was duplicated by the new division into *Gaue*, whose borderlines did not coincide with the Weimar divisions and so left citizens subject to multiple, potentially conflicting jurisdictions. Also, the Minister of the Interior was made to report to Himmler as Chief of Police, his nominal subordinate. And the responsibilities of the Foreign Office were duplicated by those of the SS.[28] The resulting confusion was not accidental but intended: only the leader's say-so determined who was responsible for what; there was no external, objective standard. Similarly, in the Soviet Union, the state, the party, and the secret police, the NKVD, were separate yet overlapping organizations. The NKVD spies on the functionaries of the state and the party, while the party has its own secret police which spies on the NKVD.[29] Again, the result is to preclude the emergence of a center of power independent of the Leader. Thus the barbarist "fluidity" is amply exemplified in both Nazism and Soviet communism. In today's (2020) United States, while we are still a democracy, any major policy statement by the president is likely to be "walked back" the next day if not sooner; fluidity reigns here and now.

This image of totalitarianism stands in striking contrast to that of the super-rational totalitarianism envisioned by Aldous Huxley in his dystopian novel *Brave New World* (1932) and, to a lesser extent, by Friedrich Hayek, in his otherwise remarkably perceptive political tract *The Road to Serfdom* (1944). The fluidity noted by Collingwood and Arendt is, however, clearly recognizable in George Orwell's *Nineteen Eighty-Four* (1948), where the nation's history is updated on a day-to-day basis so as at any time to reflect "Big Brother's" current priorities.

A. J. M. Milne has noted a similarity between civilization, as understood by Collingwood, and Karl Popper's concept of the "open society" in his eponymous *The Open Society and Its Enemies*, published in 1945. Although Popper and Collingwood were unaware of each other's work, each regarded his book as his contribution to the war effort, and in his Introduction Popper referred to the enemies of the open society as the enemies of civilization.[30] And Milne is surely right to the extent that Popper's open society, like Collingwood's civilization, is essentially a *process*, which never actually reaches an end-state, but which approximates its end asymptotically, as a limit. Unlike Collingwood, however, Popper does not distinguish between savagery, or a primeval closed society, and barbarism, that is, the effort to close an already relatively open society. Thus, Popper is not able to distinguish, except on the level of individual psychology, Plato's defense (as Popper saw it) of traditional Greek society from the project of twentieth-century totalitarianism. As in our discussion of historical explanation in Chapter 4, the contrast with Popper is drawn primarily because Popper came so tantalizingly close—perhaps closer than any of his contemporaries—to capturing Collingwood's vital insights.

While the barbarist may do considerable damage in the short run, in the long run the barbarist is bound to fail, and for two reasons. First, as we have seen, civilization is not a thing, and thus cannot be destroyed. Civilization is a *process*, and no matter how many of the fruits of that process you destroy, there is nothing to prevent the civilizing process from arising again and again. Secondly, the barbarist cannot function as a single individual; barbarists work in concert as a movement, and their cooperation is necessarily a form of civility, and hence self-defeating:

> For barbarism implies not only a quarrel between any barbarist and any civilized man; it also implies a quarrel between any one barbarist and any other; and that any state of harmony between them is merely this quarrel suspended. (NL, 41.76)

Collingwood offers four historical examples of barbarism: the Saracens, the Albigensians, the medieval Turks, and the Germans. Of the four, the last one was obviously of greatest interest in 1942. The slide into barbarism represented by Nazism was the outcome of a gradual process; like a landslide, no one can say precisely when it started (NL, 45.26). It may be dated back to Bismarck's conquests in the 1860s, or even further. At any rate, a form of herd worship appears to have been an immemorial condition of the German people, a condition which betokens a lack of civility, which has lately taken the form of a mania (NL, 45.89). Collingwood of course did not live to see the success of democratic federalism in postwar Germany, in many ways a corrective to his diagnosis.

6. Conclusion

We have reached the end of our journey. We have observed the steady, continuous evolution of Collingwood's thought, guided and inspired, but never hemmed in, by Collingwood's early discovery of the dialectical scale-of-forms analysis. Emphasizing from the start the unity of thought and action, of theory and practice, Collingwood's thought exhibits throughout a passionate concern with defending and preserving civilization against its irrationalist enemies, and to do so by promulgating an understanding of history, of art, and of politics. On the way, I hope to have conveyed, however briefly, the amazing scope and depth of Collingwood's thought, its thorough anticipation of substantive, post-analytic philosophy, and the stark, eye-opening light it sheds on today's civilization, society, and politics. Collingwood's works thus continue to be of profound and abiding value to students of history, politics, religion, and art, as well as of philosophy.

Further Reading

Peter Johnson, *R.G. Collingwood: An Introduction*, Chapter Nine.
David Boucher, *The Social and Political Philosophy of R.G. Collingwood*.
James Connelly, *Metaphysics, Method, and Politics: The Political Philosophy of R.G. Collingwood*, Part Two.

Notes

Introduction

1. Ray Monk, "How the untimely death of R.G. Collingwood changed the course of philosophy forever," prospectmagazine.co.uk, September 5, 2019. The personal power wielded by Ryle over postwar Oxford philosophy has recently been attested to by Cora Diamond in her John Dewey Lecture "Reflections of a Dinosaur," p. 93. During the Q&A Diamond made it clear that Ryle never to her knowledge abused his position of power.
2. Fred Inglis, *History Man: The Life of R.G. Collingwood*, pp. 324–5, 338–42. MacIntyre directed my own doctoral dissertation on Collingwood's metaphysics.
3. The exception is Peter Johnson, *R.G. Collingwood: An Introduction*.
4. Lionel Rubinoff, *Collingwood and the Reform of Metaphysics*.
5. James Connelly, *Metaphysics, Method, and Politics*, p. 12.

Chapter 1

1. Fred Inglis, *History Man: The Life of R.G. Collingwood*.
2. Ibid., p. 46.
3. Teresa Smith, "R.G. Collingwood's Childhood: Habits of Thought," p. 185.
4. Tony Bierly, "Collingwood as Archaeologist and Historian," esp. pp. 283–4.
5. Quoted in Jan van der Dussen, *History as a Science*, p. 192.
6. Inglis, *History Man: The Life of R.G. Collingwood*, pp. 151–2.
7. T.H. Green, *Lectures on the Principles of Political Obligation*, §228, quoted in David Boucher and Andrew Vincent, *British Idealism: A Guide for the Perplexed*, p. 126.
8. John Passmore, *A Hundred Years of Philosophy*, p. 58.
9. T.H. Green, *Prolegomena to Ethics*, p. 198, referenced by Frederick Copleston, *A History of Philosophy*, vol. VIII, p. 169.
10. D.F. Pears, *Bertrand Russell and the British Tradition in Philosophy*, p. 162.
11. F.H. Bradley, *Appearance and Reality*, p. 31, referenced by Copleston, *A History of Philosophy*, p. 203.

12 Bradley, *Appearance and Reality*, pp. 132–59, referenced by Copleston, *A History of Philosophy*, pp. 207–8.
13 J.M.E. McTaggart, *The Nature of Existence*, p. 88, quoted in Copleston, *A History of Philosophy*, p. 242.
14 Boucher and Vincent, *British Idealism: A Guide for the Perplexed*, p. 2.
15 For a detailed account, see Rik Peters, *History as Thought and Action: The Philosophies of Croce, Gentile, de Ruggiero, and Collingwood*.
16 James Patrick, "The Oxford Man," p. 235.
17 David Boucher, *The Social and Political Thought of R.G. Collingwood*, p. 21.
18 Frederick Copleston's magisterial history also does not mention Collingwood, but Copleston has the excuse that he only intended to cover British philosophy through the nineteenth century, while including Bertrand Russell as a nineteenth-century philosopher.

Chapter 2

1 Charles Peirce, *The Essential Peirce*, p. 55.
2 Jan van der Dussen has also traced the re-enactment doctrine to the earlier work; cf. *History as a Science*, p. 317.
3 H.A. Prichard, "Does Moral Philosophy Rest on a Mistake?," *Mind*, xxi, 81, Jan. 1912, reprinted in Prichard, *Moral Obligation*.
4 Lionel Rubinoff, *Collingwood and the Reform of Metaphysics*, p. 51.
5 Boucher, *The Social and Political Thought of R.G. Collingwood*, p. 16.
6 Peirce, *The Essential Peirce*, p. 52.
7 Louis Mink, *Mind, History & Dialectic*, p. 55.
8 Rubinoff, *Collingwood and the Reform of Metaphysics*, pp. 26–7. Rubinoff also notes the resemblance of *Speculum Mentis* to Hegel's Phenomenology.
9 Mink, *Mind, History & Dialectic*, p. 16.
10 Jan van der Dussen, *History as a Science*, p. 13. Van der Dussen also cites Mink's judgment.
11 James Connelly, *Metaphysics, Method and Politics*, p. 30.

Chapter 3

1 Louis Mink, *Mind, History & Dialectic*, p. 3.
2 A. J. Ayer, *Philosophy in the Twentieth Century*, p. 193.

3   Bernard Williams, "An Essay on Collingwood," pp. 32, 17.
4   Aristotle, *Posterior Analytics*, I, 1, 71b, 5.
5   Quoted in Fred Inglis, *History Man*, p. 193.
6   Boucher, *The Social and Political Thought of R.G. Collingwood*, pp. 82–4.
7   David Hume, *An Enquiry Concerning Human Understanding*, p. 211.
8   Bertrand Russell, *Logic and Knowledge*, p. 53.
9   Gilbert Ryle, "Systematically Mislesading Expressions," esp. pp. 29–30.
10 Ibid., pp. 20–1.
11 Ibid., p. 36.
12 Giueppina D'Oro, *Collingwood and the Metaphysics of Experience*, p. 11.
13 John Rawls, *A Theory of Justice*, pp. 44–5, 47–8.
14 D'Oro, *Collingwood and the Metaphysics of Experience*, p. 13.
15 Ryle, "Systematically Misleading Expressions"; Russell, *Logic and Knowledge*, p. 54.
16 Ryle, ibid., p. 16.
17 Ryle, *Mind*, XLIV, 1935, pp. 137–51.
18 Ibid., p. 147.
19 Ibid., p. 141.
20 Quoted in Alan Donagan, *The Later Philosophy of R.G. Collingwood*, p. 261.
21 T.M. Knox, Prefatory Note to *The Idea of Nature*, p. v.
22 T.S. Kuhn, *The Structure of Scientific Revolutions*.

Chapter 4

1   *Principles of History*, p. xiii.
2   Ibid., pp. liii–lvii.
3   F.H. Bradley, *The Presuppositions of Critical History*, p. 93.
4   Leo Strauss, "On Collingwood's Philosophy of History," p. 561.
5   Ibid., p. 577.
6   W.H. Walsh, *Philosophy of History*, p. 57.
7   Patrick Gardiner, *The Nature of Historical Explanation*, p. 29. For an opposing view, see William Dray, "Collingwood and the Acquaintance Theory of Knowledge".
8   Karl R. Popper, *Objective Knowledge*, p. 188.
9   Isaiah Berlin, *Three Critics of the Enlightenment*, p. 119. See also my "Collingwood and Berlin: A Comparison".
10 Leon J. Goldstein, "Collingwood's Theory of Historical Knowing," pp. 29–31.
11 Jan van der Dussen, *History as a Science*, p. 7; Hurup Nielsen, "Re-enactment and Reconstruction," pp. 3–5. Both van der Dussen and Dray have taken

"Hurup" to be a middle name, and so reference this writer as "Nielsen," whereas Rex Martin has taken it to be part of the last name. From my personal familiarity with Scandinavian names I believe Martin is right, but I have not been able to verify this.

12 Alan Donagan, "The Verification of Historical Theses," p. 203.
13 William Dray, *Laws and Explanation in History*, p. 1.
14 Alan Donagan, "The Popper-Hempel Thesis Reconsidered," p. 127.
15 Carl G. Hempel, "The Function of General Laws," p. 345.
16 Ibid., p. 346.
17 Ibid.
18 Ibid., p. 348.
19 Ibid., p. 349.
20 Ibid., p. 351.
21 Ibid., p. 352. Emphasis in the original.
22 Hurup Nielsen, "Making Sense of History," p. 482.
23 J.S. Mill, *A System of Logic*, chs. 12–14; William Dray, *History as Re-enactment*, p. 68 and n. 1.
24 Dray, *Laws and Explanation in History*, p. 8.
25 Karl R. Popper, *The Open Society and Its Enemies*, pp. 264–5.
26 Ibid., p. 364, n. 7.
27 Gardiner, *The Nature of Historical Explanation*, p. 61.
28 Ibid., p. 47.
29 Ibid., p. 49.
30 Ibid., p. 47.
31 Ibid., pp. 50, 125.
32 Dray, *Laws and Explanation in History*, pp. 32–3.
33 Ibid., p. 33.
34 Ibid., pp. 33–4.
35 Ibid., p. 36.
36 Ibid., p. 118.
37 Ibid., pp. 121–2.
38 Ibid.
39 Ibid., p. 123.
40 Ibid., p. 124.
41 Ibid., p. 125.
42 Popper, *Objective Knowledge*, p. 106.
43 Ibid.
44 Gottlob Frege, "The Thought," pp. 29, 37; Gottlob Frege, *Translations*, p. 59.

45 Popper, *Objective Knowledge*, p. 107. Emphases in the original.
46 Peter Skagestad, "Thinking With Machines," p. 167; Paul Levinson, *Mind at Large*, p. 79.
47 Popper, *Objective Knowledge*, p. 170.
48 Ibid., p. 171.
49 Ibid., p. 174.
50 Ibid., pp. 187–8; Joseph Agassi, "Towards an Historiography of Science," p. 50.
51 Popper, *Objective Knowledge*, p. 187.
52 Ibid., p. 188.
53 Ibid., p. 177.
54 Ibid., p. 178.
55 Jeremy Shearmur, "Making Sense of History"; Hurup Nielsen, "Making Sense of History," p. 478; van der Dussen, *History as a Science*, p. 320; Jan Van der Dussen, "The Philosophical Context for Collingwood's Re-enactment Theory," esp. p. 90.
56 Dray, *History as Re-enactment*, p. 109; Walsh, *Philosophy of History*, p. 50; Peter Winch, *The Idea of a Social Science*, p. 13.
57 Dray, *History as Re-enactment*, p. 110.
58 Ibid., p. 111.
59 Ibid., p. 114 and n. 7.
60 Ibid., p. 115.
61 Ibid.
62 Ibid., p. 116.
63 Ibid.
64 Ibid., p. 118.
65 Ibid., pp. 119–22.
66 Ibid., p. 126.
67 David Boucher, "The Significance of R.G. Collingwood's 'Principles of History,'" p. 327.
68 Heikki Saari, *Re-enactment*, p. 39; Dray, *History as Re-enactment*, pp. 136–7.
69 David H. Fischer, *Historians' Fallacies*, p. 127.
70 Dray, *History as Re-enactment*, p. 153.
71 Ibid.
72 Ibid., p. 157.
73 Ibid., p. 159.
74 Ibid., p. 158; Louis Mink, *Mind, History, and Dialectic*, p. 171.
75 Dray, *History as Re-enactment*, p. 163.
76 Ibid., p. 164.

77 Ibid., p. 167.
78 Ibid., p. 173.
79 Ibid., p. 175.

Chapter 5

1. Bur Arendt was in this respect anticipated by Walter Lippmann already in 1936; see his *The Good Society*, pp. 66–90.
2. Fred Inglis, *History Man*, p. 23.
3. John Dewey, *Art as Experience*, p. 49; note that there are three extant editions of this work, each—unhelpfully—with its own page-numbering; Mark Rothko, *The Artist's Reality*, p. 20; *Writings on Art*, p. 75.
4. Alan Donagan, *The Later Philosophy of R.G. Collingwood*, p. 104.
5. Reprinted in Walter Benjamin, *Illuminations*, pp. 217–51.
6. Although Collingwood's editors suggest that his essay may have been written after the appearance of the talkie *The Jazz Singer* in 1927 (PE, 291, n).
7. Mark Rothko, *Writings on Art*, p. 34.
8. Quoted in Dorothy Sieberling, "The Varied Art of Four Pioneers," *LIFE*, November 16, 1959, p. 82. In the same vein, Rothko also wrote: "Self-expression is boring. I want to talk of nothing [sic] outside of myself—a great scope of experience." *Writings on Art*, p. 128.
9. *Clyfford Still Museum Handbook*, Denver, CO, 2015, p. 25.
10. Dewey, *Art as Experience*, p. 128.
11. Nelson Goodman, *Languages of Art*, pp. 12–13.
12. Will Gompertz, *What Are You Looking At?* p. 78.
13. Goodman, *Languages of Art*, p. 14.
14. In the permanent collection of The Butler Institute of American Art in Youngstown, Ohio.
15. Richard Wollheim, "On An Alleged Inconsistency in Collingwood's Aesthetic," in Krausz, *Critical Essays on the Philosophy of R.G. Collingwood*, pp. 68–78, p. 69.
16. Donagan, *The Later Philosophy of R.G. Collingwood*, pp. 118–19.
17. Ibid., p. 105. See also David Boucher, *The Social and Political Philosophy of R.G. Collingwood*, p. 131.
18. Howard DeLong, *In the Cause of Humanity*, p. 275.
19. Mink, *Mind, History, and Dialectic*, p. 228.
20. Boucher, *The Social and Political Philosophy of R.G. Collingwood*, p. 136, citing Ludwig Wittgenstein, *Philosophical Investigations*, p. 20e, par. 43.

21 Peter Jones, "A Critical Outline of Collingwood's Philosophy of Art," in Krausz, pp. 42–67, p. 48.
22 Aaron Ridley, *R.G. Collingwood: A Philosophy of Art*, p. 33.
23 Dewey, *Art as Experience*, p. 222.
24 Ibid., p. 50.
25 E.H. Gombrich, *Art and Illusion*, Part Three: "The Beholder's Share."
26 For a perceptive and informative account of Dewey's aesthetics as a critique of modern technology, see Robert Innis, *Pragmatism and the Forms of Sense*, pp. 167–202.
27 Inglis, *History Man*, 25.
28 Ridley, *R.G. Collingwood: A Philosophy of Art*, p. 1.
29 Donagan, *The Later Philosophy of R.G. Collingwood*, p. 133; Ridley, *R.G. Collingwood: A Philosophy of Art*, p. 3.

Chapter 6

1 Prichard's 1912 paper is reprinted in his posthumous *Moral Obligation*, pp. 1–17.
2 William James, *Pragmatism*, p. 44.
3 Alan Donagan, *The Later Philosophy of R.G. Collingwood*, p. 60.
4 Ibid., p. 57.
5 Ibid., p. 58.
6 Ibid., p. 61.
7 Ibid., p. 62.
8 Mink, *Mind, History, and Dialectic*, p. 131.
9 Peter Johnson, *R.G. Collingwood: An Introduction*, p. 71.
10 Michael Beaney, "Collingwood's Critique of Oxbridge Realism," p. 260.
11 Ibid., p. 261.
12 Ibid., p. 262.
13 Ibid., p. 263.
14 Mink, *Mind, History, and Dialectic*, pp. 131–9.
15 James, *Pragmatism*, p. 58. Emphasis in the original.
16 W.V.O. Quine, "Two Dogmas of Empiricism," in *From A Logical Point of View*, p. 41.
17 T.M. Knox, "Editor's Preface" to *The Idea of History*, 1946, p. x.
18 Ibid.
19 Ibid., p. xi.
20 Ibid., p. xii.

21 Ibid., p. xvi.
22 Ibid., p. xvii.
23 Donagan, *The Later Philosophy of R.G. Collingwood*, esp. pp. 12–18.
24 Mink, *Mind, History, and Dialectic*, p. 16.
25 Lionel Rubinoff, *Collingwood and the Reform of Metaphysics*, pp. 239–40.
26 Skagestad, "R.G. Collingwood's Theory of Presuppositions," pp. 107–10.
27 Giuseppina D'Oro, *Collingwood and the Metaphysics of Experience*, pp. 81–4. See also Tariq Modood, "The Later Collingwood's Alleged Historicism and Relativism," pp. 101–25.
28 James Connelly, "Collingwood Controversies," pp. 399–429.
29 Ibid., p. 408.
30 Ibid.
31 Ibid., p. 409.
32 Ibid., pp. 409–10.

Chapter 7

1 E.g. James Connelly, *Metaphysics, Method, and Politics*, p. 117.
2 Rex Martin, Introduction to *An Essay on Metaphysics*, p. xxiii.
3 Tariq Modood, "The Later Collingwood's Alleged Historicism and Relativism," p. 121.
4 Giuseppina D'Oro, *Collingwood and the Metaphysics of Experience*, p. 65.
5 Martin, Introduction to *An Essay on Metaphysics*, p. xxviii, n. 4. Martin here references Wittgenstein's *On Certainty*.
6 D'Ordo, "Unlikely Bedfellows? Collingwood, Carnap and the Internal/External Distinction."
7 Kenneth Laine Ketner, *An Emendation of R.G. Collingwood's Doctrine of Absolute Presuppositions*, p. 31, n. 67. Ketner cites a passage now found in N. Houser and C. Kloesel, eds., *The Essential Peirce*, vol. 1, p. 115. Coincidentally, Ketner's monograph appeared four months after I had submitted my doctoral dissertation on the same subject.
8 Martin, "Collingwood's Claim that Metaphysics Is a Historical Discipline," in Boucher, Connelly, and Modood, eds., *Philosophy, History, and Civilization*, pp. 204–45, pp. 211–12.
9 Ibid., pp. 222, 227.
10 Stephen Toulmin, *Human Understanding*, p. 76.
11 Ibid., pp. 80, 99.

12 Peter Skagestad, *Making Sense of History*, p. 84.
13 Martin, Introduction, loc. cit., p. xlviii.
14 See Ibid., p. xlvi.
15 Ibid., p. xlii.
16 Imre Lakatos, "Criticism and the Methodology of Scientific Research Programmes," in Lakatos and Musgrave, eds., *Criticism and the Growth of Knowledge*, p. 155.
17 Skagestad, "Collingwood and Berlin: A Comparison".
18 Isaiah Berlin, *Three Critics of the Enlightenment*, p. 118. Berlin here traces Collingwood's doctrine back to Giambattista Vico.
19 Berlin, "Two Concepts of Liberty," in *Four Essays on Liberty*, esp. pp. 121–2.
20 Ibid., pp. 128, 136.
21 Ibid., p. 127.
22 Ibid., p. 134.
23 James Patrick, "The Oxford Man," p. 244.
24 A.J. Ayer, *Language, Truth, and Logic*, for example, pp. 41, 62.
25 Heikki Saari, "Some Aspects of R.G. Collingwood's Doctrine of Absolute Presuppositions," esp. p. 65.
26 Martin, loc. cit., p. xxv.
27 See D'Oro, *Collingwood and the Metaphysics of Experience*, p. 65.
28 As noted by Jan van der Dussen, who also observed that Collingwood was not even mentioned in Copleston's earlier multivolume *History of Philosophy*; cf. "The Philosophical Context of Collingwood's Re-enactment Theory," p. 81.
29 A.J. Ayer, *Philosophy in the Twentieth Century*, p. 198.
30 Ibid., p. 201.
31 Ludwig Wittgenstein, *Tractatus Logico-Philosophicus*, para. 1.1.
32 W.B. Gallie, *Philosophy and the Historical Understanding*, p. 158.
33 Ibid., p. 161.

Chapter 8

1 David Boucher, Introduction to EPP, p. 7.
2 Ibid., p. 18.
3 Ibid., pp. 24 ff; James Connelly, *Metaphysics, Method, and Politics*, pp. 182–3.
4 Guido de Ruggiero, *The History of European Liberalism*, pp. 351–2. I personally encountered this work before embarking on my study of Collingwood, as it was on the list of required readings for my PhD qualifying examinations.

5 Ibid., p. 353.
6 Ibid., p. 357.
7 Ibid., p. 361.
8 Ibid., p. 379.
9 Ibid., p. 392.
10 A.J.M. Milne, "Collingwood's Ethics and Political Theory," p. 318.
11 W.D. Ross, *The Right and the Good*, p. 143.
12 Ibid.
13 Jean-Paul Sartre, *Existentialism and Human Emotions*, pp. 24–7.
14 Boucher, *The Social and Political Thought of R.G. Collingwood*, p. 64.
15 Ibid., p. 68.
16 Ibid., p. 80.
17 Ibid., pp. 69–71.
18 Ibid., p. 122.
19 Ibid., pp. 95–6; Connelly, *Metaphysics, Method, and Politics*, p. 42, n. 104.
20 Boucher, *The Social and Political Thought of R.G. Collingwood*, p. 160.
21 Ibid., p. 230.
22 Connelly, *Metaphysics, Method, and Politics*, p. 220.
23 John Dewey, *Liberalism and Social Action*, p. 81.
24 Boucher, *The Social and Political Thought of R.G. Collingwood*, pp. 223–4.
25 Oliver Goldsmith, *The Deserted Village*, 1770.
26 Hannah Arendt, *The Origins of Totalitarianism*, p. 391.
27 Ibid., p. 395.
28 Ibid., pp. 396–7.
29 Ibid., pp. 402–3.
30 A.J.M. Milne, "Civilization and the Open Society: Collingwood and Popper," p. 300.

Select Bibliography

Works by Collingwood

Books

Religion and Philosophy, London: Macmillan, 1916.

Speculum Mentis, Oxford: Clarendon Press, 1924.

Outlines of a Philosophy of Art, London: Oxford University Press, 1925 (Reprinted in Donagan, 1964).

An Essay on Philosophical Method, Oxford: Clarendon Press, 1933, new edition with an Introduction and additional material edited by James Connelly and Giuseppina D'Oro, Oxford: Oxford University Press, 2005.

Roman Britain and the English Settlements, with J.N.L. Myre, second edition, Oxford: The Clarendon Press, 1937.

The Principles of Art, Oxford: Clarendon Press, 1938.

An Autobiography, London: Oxford University Press, 1939, reprinted with a new Introduction by Stephen Toulmin, 1978, new edition: *An Autobiography & Other Writings with Essays on Collingwood's Life and Work*, edited by David Boucher and Theresa Smith, Oxford: Oxford University Press, 2013.

An Essay on Metaphysics, Oxford: Clarendon Press, 1940, revised edition with an Introduction and additional material edited by Rex Martin, Oxford: Oxford University Press, 1998.

The First Mate's Log, London: Oxford University Press, 1940.

The New Leviathan, Oxford: Clarendon Press, 1942, revised edition with an Introduction and additional material edited by David Boucher, Oxford: Oxford University Press, 1992. Following established convention, references to this work cite paragraph numbers, rather than page numbers.

The Idea of Nature, Oxford: Clarendon Press, 1945.

The Idea of History, Oxford: Clarendon Press, 1946, revised edition with Lectures 1926–28, edited with an Introduction by Jan van der Dussen, Oxford: Oxford University Press, 1994.

The Principles of History and Other Writings in Philosophy of History, edited with an Introduction by W.H. Dray and W.J. van der Dussen, Oxford: Oxford University Press, 1999.

The Philosophy of Enchantment: Studies in Folktale, Cultural Criticism, and Anthropology, edited by David Boucher, Wendy James, and Philip Smallwood, Oxford: The Clarendon Press, 2005.

Manuscripts

"Goodness, Rightness, Utility," 1940, reprinted in the revised edition of *The New Leviathan*; page numbers will refer to this edition. This item is listed separately because *The New Leviathan* is, by established convention, referenced by paragraph numbers, not page numbers.

Collections of Articles

Boucher, David, ed., *Essays in Political Philosophy*, Oxford: Clarendon Press, 1989.

Debbins, William, ed., *Essays in the Philosophy of History*, New York: McGraw-Hill, 1966.

Donagan, Alan, ed., *Essays in the Philosophy of Art*, Bloomington: Indiana University Press, 1964.

Rubinoff, Lionel, ed., *Faith & Reason: Essays in the Philosophy of Religion*, Chicago: Quadrangle Books, 1968.

Works by Others

Agassi, Joseph, "Towards a Historiography of Science," *History and Theory*, Beiheft 2, 1963.

Arendt, Hannah, *The Origins of Totalitarianism*, 1951, second edition, Cleveland: World Publishing Company, 1958.

Aristotle, *The Basic Works of Aristotle*, edited and with an Introduction by McKeon Richard, New York: Random House, 1945.

Ayer, Alfred Jules, *Language, Truth and Logic*, 1936, second edition, London: Victor Gollantz, Ltd., 1946.

Ayer, Alfred Jules, *Philosophy in the Twentieth Century*, New York: Random House, 1982.

Beaney, Michael, "Collingwood's Critique of Oxbridge Realism," in *An Autobiography & Other Writings*, edited by David Boucher and Theresa Smith, Oxford: Oxford University Press, 2013, 247–69.

Benjamin, Walter, *Illuminations: Essays and Reflections*, edited and with an Introduction by Hannah Arendt, New York: Shocken Books, 1968.

Berlin, Isaiah, *Four Essays on Liberty*, Oxford: Oxford University Press, 1969.
Berlin, Isaiah, *Three Critics of the Enlightenment: Vico, Hamann, Herder*, edited by Henry Hardy, Princeton: Princeton University Press, 2000.
Birley, Tony, "Collingwood as Archaeologist and Historian," in *An Autobiography and Other Writings*, edited by David Boucher and Theresa Smith, Oxford: Oxford University Press, 2013, 271–304.
Boucher, David, *The Social and Political Thought of R.G. Collingwood*, Cambridge: Cambridge University Press, 1989.
Boucher, David, "The Significance of R.G. Collingwood's Principles of History," *Journal of the History of Ideas*, vol. 58, no. 2, 1997, 309–30.
Boucher, David and Vincent, Andrew, *British Idealism: A Guide for the Perplexed*, London: Continuum, 2012.
Boucher, David, Connelly, James, and Modood, Tariq, eds., *Philosophy, History and Civilization: Interdisciplinary Perspectives on R.G. Collingwood*, Cardiff: University of Wales Press, 1995.
Bradley, F.H., *Ethical Studies*, second edition, with an Introduction by Richard Wollheim, Oxford: Oxford University Press, 1962.
Bradley, F.H., *The Presuppositions of Critical History*, edited with an Introduction and Commentary by Lionel Rubinoff, Chicago: Quadrangle Books, 1968.
Carr, Edward Hallett, *What Is History?* New York: Vintage Books, 1961.
Connelly, James, *Metaphysics, Method and Politics: The Political Philosophy of R.G. Collingwood*, Exeter: Imprint Academic, 2003.
Connelly, James, "Collingwood Controversies," in *An Autobiography & Other Writings*, edited by David Boucher and Theresa Smith, Oxford: Oxford University Press, 2013, 399–425.
Copleston, Fredrick, *A History of Philosophy, Volume VIII: Bentham to Russell*, New York: Doubleday, 1965.
DeLong, Howard, "The Development of R.G. Collingwood's Theory of History," Ph.D. dissertation, Princeton University: Princeton, New Jersey, 1960.
DeLong, Howard, *In the Cause of Humanity*, third edition, West Hartford, CT: Belcrest Press, 2015.
Dewey, John, *Art as Experience*, 1934, New York: Penguin Group, 1980.
Dewey, John, *Liberalism & Social Action*, 1935, New York: G.P. Putnam's Sons, 1963.
Dharamsi, Karim, D'Oro, Giuseppina, and Leach, Stephen, eds., *Collingwood on Philosophical Methodology*, Cham, Switzerland: Palgrave Macmillan, 2018.
Diamond, Cora, "Reflections of a Dinosaur," *Proceedings and Addresses of The American Philosophical Association*, vol. 93, November 2019, 87–104.
Donagan, Alan, "The Verification of Historical Theses," *The Philosophical Quarterly*, vol. 6, no. 24, 1956, 193–208.

Donagan, Alan, *The Later Philosophy of R.G. Collingwood*, Oxford: Clarendon Press, 1962.

Donagan, Alan, "The Popper-Hempel Thesis Reconsidered," *History and Theory*, vol. 4, no. 1, 1964, 3–26, reprinted in Dray, *Philosophical Analysis and History*, 127–59.

D'Oro, Giuseppina, *Collingwood and the Metaphysics of Experience*, London: Routledge, 2002.

D'Oro, Giuseppina, "Unlikely Bedfellows? Collingwood, Carnap and the Internal/External Distinction," *British Journal for the History of Philosophy*, vol.23, no.4, June 18, 2015, 802–17.

Dray, William, *Laws and Explanation in History*, Oxford: Oxford University Press, 1957.

Dray, William, "R.G. Collingwood and the Acquaintance Theory of Knowledge," *Revue Internationale de Philosophie*, vol. 11, no. 42, 1957, 420–32.

Dray, William, ed., *Philosophical Analysis and History*, New York: Harper & Row, 1966.

Dray, William, *History as Re-Enactment: R.G. Collingwood's Idea of History*, Oxford: Clarendon Press, 1995.

Fischer, David Hackett, *Historians' Fallacies: Towards a Logic of Historical Thought*, London: Routledge, 1971.

Flew, Antony, ed., *Logic and Language* (First Series), Oxford: Oxford University Press, 1955.

Frege, Gottlob, *Translations from the Philosophical Writings of Gottlob Frege*, edited by Peter Geach and Max Black, Oxford: Basil Blackwell, 1966.

Frege, Gottlob, "The Thought: A Logical Inquiry," *Philosophical Logic*, edited by P.F. Strawson, London: Oxford University Press, 1967.

Gallie, W.B., *Philosophy and the Historical Understanding*, second edition, New York: Shocken Books, 1968.

Gardiner, Patrick, ed., *Theories of History*, New York: The Free Press, 1959.

Gardiner, Patrick, *The Nature of Historical Explanation*, Oxford: Oxford University Press, 1961.

Goldstein, Leon J., "Collingwood's Theory of Historical Knowing," *History and Theory*, vol. 9, no. 1, 1970, 3–36.

Gombrich, E.H., *Art and Illusion: A Study in the Psychology of Pictorial Representation*, second edition, Princeton: Princeton University Press, 1961.

Gompertz, Will, *What Are You Looking At? The Surprising, Shocking, and Sometimes Strange Story of 150 Years of Modern Art*, New York: Penguin Group, 2012.

Goodman, Nelson, *Languages of Art: An Approach to a Theory of Symbols*, second edition, Indianapolis: Hackett, 1976.

Hempel, Carl G., "The Function of General Laws in History," 1942, reprinted in Gardiner, *Theories of History*, 344–56.

Hume, David, *An Enquiry Concerning Human Understanding*, 1748, Oxford Philosophical Texts edited by Tom Beauchamp, Oxford: Oxford University Press, 1999.

Hurup Nielsen, Margit, "Making Sense of History: Skagestad on Popper and Collingwood," *Inquiry*, vol. 22, 1979, 477-89.

Hurup Nielsen, Margit, "Re-Enactment and Reconstruction in Collingwood's Philosophy of History," *History and Theory*, vol. 20, 1981, 1-31.

Inglis, Fred, *History Man: The Life of R.G. Collingwood*, Princeton: Princeton University Press, 2009.

Innis, Robert, *Pragmatism and the Forms of Sense*, University Park: The Pennsylvania State University Press, 2002.

James, William, *Pragmatism: A New Name for Some Old Ways of Thinking*, New York: Longmans, Green, and Co., 1907.

Johnson, Peter, *R.G. Collingwood: An Introduction*, Bristol: Thoemmes Press, 1998.

Ketner, Kenneth Laine, *An Emendation of R.G. Collingwood's Doctrine of Absolute Presuppositions*, Lubbock: Graduate Studies, Texas Tech University, no. 4, July 1973.

Knox, T.M., "Editor's Preface" to *The Idea of History*, first edition, 1946. Not reprinted in the revised edition, and now out of print.

Krausz, Michael, ed., *Critical Essays on the Philosophy of R.G. Collingwood*, Oxford: Clarendon Press, 1972.

Kuhn, Thomas, *The Structure of Scientific Revolutions*, second edition, Chicago: University of Chicago Press, 1970.

Lakatos, Imre, "Falsification and the Methodology of Scientific Research Programmes," in *Criticism and the Growth of Knowledge*, edited by Imre Lakatos and Alan Musgrave, Cambridge: Cambridge University Press, 1970, 91-195.

Levinson, Paul, *Mind at Large: Knowing in the Technological Age*, Greenwich, CT: JAI Press, 1988.

Lippmann, Walter, *The Good Society*, 1936, new edition, New York: Grosset & Dunlap, 1943.

Martin, Rex, "Collingwood's Claim that Metaphysics Is a Historical Discipline," in *Philosophy, History and Civilization: Interdisciplinary Perspectives on R.G. Collingwood*, edited by David Boucher, James Connelly, and Tariq Modood, Cardiff: University of Wales Press, 1995, 203-45.

Martin, Rex, "From Method to Metaphysics," in *An Autobiography & Other Writings*, edited by David Boucher and Theresa Smith, Oxford: Oxford University Press, 2013, 353-75.

Milne, A.J.M., "Collingwood's Ethics and Political Theory," in *Critical Essays on the Philosophy of R.G. Collingwood*, edited by Michael Krausz, Oxford: Clarendon Press, 1972, 296-326.

Milne, A.J.M., "Civilization and the Open Society: Collingwood and Popper," in *Philosophy, History and Civilization: Interdisciplinary Perspectives on R.G. Collingwood*, edited by David Boucher, James Connelly, and Tariq Modood, Cardiff: University of Wales Press, 1995, 300-29.

Mill, John Stuart, *A System of Logic: Ratiocinative and Inductive*, New York: Harper & Brothers, 1864.

Mink, Louis, *Mind, History & Dialectic: The Philosophy of R.G. Collingwood*, Bloomington: Indiana University Press, 1969.

Modood, Tariq, "The Later Collingwood's Alleged Historicism and Relativism," *Journal of the History of Philosophy*, 27, 1989, 101–25.

Monk, Ray, "How the Untimely Death of R.G. Collingwood Changed the Course of Philosophy Forever," prospectmagazine.co.uk, September 5, 2019.

Passmore, John, *A Hundred Years of Philosophy*, Harmondsworth: Penguin Books, 1966.

Patrick, James, "The Oxford Man," in *An Autobiography & Other Writings*, edited by David Boucher and Theresa Smith, Oxford: Oxford University Press, 2013, 213–45.

Pears, D.F., *Bertrand Russell and the British Tradition in Philosophy*, London: The Fontana Library, 1967.

Peirce, Charles Sanders, *The Essential Peirce*, vol. 1, edited by Nathan Houser, and Christian Kloesel, Bloomington: Indiana University Press, 1992.

Peters, Rik, *History as Thought and Action: The Philosophies of Croce, Gentile, de Ruggiero and Collingwood*, Exeter, UK: Imprint Academic, 2013.

Popper, Karl R., *The Open Society and Its Enemies*, vol. 2, 1945, New York: Harper & Row, 1963.

Popper, Karl R., *The Poverty of Historicism*, 1957, New York: Harper & Row, 1964.

Popper, Karl R., *Objective Knowledge: An Evolutionary Approach*, Oxford: Clarendon Press, 1972.

Prichard, H.A., *Moral Obligation*, Oxford: Oxford University Press, 1968.

Quine, Willard Van Orman, *From a Logical Point of View*, Cambridge: Harvard University Press, 1953.

Rawls, John, *A Theory of Justice*, Cambridge, MA: Harvard University Press, 1971.

Ridley, Aaron, *R.G. Collingwood: A Philosophy of Art*, New York: Routledge, 1997.

Ross, David, *The Right and the Good*, 1930, new edition, edited with Introduction by Philip Stratton-Lake, Oxford: The Clarendon Press, 2002.

Rothko, Mark, *The Artist's Reality*, edited by Christopher Rothko, New Haven: Yale University Press, 2004.

Rothko, Mark, *Writings on Art*, edited by Miguel Lopez Remiro, New Haven: Yale University Press, 2006.

Russell, Bertrand, "On Denoting," *Mind*, 1905, reprinted in *Logic and Knowledge: Essays 1901–1950*, edited by Robert C. Marsh, New York: Allen & Unwin, 1956.

Rubinoff, Lionel, *Collingwood and the Reform of Metaphysics: A Study in the Philosophy of Mind*, Toronto: University of Toronto Press, 1970.

Ryle, Gilbert, "Mr. Collingwood and the Ontological Argument," *Mind*, vol. XLIV, 1935, 137–51.

Ryle, Gilbert, "Systematically Misleading Expressions," *Mind*, 1931, reprinted A. Flew, ed., *Logic and Language* (First Series), Oxford: Oxford University Press, 1955, 11–36.

Saari, Heikki, "Some Aspects of R.G. Collingwood's Doctrine of Absolute Presuppositions," *International Studies in Philosophy*, vol. 23, no. 1, 1991, 61–73.

Sartre, Jean-Paul, *Existentialism and Human Emotions*, New York: Citadel Press, 1957.

Shearmur, Jeremy, "Making Sense of History: Skagestad on Popper and Collingwood," *Inquiry*, vol. 22, 1979, 459–77.

Skagestad, Peter, "R.G. Collingwood's Theory of Presuppositions," Ph.D. dissertation, Brandeis University: Waltham, Massachusetts, 1973.

Skagestad, Peter, *Making Sense of History: The Philosophies of Popper and Collingwood*, Oslo: Universitetsforlaget, 1975.

Skagestad, Peter, "Thinking with Machines: Intelligence Augmentation, Evolutionary Epistemology, and Semiotic," *Journal of Social and Evolutionary Systems*, vol. 16, no. 2, 1993, 157–80.

Skagestad, Peter, "Collingwood and Berlin: A Comparison," *Journal of the History of Ideas*, vol. 66, no. 1, 2005, 99–112.

Smith, Teresa, "R.G. Collingwood's Childhood: Habits of Thought," in *An Autobiography and Other Writings*, edited by David Boucher and Theresa Smith, Oxford: Oxford University Press, 2013, 175–212.

Strauss, Leo, "On Collingwood's Philosophy of History," *The Review of Metaphysics*, vol. 5, no. 4, 1952, 559–86.

Strawson, P.F., ed., *Philosophical Logic*, London: Oxford University Press, 1967.

Toulmin, Stephen, *Human Understanding*, vol. 1, Princeton: Princeton University Press, 1972.

Van der Dussen, Jan, *History as a Science: The Philosophy of R.G. Collingwood*, The Hague: Nijhoff, 1981.

Van der Dussen, Jan, "The Philosophical Context of Collingwood's Re-Enactment Theory," *International Studies in Philosophy*, vol. 27, no. 2, 1995, 81–99.

Walsh, W.H., *Philosophy of History: An Introduction*, second edition, New York: Harper & Row, 1958.

Williams, Bernard, "An Essay on Collingwood," in *Collingwood on Philosophical Methodology*, edited by Karim Dharamsi, Giuseppina D'Oro and Stephen Leach, Cham, Switzerland: Palgrave Macmillan, 2018, 15–34.

Winch, Peter, *The Idea of a Social Science*, London: Routledge, 1958.

Wittgenstein, Ludwig, *Philosophical Investigations*, third edition, New York: The Macmillan Company, 1953.

Wittgenstein, Ludwig, *Tractatus Logico-Philosophicus*, 1922, new translation by D.F. Pears and B.F. McGuinness, London: Routledge, 1961.

Wittgenstein, Ludwig, *On Certainty*, edited by G.E.M. Anscombe, and G.H. von Wright, Oxford: Blackwell, 1969.

Wollheim, Richard, "On An Alleged Inconsistency in Collingwood's Aesthetic," in *Critical Essays on the Philosophy of R.G. Collingwood*, edited by Krausz, Oxford: Clarendon Press, 1953.

Index

Absolute, the   10, 13
Absolute Idealism   10–12
absolute presuppositions   131–44,
    148–51. *See also* presuppositions;
    relative presuppositions
  changes in   127, 129, 140
  defined   133–5
  metaphysics the science of   137–9
  and propositions   135–6, 148
  and science   138–9, 141–2
  unawareness of   133, 140
Abstract Expressionism   102–3
action   18–19, 69
  individual   88
  "inside-outside" metaphor   65–70, 77
  rational   84–5
  reflective   83
  and thought   18–19
Agassi, Joseph   81
amusement
  and art   99–101
  and magic   99
analytic philosophy   1, 14, 22, 51–3
Anselm of Canterbury   50. *See also*
    Ontological argument; God,
    existence of
anthropology   89–90, 97
anti-metaphysics   145–6, 148
  irrationalist   146
  progressive   145
  reactionary   145
archaeology   7, 65, 116–17
Arendt, Hannah   93, 177
Aristotle   38–9, 94, 137, 138, 150
art   17, 27, 29–31, 93–114
  and amusement   99–101
  and crafts   94–7
  as expression   101–3
  history of   86
  as imagination   103–6
  as language   108–10
  and magic   97–9
  and mechanical reproduction   100–1

assertions   136
Ayer, A.J.   14, 37, 147–50

Bacon, Francis   117–18
barbarism   177–9
Beaney, Michael   124–5
Benjamin, Walter   101
Bentham, Jeremy   10, 164
Berenson, Bernard   104
Berlin, Isaiah   70, 142–4
body politic   167–71
Bosanquet, Bernard   10, 12
Boucher, David   14–15, 85, 109
  on education   174
  on Idealism   12, 27, 44
  on *The New Leviathan*   162
  on re-enactment   138
  on the scale of forms   165
  on social and political philosophy
    153, 154, 169
Bradley, F.H.   10–11, 13, 22, 44, 67, 161
British Idealism   10–13

Caesar   65, 74, 75
Carr, Edward Hallett   88
Cézanne, Paul   21, 104–5
civility   172–3
civilization   171–4
Code, Lorraine   138
Coleridge, Samuel Taylor   93, 102
Collingwood, Molly   5
Collingwood, William Gershom   5, 7
community   166–7
concepts   40–4. *See also* philosophical
    concepts
Connelly, James   15, 36, 169
  on *An Essay on Philosophical Method*   46
  on politics   154
  on the radical-conversion hypothesis
    4, 127–9
  on the scale of forms   165
consciousness   13, 19, 106–8, 162–5.
    See also corruption of consciousness

continental liberalism   154–6
Copleston, Frederick   10
corruption of consciousness
    106–8, 110, 114
  art and   110
  and bad faith   108
  and repression   108
covering-law model   74–6. *See also*
    historical explanation
craft
  and art   94–7
critical philosophy   51–3, 116
Croce, Benedetto   6, 9, 13, 22–3, 44, 93

Debbins, William   64
DeLong, Howard   107
democracy   155, 157, 169–70
Descartes, René   26, 50, 53, 117–18, 147
Dewey, John   97, 105, 111, 113, 126, 173
dialectic   26, 161
  Hegel's concept of   28–9
  Plato's concept of   39
  and political discourse   168, 176
  and the scale of forms   35–6, 44, 131
Dilthey, Wilhelm   22, 70
Donagan, Alan   14, 106, 113
  on the logic of question and answer
    120, 123–4
  on the radical-conversion hypothesis
    4, 127–8
  rebuttal of Weitz   97
  on re-enactment   73–4, 87
D'Oro, Giuseppina   46, 55,
    127, 128, 136
Dray, William   76–79, 83–8
Duhem, Pierre   33, 126
Duhem-Quine Hypothesis   126
Dussen, Jan van der   14, 36, 73, 82
duty   159, 161

education   167, 174
Edwardes, Kathleen   9
Eliot, T.S.   21, 111, 113
emotion   85, 101–3
empiricism   13
essentially contested concepts   151
Euclid   70
evidence   67–8
explicit   26, 34, 36. *See also* implicit-
    explicit distinction

expression
  art as   101–3, 108–10
expressionism, *see* Abstract Expressionism

fascism   93, 114, 115, 154, 157–8
feeling   162–5
first-order thought   21, 34, 36
Folklore   5, 89–90
forms   35–6. *See also* Scale of forms
Frazer, James   89, 97
freedom   143–4, 155, 166
Frege, Gottlob   79–80, 82, 123
Freud, Sigmund   90, 163

Galileo   80–2
Gallie, W.B.   151
Gardiner, Patrick   70, 76–7
Gentile, Giovanni   13, 27
God, existence of   25–6, 50–1,
    57–8, 149–51
Goldsmith, Oliver   176
Goldstein, Leon   72–3, 83
Gombrich, Ernst   112
good   42, 159–61
Goodman, Nelson   105
Goya, Francisco   112
Graham, Ethel Winifred   8
Green, Thomas Hill   10–11

Haddock, Bruce   138
Haverfield, F.J.   7
Hegel, G.W.F.
  Ayer's rejection of   147
  and dialectic   13, 28–9
  influence of   10, 35, 44, 142
  and objective spirit   79
  opposition to Kant   12, 57
  and progression of consciousness
    61, 162
Hempel, Carl G.   74–7
hermeneutics   124
Herodotus   65
historical explanation   74–9
historical understanding   63–90
historicism   126–9. *See also* radical-
    conversion hypotheses; relativism
history   17, 27, 33–4, 63–90
  and art   86
  and nature   65, 86
  and philosophy   63, 121–9

scientific   63, 66-7
scissors-and-paste   63, 66
and society   88
history of philosophy   121-2
Hobbes, Thomas   120-1, 162, 164, 167
Hockney, David   105
Hume, David   44, 76
Hume's Fork   44-5, 46, 147
Hurup Nielsen, Margit   73, 76, 82

idealism   1, 10-13. *See also* Absolute Idealism; British Idealism
identified coincidents, fallacy of   44
imaginary   105-6
imagination
   art as   103-6
implicit   26, 34, 36
implicit-explicit distinction   26, 36, 43
individualism   88
Inglis, Fred   1, 5, 113
intellectualism   83-4

James, William   18, 19, 118-19, 126
Johnson, Peter   124
Joseph, H.W.B.   12, 21, 147
judgments   46-51. *See also* philosophical judgments

Kant, Immanuel
   and autonomy   155, 160
   and the Categorical Imperative   55
   and the *Groundwork*   6, 44
   and Hegel   10, 12
   and metaphysics   138, 149
   and the ontological argument   57
Ketner, Kenneth L.   136
Knox, T.M.   4, 9, 59, 64, 126-9, 153
Kuhn, Thomas   1, 60, 141, 142

Lakatos, Imre   142
language
   art as   108-10
law, rule of   176-7
laws of politics   169
Leibniz, G.W.   122, 138
liberalism   154-6. *See also* continental liberalism
liberty. *See also* freedom
   negative *vs.* positive   143-4
Lindsey, A.D.   140, 154

logical positivism   147
logic of question and answer   117-22, 136. *See also* question and answer

MacIntyre, Alasdair   1, 12
McTaggart, J.M.E.   10-12
magic   89-90
   art and   97-9
Manet, Edouard   112
Martin, Rex   136, 138, 141, 142, 148
Marx, Karl   153-4, 165-6
meaning   118-19, 125-6
metaphysics. *See also* anti-metaphysics; pseudo-metaphysics
   history of   138
   as science of absolute presuppositions   137, 148
   as science of pure being   137
method   38-40, 48
Mill, John Stuart   10, 47, 76, 143, 164
Milne, A.J.M.   156-7, 178
mind   19-20
Mink, Louis   14
   on historical understanding   87
   on the logic of question and answer   124-5
   on *The New Leviathan*   162
   on parallel with Wittgenstein   109
   on the radical-conversion hypothesis   127
   on *Speculum Mentis*   35-6
Modood, Tariq   136
Monk, Ray   1
Moore, G.E.   12, 22, 52, 116, 158
moral philosophy   158-62

Nazism   93, 114, 115, 157-8
Nelson, Lord   71-2, 121, 122
Nietzsche, Friedrich   71, 85

ontological argument   50-1, 57-8, 149-51
Oxford   1, 6, 9, 12, 116

past, knowledge of   68
Peirce, Charles Sanders   13, 19, 80, 123, 137
philosophical concepts   40-4
philosophical judgments   46-51
philosophy   17, 27, 34-5
philosophy and history   59, 121-2, 127-9

Plato   48, 127, 179
   and art   94
   and dialectical *vs.* eristic discussion   168
   and God   50
   and the state   120–1
   and the world of ideas   79
political action   156
political philosophy   153, 167–71
politics   153–7, 167–71. *See also* body politic; laws of politics
Popper, Karl R.
   and falsificationism   142
   and historical explanation   76–7
   and re-enactment   71
   and situational analysis   79–82
   and totalitarianism   93, 178–9
pragmatism   13
precarious margins, fallacy of   41
presuppositions   127, 129, 131–44, 148–51. *See also* absolute presuppositions; relative presuppositions
Prichard, H.A.   6, 12, 21, 116, 147, 158
principle of propositional logic   123, 125
   and Socratic principle   125
propositional logic   119
propositions   135–6
psychology   162–5
   as anti-metaphysics   146

question and answer   117–22
Quine, W.V.O.   126

radical-conversion hypothesis   4, 59, 126–9. *See also* historicism; relativism
Raffael, Joseph   105
rational explanations   78
rationalism   84–5
Rawls, John   22, 54
Realism   21–2, 26, 116
Realists   6, 10, 12, 21, 52, 116, 121, 124
re-enactment, history as   4, 19–20, 69–74, 83–90
   and art   86
   and emotions   89–90
   and empathy   70–2, 81–2
   and explanation   74–9
   and metaphysics   138
   and situational analysis   79–82
relative presuppositions   134

relativism   68, 126–9, 140–1. *See also* historicism, radical-conversion hypothesis
religion   17, 25–7, 31–2
representation in art   97
Ridley, Aaron   110, 113
right   159–61
Roman Britain   7, 64
Ross, W.D.   22, 158–9
Rothko, Mark   97, 102–3
Rubinoff, Lionel   3, 14, 27, 35–6, 127–8
Ruggiero, Guido de   8, 9, 13, 129
ruled   168–70
Rule of law   176–7
rulers   168–70
Ruskin, John   5, 6, 93, 135
Russell, Bertrand
   and analytic philosophy   52
   and logic   127
   and the ontological argument   57
   and Realism   12, 116
   and the Theory of Descriptions   45–6, 147
Ryle, Gilbert   1, 12, 45–6, 57–8, 147

Saari, Heikki   88
Sartre, Jean-Paul   108, 161
scale of forms   35–6, 38, 42–4, 57, 165
   modified scale of forms   142
science   17, 27, 32–3
scientific history   63, 66–7
scissors-and-paste history   63, 66
second-order thought   21, 34, 36
self-control, freedom as   155
self-knowledge, history as   64–5
Shakespeare, William   19, 112
Shearmur, Jeremy   82
situational analysis   79–82
Smith, J.A.   6, 8
Smith, Teresa   6
society   165–7
   and community   166–7
Socrates   38–9, 110
Socratic principle   47, 125
Spinoza, Baruch de   162, 164
Stebbing, L.S.   45, 52
Still, Clyfford   103
Stout, G.F.   124
Strauss, Leo   68–9, 127
system   55–7

Tacitus 66, 72
technical theory of art 94–7
Theodosian Code 69–70, 73, 81
Theory of Descriptions 45–6, 147
thought 18–19
Thucydides 65, 122
totalitarianism 93
Toulmin, Stephen 140–1
truth 119–20, 124–6

utilitarianism 10, 160
utility 159–60

verifiability 147–9
Vico, Giambattista 6, 64, 88, 93
Villeneuve, Pierre-Charles 121

Vincent, Andrew 13
visual experience 104–5

Walsh, W.H. 70, 83
Warnock, G.J. 14
wealth 175–6
Weitz, Morris 97
White, Morton 76
Whitehead, Alfred North 123
Williams, Bernard 37
Wilson, John Cook 6, 21, 37, 116, 124
Winch, Peter 83
Wittgenstein, Ludwig 1, 97, 109, 136, 151
Wollheim, Richard 105
work of art 104–5, 111

www.ingramcontent.com/pod-product-compliance
Lightning Source LLC
Chambersburg PA
CBHW072236290426
44111CB00012B/2116